Jackie Robinson
A Spiritual Biography

Jackie Robinson
A Spiritual Biography

The Faith of a Boundary-Breaking Hero

MICHAEL G. LONG AND CHRIS LAMB

WESTMINSTER
JOHN KNOX PRESS
LOUISVILLE · KENTUCKY

First edition
Published by Westminster John Knox Press
Louisville, Kentucky

17 18 19 20 21 22 23 24 25 26—10 9 8 7 6 5 4 3 2 1

Book design by Drew Stevens
Cover design by Marc Whitaker / MTWdesign.net

Library of Congress Cataloging-in-Publication Data

Names: Long, Michael G., author.
Title: Jackie Robinson : a spiritual biography : the faith of a
  boundary-breaking hero / Michael G. Long and Chris Lamb.
Description: Louisville, KY : Westminster John Knox Press, 2017. |
  Includes bibliographical references and index.
Identifiers: LCCN 2016052017 (print) | LCCN 2016056614 (ebook) | ISBN
  9780664262037 (pbk. : alk. paper) | ISBN 9781611648010 (ebk.)
Subjects: LCSH: Robinson, Jackie, 1919-1972. | Robinson, Jackie,
  1919-1972--Religion. | African American baseball players--Biography. |
  Discrimination in sports--United States--History--20th century. |
  United States--Race relations--History--20th century.
Classification: LCC GV865.R6 L66 2017 (print) | LCC GV865.R6 (ebook) |
  DDC 796.357092 [B] --dc23
LC record available at https://lccn.loc.gov/2016052017

Most Westminster John Knox Press books are available at special quantity discounts when purchased in bulk by corporations, organizations, and special-interest groups. For more information, please e-mail SpecialSales@wjkbooks.com.

For Bob, Karin, and Sharon,
who guided me through the night.
—MGL

For Jean Lamb (1925–2016),
whose faith inspired me to write this book.
—CL

*The Good Lord has showered blessings on me and this country
and its people, black and white, have been good to me.
But no matter how rich or famous I might become,
no matter what luxuries or special privileges I might achieve,
no matter how many powerful friends I might make,
I would never be the man I want to be until my humblest brother, black
and white, becomes the man he wants to be.
So I must be involved in our fight for freedom.*

—JACKIE ROBINSON

Contents

Acknowledgments

We are deeply grateful to the following individuals and institutions: Rachel Robinson, who kindly met with Michael to talk about her husband's faith; Lee Lowenfish, author of *Branch Rickey: Baseball's Ferocious Gentleman*, for his valuable comments on the manuscript; the staff at the Manuscripts Division of the Library of Congress; the National Baseball Hall of Fame; the Special Collections Department staff at Ohio University Western Libraries; Tim Tanton, executive director of global voices, news, and information at United Methodist Communications; the microfilm staff at Pattee and Paterno Library of the Pennsylvania State University; Sylvia Morra and the staff of High Library at Elizabethtown College; Dean Fletcher McClellan of Elizabethtown College; Tom Davis, dean of the School of Liberal Arts, and Jonas Bjork, chair of the Department of Journalism and Public Relations at Indiana University–Purdue University, Indianapolis; Sharon Herr; Karin, Jackson, and Nate Long; Lesly and David Lamb; and the wonderful staff at Westminster John Knox Press, especially Jessica Miller Kelley and Julie Tonini.

Introduction

"God Is with Us in This, Jackie": The Meeting of the Methodists

Jackie Robinson met Brooklyn Dodgers president Branch Rickey for the first time shortly after 10:00 a.m. on August 28, 1945, in Rickey's fourth-floor office at 215 Montague Street in Brooklyn, New York. Rickey sat in a leather swivel chair behind a large mahogany desk. Rickey, bulky and rumpled, was wearing a sport coat and bow tie and holding a cigar. Light gleamed off his glasses. An extensive file on Robinson lay on his desk.

Robinson entered the office with Clyde Sukeforth, a Brooklyn scout, who had joined him outside the Montague Street building. A few days earlier, Sukeforth had introduced himself to Robinson, a shortstop on the Kansas City Monarchs in the Negro leagues, after a game in Chicago. Sukeforth said he was there on behalf of Rickey, who wanted to talk to the ballplayer about joining a black team Rickey was creating, the Brooklyn Brown Dodgers.[1]

Robinson was unaware that Rickey had been scouting him for several months. Rickey had learned everything he could about Robinson, including his time at the University of California, Los Angeles (UCLA), in the US Army, and with the Monarchs. Rickey's announcement that he was creating a team for a new Negro league worked as a smoke screen to hide his real intentions.[2]

Robinson's eyes quickly scanned the inside of Rickey's office. On one wall was a blackboard with the names of the baseball personnel at all levels in the Brooklyn organization. On another was a portrait of Abraham

1

Lincoln, the Great Emancipator. There were photos of Brooklyn's tempestuous manager, Leo Durocher, Rickey's granddaughters, and the late Charley Barrett, who had been one of Rickey's closest friends.

Goldfish swam nervously in a fish tank off to the side of the office, demonstrating an uneasiness that Robinson later said captured his own.

"Hello, Jackie," said Rickey as he stood up, reached across his desk, and warmly shook Robinson's hand.[3]

Rickey did not immediately say anything else.

"He just stared and stared," Sukeforth recalled. "That's what he did with Robinson—stared at him as if he were trying to get inside the man. And Jack stared right back at him. Oh, they were a pair, those two. I tell you, the air in the office was electric."[4]

Rickey then began asking Robinson about his personal life.

"Do you have a girl?" he said.

Robinson told Rickey he was engaged to Rachel Isum, whom he met while attending UCLA.

"Well, marry her," Rickey said. "When we get through today you may want to call her up, because there are times when a man needs a woman by his side."[5]

The personal questions continued.

Rickey asked Robinson about his religious affiliation. Robinson said he was a Methodist. This pleased Rickey, a lifelong Methodist whose name, Wesley Branch Rickey, came from John Wesley, the founder of Methodism.

Shortly before his meeting with Robinson, Rickey had visited the office of the Rev. L. Wendell Fifield, his pastor at Plymouth Church of the Pilgrims in Brooklyn.

"Don't let me interrupt you. I can't talk with you," Rickey said. "I just want to be here. Do you mind?"

The minister agreed, and for the next forty-five minutes Rickey frantically paced about Fifield's office.

"I've got it," Rickey finally yelled as he pounded the minister's desk.

"Got what, Branch?" Fifield replied.

Rickey plopped down on the minister's couch and offered a brief explanation. "This was so complex, fraught with so many pitfalls but filled with so much good, if it was right, that I just had to work it out in this room with you. I had to talk to God about it and be sure what He wanted me to do. I hope you don't mind.

"Wendell," Rickey said, "I've decided to sign Jackie Robinson!"

Rickey then straightened his trademark bow tie and thanked his pastor.

"Bless you, Wendell," he said, and left the room.[6]

In later years, Rickey said, "Surely, God was with me when I picked Jackie Robinson as the first Negro player in the major leagues."[7]

The late August 1945 meeting between the two Methodists, Rickey and Robinson, ultimately transformed baseball and America.

Rickey knew Robinson was a good athlete who had lettered in four sports at UCLA. He earned honorable mention on the all-American football team. He led the conference in scoring in basketball and finished first in the long jump at the NCAA national track and field championship. His worst sport was baseball.

But Rickey wanted to know more about Robinson as a man. He asked him if he drank alcohol. Robinson said he did not. Jackie, in fact, had openly scorned his whiskey-drinking teammates on the Kansas City Monarchs, once tossing a glass of scotch into a lighted fireplace to demonstrate the lethality of liquor.

Robinson did not tell Rickey this story. But if he had, it would have brought a smile to Rickey's face. Rickey, too, often used dramatics to make a point.

As Rickey looked at Robinson, he saw the intensity in Robinson's face. The ballplayer was twenty-six, old for someone without any experience in what was called "organized professional baseball."

Robinson's birthday was January 31, 1919. The date resonated with Rickey. His own son, Branch Rickey Jr., was born on January 31, 1914. Both men, Robinson and Rickey Jr., as it turned out, would die relatively young from complications from diabetes.

Rickey's line of questioning thus far must have confounded Robinson, who still did not know what he was doing in the office on Montague Street.

Rickey asked Robinson if he was under contract with the Monarchs. Robinson said he was not. Rickey then asked if Robinson had any agreement with the Monarchs.

"No, none at all. Just pay day to pay day," Robinson said.[8]

Finally, Rickey asked Robinson if he knew why he had been brought to the office.

"To play on a black team," Robinson responded.

Rickey shook his head.

He told Robinson he wanted to sign him for the Brooklyn Dodgers organization. Rickey told Robinson he would start with the Montreal Royals, the organization's top minor-league team, and then, if he was good enough, be promoted to the Dodgers.

Robinson was being asked if he was interested in breaking baseball's color line, which had existed since the nineteenth century.

Robinson tried to grasp the totality of the moment.

Rickey's booming voice interrupted Robinson's thoughts.

"I want to win the pennant and we need ball players!" Rickey thundered as he whacked his desk. "Do you think you can do it?"

Robinson waited before answering.

"Jack waited, and waited, and waited before answering," Sukeforth remembered.

"Yes," Robinson said.[9]

Rickey's scouts told him that Robinson was a good baseball player, maybe not the best player in black baseball, but better than most. Rickey liked the fact that Robinson had played against white athletes in college and that he had been an officer in the army. He liked what he heard about Robinson's athleticism, his intelligence, his speed, and his competitiveness. Rickey liked just about everything he heard about Robinson.

Except his temper.

Rickey knew that Robinson's temper was particularly explosive when he was confronted with racial bigotry—whether as a teenager on the streets of Pasadena, during athletic competitions, or while serving as a soldier. Lieutenant Robinson had been court-martialed for insubordination after refusing to move to the back of a military bus in Fort Hood, Texas.

Robinson was cleared of the charges and discharged from the army in late November 1944. He began playing the next spring with the Monarchs. He did not like the Negro leagues and the ways black baseball perpetuated Jim Crowism. He hated the long bus rides, the Jim Crow hotels and restaurants, the poor umpiring, and the carousing of his teammates. His feelings on drinking and sexual abstinence put him at odds with his teammates.

Robert Abernathy played with Robinson for the Monarchs during the summer of 1945.

"Jackie Robinson, he was a good player, but he had some temper—temper like a rattlesnake," Abernathy said. "The umpire would call a strike or a bad call on him and he wanted to argue. And then he'd get in there and he'd knock the cover off the ball.

"Jackie said, 'Ab, you're a good ballplayer' and I'd say, 'So are you—just control your temper.' And he said, 'Well, I ain't gonna take no mess.'"[10]

Reports about Robinson's temper got back to Rickey, who was clearly worried about Robinson's ability to control his anger.

For Robinson to succeed, Rickey knew, he could not respond to the indignities that would be piled onto him, or he would give credence to the segregationists who said blacks were too temperamental to play in the major leagues. Segregationists had long said that mixing blacks and whites on baseball diamonds inevitably would lead to fistfights on the field and race riots in the bleachers.[11]

Rickey needed to know what was inside Robinson.

"I know you're a good ballplayer," Rickey told him. "What I don't know is whether you have the guts."

Rickey's words stung Robinson, whose fists clenched while anger stirred in his stomach. Nobody had ever questioned Robinson's guts. He started to respond. But Rickey cut him off.

"I'm looking for a ballplayer with guts enough not to fight back," Rickey said.

Rickey did not immediately say anything more.

He took off his coat and transformed himself from baseball executive to method actor. First, he was a white hotel clerk refusing the black Robinson a room, then a white waiter denying Robinson service, and then a white train conductor sticking a finger in Robinson's face and calling him "boy."

Rickey then became a foulmouthed opposing player who, as Robinson later recalled, derided "my race, my parents, in language that was almost unendurable."

And finally, Rickey became a vindictive base stealer who slid into Robinson with his spikes high in the air, hoping to bloody the infielder trying to tag him out.

"How do you like that, nigger boy?" the base stealer said.

Rickey, the base stealer, swung his fist at Robinson's head.

Robinson did not flinch. He did not respond.[12]

Rickey opened a book published in 1921, Giovanni Papini's *Life of Christ*, and read Jesus' words from the Sermon on the Mount in the Gospel of Matthew: "Ye have heard that it hath been said, An eye for an eye, and a tooth for a tooth: But I say unto you, That ye resist not evil: but whosoever shall smite thee on thy right cheek, turn to him the other also. And if any man will sue thee at the law, and take away thy coat, let him have thy cloke also. And whosoever shall compel thee to go a mile, go with him twain" (Matt. 5:38–41 KJV).

Robinson recognized the text and the point Rickey was making, and what was required of him.

"I have two cheeks, Mr. Rickey," Robinson replied. "Is that it?"[13]

Rickey nodded and then smiled. Robinson's words were just what Rickey hoped to hear.

"Well, I thought the old man was going to kiss him," remembered Clyde Sukeforth, who witnessed the exchange.[14]

But Rickey had to make sure that Robinson understood what he was getting himself into.

"We can't fight our way through this," Rickey said. "We've got no army. There's virtually nobody on our side. No owners, no umpires, very few newspapermen. And I'm afraid that many fans will be hostile."[15]

Rickey asked Robinson for his assurance that he would restrain himself from responding to any verbal or physical confrontation, on or off the field. He told Robinson that if he lost his temper, it would vindicate those who believed blacks did not belong in white baseball. Rickey told Robinson he would have to be "a man big enough to bear the cross of martyrdom."[16]

Robinson agreed.

Rickey signed Robinson to a contract with the Montreal Royals. It included a bonus of $3,500 and a salary of $600 a month.

He insisted that Robinson keep the news to himself. Robinson told neither Rachel nor his mother, Mallie. As Robinson got to know Rickey, he found that the white baseball executive reminded him of his mother because both possessed a deep and uncompromising faith in God.

"I am not the most religious person in the world. I believe in God, in the Bible and in trying to do the right thing as I understand it," Robinson once said. "I am sure there are many, many better Christians than I. Yet, it has always impressed me that two of the people who had the greatest influence on my life—my mother and Branch Rickey—had such deep faith in the existence of a Supreme Being. It is one thing to express faith. It is another thing to do as these two people did—to practice faith every day of one's life."[17]

The next two months were anxious ones for Robinson. He did not know Rickey well enough yet to fully believe him. He tried to go on with his life as it was, but he could not stop thinking about the opportunity ahead for him. Nor could he help but wonder whether this would become another deferred dream for another black person.

Two months later, on October 23, Brooklyn announced it had signed Robinson for its Montreal team. By doing so, Rickey fulfilled a promise he had made to himself decades earlier, when he was the baseball coach at Ohio Wesleyan University, a private Methodist-affiliated school in Delaware, Ohio.

In 1903, the Ohio Wesleyan team traveled to South Bend, Indiana, for a game against the University of Notre Dame. The hotel clerk denied a room to Charles "Tommy" Thomas, the team's only black player. Rickey asked if Thomas could sleep on a cot in his room. The clerk agreed.

Later that evening, Rickey said, he saw Thomas sobbing and rubbing his hands, saying, "Black skin. Black skin. If only I could make them white."

Rickey said the scene haunted him.

"I vowed," Rickey told the Associated Press after he signed Robinson, "that I would always do whatever I could to see that other Americans did not have to face the bitter humiliation that was heaped upon Charles Thomas."[18]

Rickey could not make good on the promise he made to Thomas by himself. He needed the right man—and in Robinson he found him.

Rickey, it appears, did not tell Robinson the story of Charles Thomas. But, as Robinson later explained in an article he wrote for *Guideposts* magazine, Rickey told another story as the men discussed what might happen if Robinson integrated baseball.

"There will be trouble ahead—for you, for me, for my people, for baseball," Robinson told Rickey.

"Trouble ahead," Rickey said, repeating Robinson's words. "You know, Jackie, I was a small boy when I took my first train ride. On the same train was an old couple, also riding for the first time. We were going through the Rocky Mountains. The old man sitting by the window looked forward and said to his wife, 'Trouble ahead, Ma! We're high up over a precipice and we're going to run right off!'

"To my boyish ears the noise of the wheels repeated, 'Trouble a-head, trouble-ahead. . . .' I never hear train wheels to this day but that I think of this. But our train course bent into a tunnel right after the old man spoke, and we came out on the other side of the mountain. That's the way it is with most trouble ahead in this world, Jackie—if we use the common sense and courage God gave us. But you've got to study the hazards and build wisely."[19]

Robinson said he never forgot that story. He also did not forget that Rickey told him he would not be alone.

"God is with us in this, Jackie," Rickey told Robinson. "You know your Bible. It's good, simple Christianity for us to face realities and to recognize what we're up against. We can't go out and preach and crusade and bust our heads against the wall. We've got to fight out our problems together with tact and common sense."[20]

Robinson had never met anyone like Rickey. Robinson learned to be suspicious of whites. And yet he implicitly trusted Rickey. When he later remembered their first meeting, Robinson recalled how Rickey's "piercing eyes looked at me with such meticulous care. I felt almost naked." But once he got to know Rickey, Robinson learned he had no greater protector. "He was like a piece of mobile armor, and he would throw himself and his advice in the way of anything likely to hurt me."[21]

Nobody in sports had more at stake, and no one ever suffered more than Robinson. Opposing pitchers threw at him. Opposing base runners spiked him. Fans screamed the vilest of racial epithets. He routinely received death threats.

If he failed, he affirmed the belief of many whites that blacks were inferior. If he lost his temper, he affirmed the belief of those who thought blacks did not have the temperament to play white baseball. It was not enough for him to be good enough for the major leagues; he had to be better than most of the other players, he had to beat them at their own game, and do so with grace and dignity and equanimity.

If Robinson succeeded, he succeeded for all blacks and the millions of whites who believed in racial equality. His success would inspire millions of blacks that they, too, deserved to be treated with equality and fairness. It would cure many white Americans of their belief that blacks were inferior, and convince many others that blacks should have the same opportunities as whites—not just in baseball but also in jobs, housing, and education.

Through it all, Robinson remained steadfast, firmly convinced that God was guiding him, that God was on his side, and that God would sustain him. Trusting God as his constant companion, Robinson exemplified redemptive suffering on the baseball diamond: he turned the other cheek in the face of viciousness.

Robinson succeeded, he felt, because God sides with right, not might. Robinson had no doubt that God favored the cause of racial justice over the forces of bigotry and discrimination. God was on his side, fighting for equality, and not with the bigots who tormented him or with those who indifferently turned their backs on injustice.

While Robinson occasionally made public statements about his faith, he expressed his faith in these early baseball years mostly in the quiet of the night. His prayer time was intensely private, according to Rachel Robinson, who left her husband alone as he prayed for strength and courage to face the next day's trials and tribulations. Rachel knew that turning the cheek did not come naturally to her husband. He was not nonviolent by nature, and felt he needed all the help he could get through his nightly ritual of prayer.

Robinson's strength in the face of those threats and unspeakable obscenities demonstrated his Christian faith. He succeeded in no small part because of his strong faith in God, which was instilled in him through his mother, Branch Rickey, and his own prayers. "I can testify to the fact that it was a lot harder to turn the other cheek and refuse to fight back than it would have been to exercise a normal reaction," Robinson once wrote. "But it works, because sooner or later it brings a sense of shame to those who attack you. And that sense of shame is often the beginning of progress."[22]

From their first meeting, Rickey put his faith in Robinson, and Robinson remained steadfast in that faith. Robinson repeatedly observed how Rickey anticipated difficulties before they happened and then informed the ballplayer and instructed him how he should act. This would repeat itself during Robinson's season with the Montreal Royals in 1946 and during his career with the Dodgers.

Robinson was convinced that Rickey was being directed by a higher power.

"It was impossible for me to believe otherwise," Robinson said. "The first few times he did it, I waved it away as coincidences. But the evidence kept piling up until I realized that I was dealing with a man who had found a way to project himself into the future. I began to accept the fact that Branch Rickey was receiving the kind of help which is above and beyond the understanding of man. It was most valuable to me to know that he had that kind of help. For, when I came to believe that God was working with and guiding Mr. Rickey, I began to also believe that he was guiding me."[23]

The famous meeting of the Methodists is depicted in *42*, the 2013 biographical movie starring Chadwick Boseman as Jackie Robinson and Harrison Ford as Branch Rickey. Then the movie turns to the familiar, inspiring saga of Robinson's courageous fight against racism in baseball and society.

What is overlooked in *42* is that Robinson was a deeply religious man and that the story of his life was spiritual at its core.

Robinson's faith in God, as he attested, carried him not only through the torment of integrating the major leagues but also through the difficult years of advancing civil rights after he left the baseball diamond.

The purpose of this book is to take Robinson at his word and help readers recognize and understand the indispensable role that Christian faith played throughout his life.

The importance of faith for Robinson may come as a surprise to readers. Brian Helgeland, the screenwriter of *42*, is far from alone in largely ignoring Robinson's Christianity.[24] It's all too easy to read one of the numerous books about Robinson without coming across one word about his religious convictions.

Arnold Rampersad, who has written the best biography of Robinson, nicely captured Robinson's reliance on faith in his fight for freedom in Major League Baseball and in the wider society.

This book will use and build upon Rampersad's important work by looking at Robinson's life through the lens of faith.

Doing so, the book will show that to ignore Robinson's faith is to take away the very foundation on which he stood as he shattered the color barrier in baseball and became a leading figure in the civil rights movement after baseball.

It is simply impossible to understand Robinson in depth without tending to his Christian belief in God. Only when we see faith in every part of Robinson's life—from his birth to his death—will we understand that Robinson was a man for whom Christian faith acted as a source of inspiration and motivation, comfort and strength, wisdom and direction.

Jackie Robinson was a Hall of Famer and a civil rights leader, to be sure. But first and foremost, he was a Christian believer.

PART ONE

The Exodus

1

"I Put My Trust in God and Moved"

The Active Faith of Mallie Robinson

Mallie Robinson refused ether when Jackie was born at the Robinson home in Cairo, Georgia, on the evening of January 31, 1919. The visiting doctor wanted to administer the drug, but she had heard of a white woman who had fallen asleep after receiving ether and never regained consciousness. Fearing the same would happen to her, Mallie firmly resisted the doctor's entreaties, experiencing every ounce of pain that came with delivering Jack Roosevelt Robinson.

While she cradled her newborn son—named for President Theodore Roosevelt—Mallie's husband, Jerry, her brother, and her brother-in-law busied themselves making "sugar teats," lard and sugar wrapped in cheesecloth to resemble nipples that would ease Jackie's entrance into his new world. Lots of lard ended up on the floor, and as Mallie surveyed the hapless men and the sparse surroundings, she looked at her newborn and whispered a blessing. "Bless you, my boy," she said. "For you to survive all this, God will have to keep his eye on you."[1]

Little did she know how true this would be.

Mallie McGriff first met Jerry Robinson at a Christmas party in 1903 on the Jim Sasser plantation just outside Cairo, where Jerry's parents lived and labored. Mallie's father, a former slave, was not impressed when he learned that his fourteen-year-old daughter and Jerry had walked home together after the party and, worse, had made plans to go to church together the following Sunday.

Mallie's father said his daughter would be available for dating only when she was allowed to lower her dress below her knees, adding, "I ain't turned you out yet."[2]

Her parents wanted her to date a young man living in "the best house" on the Sasser plantation, but Mallie was fiercely independent and determined to continue dating Jerry. Despite the efforts to break them up, the young couple married in November 1909, just before the plantation's hog-butchering season. "I loved my husband very much," she later recalled. "I said, 'Now let's prove to the world what we can do.'"

But moving onto the Sasser plantation proved difficult for Mallie. She was accustomed to better living conditions than those Sasser provided for his black employees.

As a plantation laborer, Jerry Robinson earned twelve dollars a month, barely enough to feed him and Mallie, let alone any children on the way. And economical shopping on the plantation was impossible. Sasser owned the store where his workers had to purchase overpriced basic goods, often against the next year's salary.

Mallie grew especially upset when she discovered during butchering season that Sasser would not allow his black workers to take home anything except the hog's lungs, liver, and other organs. "Slavery is over," she told Jerry, vowing to change the plantation's oppressive economic system.

A turning point for the Robinsons occurred less than two months after their wedding. Unable to make ends meet as Christmas approached, Jerry asked to borrow fifteen dollars, more than a month's pay, against his salary in the new year. Sasser readily agreed—such borrowing and lending served his plan to keep workers bound to the plantation—but Mallie was far from agreeable when Jerry handed her five dollars from next year's paycheck to spend for this year's Christmas. "My husband worked for wages for years," she recalled, "and did not have anything to show for it at the end of the year."

Stuck in poverty and debt, Mallie concocted a plan. She knew her hardworking husband was an extremely valuable laborer on the Sasser plantation. "So I asked him to try and farm for himself," she said. It took some convincing and prodding on her part, but Jerry eventually informed Sasser he would leave the plantation unless he could half-crop—keep half the crops he farmed on the owner's land.

Unwilling to face the loss of Jerry's contributions, Sasser relented, granting Jerry sharecropper status and freeing him and Mallie to start their own farming venture and climb out of debt. "Well," Mallie recalled, "we made fine crops, plenty of everything, so I was a happy woman [with] a fine farmer for a husband."

Although Jackie Robinson never knew his father, he grew up intimately familiar with his mother's story of Jerry's transition into sharecropping, and as an adult Jackie shared the story publicly to praise his mother's faith and explain his own spiritual roots.

In Jackie's version, his father was "too afraid" to approach Sasser with Mallie's plan because he knew Sasser could throw him off the land for even daring to make such a bold request. Mallie conceded the same possibility. "In spite of this knowledge," Jackie recounted, "she had that strength and determination which has been characteristic of so many Negro women of the South. She had faith and trust in God, and she believed that God wants human beings to work and speak for the freedom and equality which is rightfully theirs, even if they must suffer because they do this."[3]

The faith of Mallie Robinson, as her son attested, was not the type of faith that encouraged slaves to be obedient to their masters or that stressed the need to be content with one's earthly status. That counsel was far from helpful. Nor was it the passive type of faith that waited for divine action to make things right or that merely prayed for the second coming of Jesus to free the oppressed from their bondage.

Mallie Robinson's faith was an active faith that took its cues directly from the biblical Jesus who declared at the outset of his ministry that he had come to set the oppressed free. Unlike submissive Christians waiting for "the pie in the sky," Mallie fervently believed that those who follow Jesus must act right here and now—that they must fight for the freedom and equality that God desires for everyone, even if doing so requires suffering along the way. In her view, the people of God will no doubt suffer as they confront oppression, but if they keep their eyes focused on God's will, they will see that suffering can be redemptive—it can redeem individual lives and establish freedom and equality.

"My mother's faith paid off," Robinson said. After Sasser granted his father's request, "there was more food for the Robinson family, more clothes and a lot more respect." Her faith, he said, "changed my father from a slave worker into a man of pride."[4]

But the uptick in finances and pride came with a price. As Mallie herself put it, Jerry proved too weak when the extra food and money attracted female attention. "He could not take it," she said, "he began to neglect, gave away what we had, until things began to get bad."[5]

Mallie felt unstable. "I talked and prayed and begged him to change," she said. When a lack of funds meant she and Jerry could not hire the extra help required for farming, she and their five children—Mack, Willa Mae, Edgar, Frank, and Jackie—took to the fields, with the older children pulling crabgrass and catching insects that would damage the crops.

It was far from ideal, and when the weather wore down the children, Jerry suggested they all move into town. "Nothing doing," Mallie replied, suggesting that it was difficult enough keeping watch over her straying husband on a rural farm, let alone in a busy town.

"So things went on," Mallie recalled. "I had a fine chicken crop, turkey, lots of hogs. We were just living as I wanted to live, only his love [was] drifting away."

Jerry had been straying for some time over the course of their nine-year marriage. "We been separated three or four times," Mallie recalled, "and every time we go back together, I got another child." Jackie arrived during one of those brief periods of reconciliation.

With Jerry's love adrift, Mallie relied on the one constant in her life. "I always lived so close to God till he would tell me things, what would happen," she explained.

Mallie's God was not the immortal and invisible God that white Christians sang about. Her God was not wholly other—transcendent, inaccessible, and unmovable. Mallie's God was always close by; he traveled with her, next to her, even inside her.

And she certainly did not need an ordained priest or minister, let alone sacraments in expensive fonts and chalices, to access her closest companion; she just needed to listen. Mallie's God spoke to her directly—in conversations, in prayers, in dreams.

Mallie believed that through her dreams God was telling her that serious trouble was ahead, that Jerry would soon be leaving her and their family. "I would tell [Jerry] about it," she explained, "and he would say that was the Devil, not God." But Mallie had the perfect reply. "Well, if the Devil loves me that good as to warn me of trouble," she said, "I had the Devil and God both on my side."

Her recurring dreams were troubling enough, but far worse was Jerry's very real wandering. Six months after the birth of Jackie, Jerry announced he was going to visit his brother in Texas, that he wanted to take their daughter Willa Mae with him, and that he would later send for the rest of the family. In the meantime, Mallie was to finish farming and use funds from the hay harvest to meet the family's needs.

"Well, I did not fall for that," she recalled. She had discovered that her husband was not planning on going to Texas but rather that he had promised to go away with another woman and begin a new life with her. "I was warned in my dreams about all of this," Mallie explained.

Armed with God's warning, Mallie had had enough, so she opened the door and invited her husband to leave. "I finally decided for him to go, only I told him he was not going to Texas. I knew just what he was up to, so I got his suitcase packed, and then I said, 'Now let's go and make a lunch.'" Mallie made sure her departing husband had something to eat as he walked out the door; she would not be vengeful in their last moments together.

On July 28, 1919, Jerry Robinson hopped aboard train number 230 and went to Florida with another woman.

Jerry left in the middle of the crop year, and Mallie was now in dire straits. Her brother offered to help harvest the crops so that she could get her fair share, but Sasser was too angry to talk about sharing anything and faulted Mallie for the loss of one of his best farmers. "You might as well go," Sasser declared. "I ain't gonna give you nothing. You knew he was leaving [and] didn't tell me."

Sasser eventually suggested that Mallie become a cook in his house, but she refused the offer because of her inability to arrange for child care. When she failed to accept another unattractive job offer, Sasser punished her.

He kicked her and the children out of their house, forcing them to move to a dilapidated property on the plantation. "I cried, but that did not do any good," she recalled. "So the neighbors came and helped me, [and] I got that fixed very nicely." But Sasser evicted her out of that one too, telling her she would have to move into "a house at the sawmill where lots of men lived."

Unable to bear the thought of rearing her children in such a cramped, dirty place full of men, Mallie resolved to leave the Sasser plantation for good. As she walked off the land, she lost her fair share—four bales of cotton, fifteen hogs, four barrels of syrup, and acres of peanuts, peas, beans, and potatoes—but not before delivering a biblical warning to Sasser: "Ye shall reap what ye sow."

"Well, I put my trust in God and moved," Mallie recalled. Though fraught with peril and uncertainty, walking away from Sasser left her feeling exhilarated and empowered, and she happily shared that taste of freedom in her prayers.

"No one, God, can outdo me," she prayed.

In her mind, she had successfully battled the forces of evil. "I was a lucky lady—out of the hands of the Devil," she said.

Mallie Robinson was free at last. And poor. Although she found work as a domestic among wealthy whites, living conditions were incredibly difficult for her and the children. Coupled with their horrible economic circumstances was a marked rise in racial violence throughout the South. The Ku Klux Klan was conducting terror campaigns with impunity, lynching was an accepted form of white justice, and race relations in the form of Jim Crow laws were increasingly vicious.

Mallie sensed nothing but a dangerous future in Georgia and believed that the time was ripe to escape the South. She became inspired all the more when her half brother, Burton Thomas, visited her and encouraged her to move to the land he had migrated to a number of years earlier. "If you poor Georgia folks want to get a little closer to heaven, come on out to California," he said.[6]

Mallie took his advice to prayer, and after long talks with God she resolved to put her faith in action again, this time by moving her young family about as far from the South as she could get without leaving the country. On May 21, 1920, an inspired Mallie and her five children, along with members of her extended family, headed to Cairo to catch a train to New Orleans and from there to California. She called it the Freedom Train.

Jerry Robinson, back in Cairo, was not pleased when he learned of the planned exodus. He was so upset that he called the local police and asked them to try to block Mallie's departure. The police were not accustomed to responding to requests from local blacks, but they could easily make an exception when asked to harass "uppity" blacks daring to leave behind white plantations and the Southern way of life. So they went to the station, kicked a few suitcases, and checked and double-checked tickets, but in the end they opted not to prevent Mallie and her children from boarding the midnight train. Deeply relieved, Mallie settled her tired children, including Jackie, one year and four months old, for the long trip west.

As an adult, Jackie marveled at his mother for demonstrating such faith-filled courage and resolve, describing her move to California as rooted in the same spirit that had liberated his father from virtual slavery. "This same spirit," he said, "gave her the courage to take her family out of the South, even though she was penniless and had no guarantee that she would be able to earn a living on the West Coast. In a sense, she was like those courageous pioneers who went into the West in search of a new life."[7]

Robinson had no doubt that his mother's quest for freedom had effectively transformed his life too. "I often wonder," he said, "what would have happened to the baby in whose ear she whispered on a January day in 1919, if she hadn't had that spirit—if she had been afraid to break away from a land of hopelessness and to go forth to a place where there was a better chance of survival."[8]

But she did have that spirit—a spirit of liberation fueled by her belief that God wants people to fight for their God-given freedom and equality, even if they must suffer along the way.

The Robinson clan certainly did not escape suffering when they arrived in Pasadena, California, in June 1920. Their first apartment had three rooms and a kitchen, but because they had to share the space with other relatives, Mallie and her five children slept in just one room. As the youngest, lucky Jackie got to share the bed with his mother, and the other children scattered here and there on the floor.

Three days after arriving, Mallie found employment as a domestic with a wealthy white family. Accustomed to working from sunup to sundown, she was shocked when she learned her work hours ran only from 8:00 a.m. to 4:00 p.m. But the job did not last long; the wealthy family soon moved away, and Mallie was deprived of her salary of eight dollars a week.

Desperate for work, she decided to place an employment advertisement in the *Pasadena Star-News*, and on the long walk there she stopped for directions in a building with a sign saying "Welfare." After Mallie described her situation, the woman behind the counter explained that not only could the welfare office help feed and clothe the Robinson children during this difficult period but also that Mallie could right then and there help herself to the clothes she needed. Shocked, relieved, and grateful, Mallie walked home wearing a fur-lined coat.

The welfare office helped considerably, but Mallie was a worker at heart, and it did not take her long to find stable employment with another white family, the Dodges, for whom she would work for the next twenty-seven years. With ongoing assistance from public welfare, she saved as much as she could, and just two years after arriving in Pasadena, Mallie became part owner of a large house at 121 Pepper Street. The house had five bedrooms, two baths, and, perhaps best of all, a yard with fruit trees and plenty of space for chickens and a garden.

One of the earliest struggles Mallie faced in the new home was getting Jackie, now around three years old, to stop sleeping with her in her first-floor bedroom. She tried offering him twenty-five cents a week to make the move upstairs, but Jackie was uncooperative, finding his mother's warmth too difficult to surrender. Characteristically, Mallie turned to prayer. "Lord," she said, "You never failed me yet. It's time for Jackie to stop being a baby."[9]

Not long after her prayer, according to Mallie, Jackie woke up in the middle of a nightmare. "Mama," he said, "I dreamed a man came through the window to steal me." Mallie prayed again, "Lord, you're answering my prayer," before telling Jackie, "The best thing for you is to go upstairs. Nobody could climb up there, and if they did, your brother Edgar is such a light sleeper he'd wake up." Little Jackie agreed, adding, "And Edgar's strong. He could knock out anyone."[10]

But a much larger problem than Jackie's sleeping preference loomed outside, in her pretty new neighborhood. While Mallie and her children were delighted with their new home, the neighbors on the all-white, working-class block were not.

Pasadena was no stranger to race-related tension in the 1920s. Jim Crow customs had established firm boundaries between blacks and whites. White-owned businesses, white-run trade unions, and white-friendly public policies made blacks into second-class citizens. One of the more painful policies experienced by the Robinsons was the Jim Crow rule that allowed blacks to swim in the public pool only one day a week, after which it would be drained and refilled for whites for the rest of the week. Pasadena's police department also firmly resisted calls to hire black officers, even though nearby communities had begun to shatter this barrier.

With Jim Crow on their backs, blacks in Pasadena knew their place and condition all too well: they were unemployed or underemployed, comparatively poor, and often segregated from whites. Blacks certainly knew they were not supposed to live on all-white blocks. But Mallie never cared much for customs or laws that trampled on her freedom, and she was not about to start doing so in her new life outside the South. So it was virtually unremarkable, at least to those who knew her well, when she boldly stepped over the red real estate lines drawn by Jim Crow.

She faced immediate and fierce resistance from many of her white neighbors. They initially sought to buy her out, but that plan failed miserably when Clara Coppersmith, the only person with the financial wherewithal to execute it, threw her support behind Mallie, who quickly made sure that the Robinson children did chores for Coppersmith without pay.

The neighbors, refusing to surrender, then burned a cross in the Robinsons' front yard, but that neither scared Mallie away nor forced her to restrict her children to the house and the yard. Fearful of blacks wandering freely, neighbors then called the police to report on the travels of the Robinson children. One of the neighbors even told the police that his wife was so afraid of blacks that she had not come out of their house since the Robinson family had moved into the neighborhood. When the white police officer passed this troubling news on to Mallie, she replied ever defiantly, "I'm afraid she'll be in that house a lifetime."[11]

Living at 121 Pepper Street, as far as Mallie was concerned, was nothing less than God's will for her life. "Take one step toward God, and he'll take two toward you" was one of her favorite expressions, and in her mind she had taken that one step when she had purchased the house. Having taken two steps toward her, God was now her constant companion as she endured the suffering caused by her neighbors, and because she felt God was always by her side, she also trusted that everything would one day be OK. Mallie Robinson's faith made her an eternal optimist.

With confidence in God, Mallie stayed put, demonstrating the importance of standing up for what is right, and even followed the biblical counsel to overcome evil with good, a tactic that proved relatively successful. Jackie Robinson biographer Arnold Rampersad suggests that the white residents of Pepper Street eventually accepted the Robinson family because of Mallie's generous response to their own economic needs. "At one point," he writes, "she even made the Robinson home a relief center," sharing leftovers that a local bakery and milkman regularly gave the Robinson family.[12] In the face of such free bounty, Mallie's neighbors found it increasingly difficult to demand that she leave the neighborhood.

That did not happen overnight, of course, and Mallie sometimes resorted to other methods, as she did when confronting a cranky neighbor who kept the balls that young Jackie and his friends accidentally kicked or hit into her yard. The neighbor insisted that all balls that landed in her yard were now her property. Mallie agreed that the boys had no business knocking the ball into the woman's yard, but she also called the wrath of God down upon her prickly neighbor. "You treat children this way," Mallie warned, "and one day God's going to knock you out of your senses."[13]

Mallie also made sure to fortify her children with racial pride. Underlying her own resolve to stay put on Pepper Street was a deep sense of confidence in the color of her skin—a fervent spiritual conviction that God had made her black, that God wanted her to be black, and that her divinely created blackness was a wholly positive characteristic. She sought to instill this same pride in her children so they could withstand the racist taunts and jeers that came their way on Pepper Street and elsewhere in Pasadena.

She bequeathed racial pride to her children mostly by modeling and teaching, with one of her more creative lessons centering on the story of Adam and Eve. In Mallie's telling, Adam and Eve were originally black but "turned pale" when God caught them eating the forbidden apple in the garden of Eden.[14] After God scared them so much they turned white as ghosts, Adam and Eve gave birth to two sons, one black and the other white. The skin color of the black child, of course, witnessed to God's original hopes for humanity.

Under Mallie's spiritual guidance, young Jackie grew proud of the color of his skin, believing that God had intentionally created him black and that his blackness was no reason for shame. Like his mother, Jackie also stood up for himself, though in different ways, in the face of discrimination and prejudice. At the age of eight, for example, he responded in kind to a girl from across the street who shouted "Nigger! Nigger! Nigger!" while he was sweeping the sidewalk.[15] The words stung sharply, and Jackie yelled back that she was "nothing but a cracker," a reply that prompted the girl's father to burst through their front door and engage in an hour-long rock battle with Jackie.[16]

Jackie did not seem inclined to kill his enemies with kindness. But Mallie continued on, determined to show Jackie another way, arguably a better way, and she eventually shared leftover baked goods and milk even with those who threw rocks at her children.

For young Jackie, Mallie Robinson was a model of strength, courage, resolve—and sacrifice. When there was little food to share among the family, and none to offer the neighbors, she would go without so that her children could eat. And when there was no food or money in the house, she would bite her lip and send Jackie and his sister Willa Mae to school without any lunches. "We would get to school so hungry we could hardly stand up, much less think about our lessons," Jackie later stated.[17] But their teachers at Cleveland Elementary School, Miss

Gilbert and Miss Haney, rose to the occasion and regularly offered Jackie and Willa Mae sandwiches for lunch.

Mallie continued to sacrifice, and on rare occasions she was able to offer her children something special. When Jackie graduated from Washington Junior High School in 1935, she celebrated his accomplishments with a special gift. As he recalled the occasion, it was "one of her happiest days . . . and through some miracle she was able to get me my first real suit." It was something Jackie had wanted, and his mother's surprise brought tears to his eyes. "I remember I cried a little when I saw it," he recalled, "and my mother said she always believed the Lord would take care of us. Right then and there I never stopped believing that."[18]

Education was important to Mallie, whose formal studies had stopped at sixth grade, and equally important was her children's religious education. Mallie made sure her children attended the local black church, Scott Methodist Church, so they could be instructed in the ways of faith. "She had me in Sunday school and church all the time," Jackie later recalled, "and she brought me up a Methodist."[19]

Her abiding hopes for all her children—that they would have faith and a solid education—were rooted in her own experiences with her father. As a slave in his childhood years, Washington McGriff had never learned to read. The lack of an education pained him, and as he grew older he dreamed of being able to read the Bible before he died. One day, he dared to share the dream with his young daughter, and when Mallie was just ten years old, she took it upon herself to give him reading lessons on the porch after school. That moving experience left her wanting to educate her own children, and to educate them in the ways of faith.

Jackie did not like attending church, and he told his mother so, suggesting that he could be a decent person without showing up for Sunday morning worship. But Mallie would have none of it. "If you plant a crop and don't cultivate it, nothing grows," she explained. "That's the way with religion; it dries up if you don't tend it." Nevertheless, Mallie was not overly forceful, and when the minister at Scott Methodist tried to arrange for Jackie to be baptized, she put the brakes on. "Jack's got to be sincere," she told her minister. "He's got to understand what this means and believe in it."[20]

In his teenage years, Jackie was more interested in the Pepper Street Gang than in formal religion. Not comparable to today's violent street gangs, the Pepper Street Gang consisted of youths from poorer

families—blacks, whites, Asians, and Hispanics—and their main purpose was to hang out together and, when not just standing around,
to engage in pranks and petty thefts. Their favorite targets were fruit
vendors and local groceries, places with food for growing boys.

As a leader of the gang, Jackie once enlisted his friends to spread
thick black tar all over the lawn of a holdout neighbor still giving the
Robinsons a tough time because of their skin color. When Mallie
learned of the prank, she was not pleased, to say the least. "God watches
whatever you do," she had often told him. "You must reap what you
sow, so sow well." And now Mallie herself had the perfect reaping in
mind: she demanded that Jackie and his friends remove the black tar
from the lawn. "How we going to get it off?" they complained. "I don't
care," Mallie said, "just get it off."[21] Like her watchful God, she super-
vised the scene as the boys cut the tarred blades with scissors or washed
them with kerosene and rags.

The pranks and thefts often landed members of the Pepper Street
Gang at the local police precinct, where Captain Hugh Morgan would
use his training in psychology to point the boys in a better direction.
Jackie first got to know the police precinct when he decided to protest
segregation at the community pool by swimming in the local reservoir,
forbidden territory for swimmers of any color.

As Jackie's confrontations with the police increased, so too did his
experiences with Jim Crow in Pasadena. Although an outstanding athlete at the integrated John Muir Technical High School, Jackie continued to experience racial segregation at the YMCA, which denied his
application for membership, and at local movie theaters, restaurants,
and businesses. Local whites enjoyed cheering for him on the sports
fields and courts, but many could still not stomach the thought of
admitting him to other shared public spaces.

Robinson, rather than exploding at the injustices, followed the example of his older brother Mack, who had placed second to Jesse Owens
in the 200-meter dash at the 1936 Berlin Olympics, and channeled
most of his anger into sports, excelling at football, basketball, track,
baseball, and tennis. In his senior year, the local newspaper reported
that there was no better athlete at Muir than Jack Roosevelt Robinson.

After graduating from Muir, Jackie enrolled at Pasadena Junior College, where the tuition was free, the facilities were integrated, and the
racial climate was relatively progressive. Jackie's athletic prowess attracted
national attention while he was a PJC student, but racial troubles continued to plague him in Pasadena's downtown. In January 1938, he

acquired a police record when he was arrested on charges stemming from an incident in which he and his friend Jonathan Nolan had angered a police officer. The details of the incident remain vague, but it seems Nolan's singing of "Flat-foot Floogie" had infuriated the officer, and the subsequent protests of the two young men resulted in a night in jail.

Yet again, Mallie was not pleased, and when she spotted Jackie walking home the next morning—she had hit the streets in search of him—she scolded him as if he were a grade-schooler. "You'd just as well bring me a switch," she said.[22] At home, Mallie picked up the phone and chewed out the police for not letting her know that Jackie was in jail all night.

Mallie worried about Jackie. She had done nearly everything she could. She had instructed him in her faith that God made all people free and equal. She had taught him about the helpfulness of constant prayer and an abiding trust that God would provide. She had stressed the importance of work and a solid education in and outside the church. She had instilled racial pride in him and showed him the value of overcoming evil with good. She had sacrificed for his material and emotional well-being and demonstrated that suffering could redeem individual lives and create freedom. She had passed along the virtues of courage and strength, perseverance and resolve, sacrifice and hope. She had even wielded the switch and thrown in a few divine threats here and there.

Jackie was not unmoved by all this. "Besides having faith in my mother," he later stated, "I came to realize through her that I had a lot of faith in God. I came to know that for sure when I was pretty young. There's nothing like faith in God to help a fellow who gets booted around once in a while."[23]

Still, Jackie worried Mallie. She feared, above all else, that his aggressive temperament would get the better of him in situations of racial injustice and that he would end up hurt. In fact, when she discovered that he had not slept in his bed and went looking for him, she found herself imagining that white students at a rival school had taken him "for a ride" in retribution for having lost both a basketball game and an on-court fight in which Jackie was the star player and fighter.[24] Her imagination turned out not to be true, but when Jackie was later sentenced to ten more days in jail, Mallie worried again, even though the presiding judge suspended her son's sentence.

But then something happened that eased her anxiety: Jackie found a best friend in the new minister of Scott Methodist Church. Her son's life was about to take a turn for the better.

2

"To Seek to Help Others"

The Spiritual Influence of Karl Downs

In January 1938, the Rev. Karl Downs stopped his car and rolled down the window at the street corner where Robinson and his friends were hanging out.

"Is Jack Robinson here?" he asked.[1]

No one answered.

Downs was only seven years older than Robinson, but he looked nothing like the Pepper Street Gang members. He was a natty dresser, the kind who wore business suits, and he had a scholarly appearance, with round glasses that heightened the effect.

He was also assertive.

"Tell him I want to see him at the junior church," he said before driving off.[2]

Karl Everett Downs was born into a pastoral home in Abilene, Texas, in 1912. His father, the Rev. John Wesley Downs, served as a minister and district superintendent for the Methodist Episcopal Church, and his mother, Lucretia Hollis Downs, made sure to steep young Karl and his nine siblings in both church and school.

Downs showed considerable talent as a student and earned a bachelor of arts degree at the all-black Samuel Huston College in Austin, Texas, where his interest in music suggested a promising career as an orchestra leader. But he chose the pulpit over the podium and earned a divinity degree from Gammon Theological Seminary in Atlanta.

While a Gammon student, Downs displayed his academic prowess and progressive politics by penning a sharply worded article for *The Crisis*, the main publication of the National Association for the Advancement of Colored People (NAACP). The pointed piece criticized college students, especially blacks, for being too timid when facing racial problems. "A downtrodden race, crushed by hardships of severity, looks ardently for its salvation to come from its best prepared men and women," Downs wrote. "The contemporary Negro students cannot hope to make any contribution to this cause unless they shake from their shoulders the shackles of timidity which have grown into their lives as a result of slavery's influence."[3]

Like other ambitious black seminarians from the South, Downs then traveled north to bolster his credentials at Boston University, where the social gospel movement, sparked by the writings of Walter Rauschenbusch, had found a welcoming home since the turn of the century. Rauschenbusch, a liberal Baptist theologian, had authored several influential books that called for Christians to leave behind a narrow focus on individual salvation in heaven and to start establishing peace and justice on earth. For Rauschenbusch and his followers, salvation was social, not just individual; it was about saving society, right here and now, from violence and economic injustice.

By the time Downs finished his master of sacred theology degree in 1937, he was theologically evangelical and socially progressive, reflecting both his black church tradition and the liberalism of Boston University.

Downs then became educational secretary of the Board of Missions of the Methodist Episcopal Church, a position that placed him in the company of nationally and internationally known Christian leaders, including the famous evangelist E. Stanley Jones, with whom he made plans to travel to India. The national position also gave Downs a number of public speaking opportunities, allowing him to polish skills that would serve him well when he accepted the pulpit at Scott Methodist Church.

He was just twenty-five years old when he became the minister at Scott, and it did not take long for Mallie Robinson to ask him to reach out to her son. Downs did not need a lot of encouraging, though, because his plans for the struggling church included a revived youth ministry that would richly benefit from Mallie's well-respected son.

Intrigued, Jackie Robinson showed up at junior church shortly after the awkward encounter at the street corner. Much to his delight, he discovered a young minister intent on tapping young people as the key resource for reviving the church. "The new minister immediately captured the imagination of the younger people because he himself was a young man," Robinson recalled.[4]

But it was not just his youth that Robinson found refreshing. "Of course, all of us know that just being young doesn't mean you are a progressive person," Robinson said. "I can testify that I have met some pretty narrow-minded young fogies. Karl Downs was just the opposite of that."[5]

Downs's progressivism faced a severe challenge a month or so after he arrived at Scott Church, when he traveled to Chicago for a conference on the future of faith and service, hosted by the United Methodist Council. The council's executive committee had asked Downs to represent Methodist youth before the four thousand attendees and to focus his speech on youth issues, not racial ones.

The committee had also instructed Downs to register at the Stevens Hotel, the location of the conference's headquarters. Although a friend had informed him that the hotel was for whites only, Downs was unable to square that troubling information with his knowledge that the Methodist Church had expressly prohibited meetings at places that practiced racial discrimination and segregation. So Downs and a white friend, Hayes Beall, reserved a room together at the hotel.

It was not intended to be a provocative act.

Beall arrived at the conference first, and the hotel clerk politely completed his reservation and granted him access to the room. But a different experience awaited Downs.

"When I called for my reservation by name and the number of my room, pandemonium broke out," he recalled.[6]

The Stevens Hotel was indeed for whites only, and the hotel staff, acting in accord with standard practices at the hotel, made numerous excuses about why it was impossible for them to give Downs his room. They could not state that race was the reason; that would expose them to a lawsuit. Nor could they claim the reserved room was otherwise occupied; Downs's white roommate had already secured the room for the two of them.

Excuses of different sorts kept coming, and Downs and his friends protested. "Each excuse was discounted upon legal and logical grounds, and the office was now in a delirium as to how they could get rid of me," he recounted.

But the hotel was expertly cunning. While the clerks dodged and delayed, maids and other workers changed the reserved room from one with twin beds to one with a double bed. With the change in place, the clerks announced: "Well, two persons cannot sleep in the same bed here unless they are married."

To make matters worse, a church leader arrived at the scene and criticized Downs in front of the hotel staff for trying to start something. "This hotel has been very nice to us," he declared. "They have given us what we wanted. We are satisfied, and you have no right to do this."

Downs was stung. "The prejudice of the hotel was not to be compared with the agony of the blow my own church leader had given me," he later stated. "Bowed in disgust and shame and seething with the human accompaniment of mental anguish, I retired from my friends as embarrassed as they were."

Downs lost the battle, left the hotel, and stewed about his next steps.

First he had to get control of his emotions. As he put it, "I had to fight back with all the 'strength of Calvary' the deep passion of hatred and despair which involuntarily boiled within me."

Next he had to figure out what to do at the conference. Should he walk out in protest? Should he recount the incident in his speech, lambasting church leaders who knowingly selected a hotel that would refuse to accommodate three hundred black delegates? Should he say nothing?

As he deliberated, Downs recounted a promise he had made to himself long before the conference: he would never allow racists or racial prejudice to defeat him.

But how should he fulfill that promise in this particular situation?

While he could easily lash out in his speech, he did not want to spoil the spirit of the conference for everyone else. Plus, even though his friends were pleading with him to share the incident publicly, he told them he had no inclination to play the role of a victimized minority. Downs also felt a keen obligation to fulfill the terms of his contract, to speak as a young Methodist, not as a black Methodist.

So the Rev. Karl Downs, the voice of young Methodism, delivered his speech without making any reference to the racism he had experienced the day before. The speech, "What We Expect of Our Church," earned him a standing ovation.

But Downs was no quietist. He took to the pen and wrote an article for *Zion's Herald*, a Boston Methodist weekly favored by progressive Methodists across the nation.

Downs said he had slept only two hours before his speech at the conference. "It was not the delivery of the speech that troubled me," he said, "but the fact that my church had led me into the agony of soul-piercing embarrassment due to the color of my skin."

The embarrassment was not warranted, according to Downs, because God had directly willed him to be a black man. As Downs put this, "No official information reached me stating that I, one of the conference speakers, whom God had willed to make a Negro, could not sleep in the hotel in Chicago."

Downs then recounted the details of the incident before faulting the church for being "timorous" in the face of racial injustice.

In its published reply to Downs, the editors of *Zion's Herald* applauded the young minister for suppressing his anger at the conference and focusing on the job at hand. "You were invited to speak in Chicago because the church recognized your ability, loved you," wrote the editors. "Its faith in you was justified—you 'made good.'"[7]

Time magazine and other national publications picked up the story, and not everyone was impressed with Downs's actions. William Jones, the managing editor of the *Baltimore Afro-American*, wrote: "It might have been more effective if the Rev. Mr. Downs had exploded, hurled the sting of religious hypocrisy into the teeth of the rest of the Christians who stood by and saw the preachment of the brotherhood and decency of human relations desecrated."[8]

Back in Pasadena, Downs probably shared the story with his congregation, emphasizing the importance of sometimes bearing one's cross in the short term in order to make an effective witness to justice in the long run. It was a strategic lesson of sacrifice and courage that would not be lost on Jackie Robinson, by now a strong supporter of the young minister.

Settling into parish ministry, Downs focused his renewed attention on attracting young people to the church, making sure to address not only their spiritual needs but also their social ones. "He started a campaign to interest the kids in the church," Robinson recalled. "He set up recreational activities within the church right on the premises; activities which brought us off the streets. Suddenly we found ourselves having dances at the church, playing on a new badminton court which was installed."[9] Scott Church also soon had a skating rink and a basketball court.

Downs's progressive ministry also sought to address the wider needs of the community. In an age when churches often ignored community needs, Downs steered his church to set up a day care, a social service ministry, and a library that loaned books and toys.

Downs also hosted interracial teas and staged a celebrity night that attracted black and white leaders known throughout the United States,

like Adam Clayton Powell Jr. of Harlem, and even the global community, like scientist Linus Pauling.

During his first year at Scott, Downs also increased his involvement with the NAACP. In June 1938 he married Marion Jackson, the
daughter of Keiffer and Lillie Jackson of Baltimore, one of the most
active and prominent families in the NAACP. A civil rights activist
with a fierce reputation, Lillie Jackson was president of the Baltimore
NAACP and worked closely with the branch's young lawyer, Thurgood Marshall, on a landmark case attacking unequal pay for black
teachers in Maryland.

Five months after his wedding, Downs spoke at the annual meeting
of the NAACP, and in a preview to his speech, the *Baltimore Afro-
American*, once critical of him, reported that since the incident in Chicago, "the Rev. Mr. Downs has been hailed as the most promising
and potent young minister today." Downs delivered a speech titled
"Wanted, Revolutionists."[10]

Downs's activism was deeply attractive to Robinson, and he began
spending much more time at Scott Church. The young minister
enlisted him to teach Sunday school, and Robinson continued in that
role even when attending Pasadena Junior College and then UCLA.
"There were so many Saturdays after a football game that my body was
so sore and aching that I didn't believe I'd be able to get out of bed on
Sunday morning and go to church and teach my class," he said. "But
you didn't let Karl down and I always made it."[11]

This experience gave Robinson a sense of purpose and transformed
him into a mentor.

He began to form a special bond with Downs. "He was more than a
pastor to me," Robinson later claimed. "He was my very close friend."
The two grew so close that he began to call Downs by his first name,
not a common practice among parishioners and pastors at this point.

Robinson respected not only Downs's activism but also his competitive character. "He had strong, vigorous ideas and the will to win," he said,
expressing pleasure that Downs's competitive streak motivated him to
outwit older Scott members who wanted their church to remain the same.

Robinson also appreciated Downs's approachability:

> I recall so many times when Rev. Downs and I went to the golf links
> together.
>   "Jack," he would say, "You know I can't beat you—but I've got
> to 'bound' you."

So we'd "bound" our dime—or something small like that. I didn't really have any money, and neither did he. But I've never had so much fun on a golf course—and I've been on plenty of them since then—as I did with my minister.

He never forgot he was a minister—not even when we were deeply engaged in golf, badminton or church dances. He was always finding a way to apply something that happened to the Bible or the Golden Rule. You had to respect him and you had to listen intently to everything he said. You see, he wasn't speaking from the outside, not viewing you from a holy distance. He was right in there with you, competing, beating you, getting beat—and proving all the while that the Christian life doesn't have to be dull or colorless. You could have fun and be a good person too. You didn't have to disappear behind some dark and dreary casement in order to be a worthwhile individual.

By his own account, Robinson felt free in Downs's presence, free to be himself and share his deepest thoughts. "Often when I was deeply concerned about personal crises, I went to him," Robinson said. "We had a lot of long talks which affected me deeply."

In one of those talks, Robinson expressed frustration with having to watch his mother work so hard for so little material reward while he attended college, largely unable to help alleviate her financial difficulties. "When I talked with Karl about this and other problems, he helped ease some of my tensions," he stated. "It wasn't so much what he did to help as the fact that he was interested and concerned enough to offer the best advice he could."[12]

Downs's effect on Robinson was spiritually significant. Arnold Rampersad, in his 1997 biography of Robinson, describes how Downs served as a father figure and became the channel through which religious faith "finally flowed into Jack's consciousness and was finally accepted there, if on revised terms, as he himself reached manhood. Faith in God then began to register in him as both a mysterious force, beyond his comprehension, and a pragmatic way to negotiate the world."[13]

But faith also began to register in Robinson as a social force capable of making one's local community, and the wider world, a better place. By protesting indentured servitude and then leaving Georgia, Mallie Robinson had taught her son the importance of struggling for one's God-given freedom. Downs supported that important lesson by showing Robinson that religion can be a resource for advancing justice for the downtrodden.

With Downs leading the way, Robinson now understood that faith was not only about praying; it was also about struggling daily to overcome social injustices and free the oppressed wherever they might be.

Robinson drew several more important life lessons from his time with Downs, and later in life he recounted them in detail.

> By deed as well as word, with friendship and companionship, Karl taught me to work for several things:
>   To be able to recognize God as the vital force in life.
>   To develop one's own self to the best of one's own ability.
>   Not only to stay out of evil—but to try to get into good.
>   To seek to help others without thinking so much of what we will get out of it, but what we are putting into it.[14]

Downs shared one more important lesson with his younger friend: that his dark skin was a gift from God. Downs strongly reinforced Mallie's lesson about racial pride, often teaching his congregation that "to be born black is more than to be persecuted; it is to be privileged."[15] God had deliberately created individuals to be black, and this act of divine creation was to be honored and celebrated.

Robinson carried that lesson with him the rest of his life. Perhaps it helped fuel his temper in September 1939, just before he was to enter UCLA, when a white man pulled up next to Robinson's car and referred to him and his friends as "niggers."

Ray Bartlett, who was riding on a running board of Robinson's car, leaned over and struck the man in the face with his baseball glove. As the man sped off, Robinson followed him to a stop and jumped out of the car, prepared to fight. But when a crowd of black youths began to form, the white man suddenly declared he was not interested in starting something and then drove off.

This did not end the situation.

A white police officer, John C. Hall, appeared on the scene and began trying to make arrests.

Robinson's friends slipped into the crowd when they saw the officer, but Robinson held his ground, refusing to skulk away.

Officer Hall pulled his gun. "I found myself up against the side of my car, with a gun barrel pressed unsteadily into the pit of my stomach," Robinson recalled. "I was scared to death."[16]

Robinson spent the night in jail, charged with resisting arrest and blocking traffic, and the officers on duty did not allow him to make any telephone calls. Help eventually came in the form of UCLA officials who arranged for Robinson to plead guilty in absentia, paid his fine for being absent, and secured a suspended sentence.

"I got out of that trouble because I was an athlete," Robinson recalled.[17]

Of course, he had also gotten into it because he was a proud, young black man who would not back down in the face of a racist jeer. That was characteristically Jackie Robinson, and when he strolled through the UCLA campus, it was clear to all who saw him that he was eminently comfortable in his skin.

With ongoing encouragement from his mentor Karl Downs, Robinson became the first four-letter man at UCLA, competing in football, basketball, baseball, and track. Along the way, the strikingly handsome athlete also caught the attention of many young women on campus, and in his senior year those admirers included first-year student Rachel Anetta Isum.

Isum, just seventeen years old, commuted to campus in an old Ford V-8 from her family home on 36th Place, a white-framed cottage in a racially integrated neighborhood. Growing up, she had experienced racial discrimination at the local movie theater and hamburger joint, but for the most part she had felt safe and comfortable in her surroundings, and especially in her church, Bethel African Methodist Episcopal Church.

"The church was central to our social activities," she recalled. Isum attended Sunday school, sang in the choir, and enjoyed more than a few church dinners. Bethel was her home away from home. "It wasn't something where you needed to have money or any social resources," she remembered. "It was available to you even as a non-religious thing."[18]

The church even served a role in Isum's budding romance with her high school boyfriend, Eddie, a tall and kind young man who faithfully walked her home from school. "I let Eddie kiss me only when he had met my two terms: I had to be sixteen, and he had to join my church," she explained. "I was sixteen, and he joined Bethel AME on 35th Street, so I let him kiss me. That's what I was like in those days!"[19]

Isum excelled as a student, and a local civic group awarded her a scholarship for university studies.

At nearby UCLA in the fall of 1940, she quickly discovered that her fellow black students, few in number, tended to hang out in Kerckhoff Hall, where Robinson held a part-time maintenance job. Isum could not help but notice him. "He was big, he was broad-shouldered, he was very attractive physically, and he had pigeon toes you couldn't miss," she recalled.[20]

There was something else she found intensely attractive. "He was clearly comfortable and proud of being a black man," she said. "In the 1940s I was very impressed by that fact. Not all of us could carry our racial identity with such pride."[21]

"Jack displayed his color by wearing white shirts," she said. "There was a kind of dignity about him and a sense of purpose that attracted me."[22]

Isum was too shy to break through the crowd that regularly gathered around Robinson, so she often arrived at the commuter parking lot early, hoping to spot him and arrange to have their paths cross. Before too long, Jackie's good friend Ray Bartlett introduced them, and much to her surprise, she sensed they shared a similar characteristic.

"I was extremely shy but I was rather pleased to see that he was also shy in that encounter," she explained. "However, my impression of him was that he had great self-confidence, and I was pleased to see that he was not arrogant. It's a trait I detest."[23] Isum had been concerned about that because when she had first spotted Robinson, during his football days back at Pasadena Junior College, she had imagined him as cocky and conceited, mostly because he stood on the sidelines with his hands on his hips.

Isum was not the only one struck in that first encounter. "I was immediately attracted to Rachel's looks and charm," Robinson remembered. But there was also something else that captured his attention. "When she left," he said, "I walked to the parking lot with her. She made me feel at ease, and I thoroughly enjoyed talking with her."[24]

Their easy conversations continued, and before long the two were seeing each other every day. In spite of their notable differences—Rachel was a serious nursing student, and Robinson was focused on sports—the two felt a deep connection. "There are few people it is easy for me to confide in," Robinson recalled, "but when I was with Rae I was delighted to find that I could tell her anything. She was always understanding and, beyond that, very direct and honest with me."[25]

Rachel and Jackie had similar values, and both had been reared in the church. That point was not lost on her mother, Zellee, when Rachel introduced her to Robinson. According to Arnold Rampersad, "Jack immediately won Zellee over; she saw him from the start as a gentle person, a gentleman, serious and religious, as well as handsome."[26]

Rachel had a similar effect on Mallie Robinson. "She thought of me the way my mother thought of Jack," Rachel said. "Here's a girl in the church, she doesn't drink or smoke, a good student, going into nursing, no other boyfriends."[27]

Jackie knew there was something special about Rachel, and the death of her father brought them closer together.

"It wasn't until her father died in 1940 that I realized I was deeply in love with her. Rae's deep grief had a profound effect on me," he said. "In this time of sorrow we found each other and I knew then that our relationship was to be one of the most important things in my life no matter what happened to me."[28]

But the bond between Jackie and Rachel, no matter how special or significant, could not keep him from leaving UCLA before he earned his diploma. The impatient Robinson had other things on his mind.

3

"You Are a Child of God"

Refusing the Back of the Bus

In early March 1941, Robinson quit college during his senior year at UCLA.[1] He had used up his eligibility in football and basketball and chose to forgo his eligibility in baseball and track. He was keenly aware of the limited opportunities for young black men in professional sports or anywhere else, regardless of whether they had a college degree. Robinson also felt it was necessary to provide financial support for his mother, Mallie.[2] His decision to leave UCLA was opposed by Mallie, Rachel, Karl Downs, his coaches, and university administrators.[3]

Robinson, who had majored in physical education, sought coaching jobs and was hired by the National Youth Association (NYA) to be an assistant athletic director on the campus of California Polytechnic Institute in San Luis Obispo, California. The NYA, which had been created by the Franklin Roosevelt administration as part of the Works Progress Administration, provided relief, jobs, and job training for people between the ages of sixteen and twenty-five.

Robinson trained NYA workers, many of whom came from underprivileged, single-parent homes and had experienced brushes with the law. He saw himself in some of the young men. "I realized that I had been no different from many of these kids, who would make good if given half a chance," he said.[4] Robinson found the work rewarding, but the job did not last. It appeared to be only a matter of time before the United States would enter World War II. The NYA was no longer viable. The war industry needed workers, and the army needed young men.[5]

Robinson again found his options limited. He might have been one of the best athletes in the country, but he was a black athlete. Professional football and baseball enforced unwritten gentlemen's agreements prohibiting blacks. Many semiprofessional leagues allowed integrated competition but paid low wages. Robinson began playing semiprofessional football in Honolulu, Hawaii, where he also did construction work near Pearl Harbor.

He left Hawaii on December 5, 1941, two days before the Japanese bombing there forced the United States into World War II, and began working at Lockheed Aircraft near Los Angeles. Back home with his mother on Pepper Street, he regularly saw Rachel, who was still attending UCLA.[6]

Robinson waited for his draft notice. He was no different from millions of other Americans who wanted to avenge the Japanese bombing on Pearl Harbor.[7] "Jack fully shared the outrage that most of America felt about the attack," Rachel remembered. "At that time he was a patriotic man and felt that he, as much as any American, owed it to his country to fight for freedom."[8]

Other black Americans felt differently. Bayard Rustin, who would become the main strategist of the modern civil rights movement, spent the war years in jail after informing his draft board that both conscription and war were inconsistent with the nonviolent teachings of Jesus. As a Christian pacifist, Rustin refused to submit to the draft, let alone to fight and kill anyone. Unlike the Quaker Rustin, Robinson did not take his cue from the nonviolence of Jesus. Love your enemies, turn the other cheek, put away your sword—this was not the type of counsel that Robinson turned to when considering his duty in the face of threats posed by Japan and Nazi Germany. He clung instead to his spiritual belief in human freedom and the need, if necessary, to fight to preserve it.

But Robinson was just like Rustin in another sense: Both were deeply troubled by a government that asked African Americans to fight for freedom abroad while denying them the same at home. The United States entered World War II partly to end racism in Europe, but while Americans fought against Germany and Japan, the country paid little attention to the racism on its home front, where blacks faced discrimination in all areas of life, including the military. African American leaders openly criticized this hypocrisy and said that if blacks were going to put their lives on the line for their country, the country should treat them as it would any other citizen—with equal justice under law.

The *Pittsburgh Courier*, the influential black newspaper, launched the "Double V" campaign that called for victory in the war but also a victory against racial discrimination in the United States.[9] Editors at the main publication of the National Association for the Advancement of Colored People (NAACP), *The Crisis*, weighed in, too. "Be it said once more that black Americans are loyal Americans," the editors wrote, "but let there be no mistake about the loyalty, it is loyalty to the democratic ideas as enunciated by America. . . . If all the people are called to gird and sacrifice for freedom, and the armies to march for freedom, then it must be for freedom for everyone, everywhere, and not merely for those under the Hitler heel."[10]

The government paid little attention. The army and navy enlisted blacks, but blacks were given little chance for promotion. German prisoners of war were allowed to drink from the same water fountains as white US soldiers; black soldiers were relegated to segregated water fountains. Black newspapers reported that the Red Cross would not accept blood from black soldiers.

Black soldiers were also sometimes shot to death by military police officers or by local police officers in towns where the soldiers were stationed. When a white police officer struck a black soldier with a nightstick in Alexandria, Louisiana, in January 1942, a riot ensued and twelve black soldiers were shot.[11] A sheriff in Centerville, Mississippi, ended a dispute between a black soldier and a white military police officer by shooting and killing the soldier.[12]

Walter White, executive secretary of the NAACP, said the discrimination and violence against blacks sent a destructive lesson to the country's white children, who were taught that the country was fighting a war for democracy. America, White said, "could not play the Star-Spangled Banner without using the black and white keys."[13]

In mid-March, Herman Hill, a correspondent for the *Pittsburgh Courier*, asked the Chicago White Sox, who spent spring training in Pasadena, if they would give a tryout to Robinson and a Negro league pitcher, Nate Moreland. Robinson impressed White Sox manager Jimmy Dykes. "I would welcome Negro players on the Sox," he said, "and so would all the other managers in the major leagues." Dykes, however, also said that baseball had an "unwritten law" that prohibited blacks. In a subsequent article, Hill wrote that Dykes had refused to pose for photographs with Robinson and Moreland and that "several White Sox players hovered around menacingly with bats in their hands."[14]

Robinson was drafted into the US Army on March 23, 1942, and sent to Fort Riley, Kansas, where he distinguished himself on the firing range. He was introduced to heavyweight champion Joe Louis. After Robinson told Louis that no black had ever been admitted to Officer Candidate School at Fort Riley, Louis interceded with the War Department, and Robinson and several other African Americans were commissioned second lieutenants. Robinson became a platoon leader and the unit's morale officer. He used his position as morale officer to confront segregation on the base. At one point he engaged in a shouting match over the phone with a white major over why blacks were not allowed access to the post exchange (PX).[15]

When Robinson showed up to play on the camp baseball team, he was told that he would have to play on the black team. Pete Reiser, who would later be Robinson's teammate on the Brooklyn Dodgers, was on the field with the white ballplayers and remembered seeing Robinson being turned away. "This was the first time I saw Jackie Robinson," Reiser said. "I can still see him slowly walking away."[16]

He was asked to play on the Fort Riley football team. But Robinson was told before a game against the University of Missouri that he had been given a two-week leave to go home, even though he had not requested one. When Robinson returned, he learned that the University of Missouri would not play the Fort Riley team if it had a black player. Robinson, furious at the army's duplicity, quit the team.[17] His commanding officer told Lieutenant Robinson he could be ordered to play. Robinson responded that he could be ordered to play, but he could not be ordered to play well.[18]

Robinson, as it turned out, did not play because of an ankle injury first suffered while playing football for Pasadena Junior College. His ankle developed a bone chip, which caused the joint to occasionally lock up. It was aggravated by sustained and vigorous physical activity, and required frequent visits to the hospital during his two and a half years in the army.[19]

In early 1944, Robinson, now a cavalry officer, was transferred to Camp Hood, forty miles southwest of Waco, Texas, where he was assigned to a segregated tank unit, the 761st Tank Battalion. There may have been no other military bases more segregated and surrounded by towns more hostile to black soldiers than Camp Hood.[20] Black soldiers lived in the least desirable section of the camp and faced Jim Crow conditions. If they went off base, they found Jim Crow customs and laws rigidly enforced by local police, who used whatever means they thought necessary. "Segregation there was so complete," one black officer said, "I even saw outhouses marked 'White,' 'Colored,' and 'Mexican'; this was on federal property."[21]

Robinson's rank did not spare him the indiginities of racial discrimination. Neither did regulations that banned segregated seating on military buses. On July 6, 1944, a month after the D-day invasion in France, Robinson was returning from the military hospital when a bus driver ordered him to the back of the bus. Robinson, who knew about the federal policy ending segregation, did not move. An argument with the driver followed. Things escalated when the bus stopped at its next stop. The military police (MP) escorted Robinson to the police station for further investigation.

When Robinson and the MPs approached the station to meet with the camp's assistant provost marshal, a white MP, hearing about the confrontation, inquired whether they had "the nigger lieutenant" with them. Robinson exploded with rage, threatening to "break in two" anyone who referred to him with that word. Inside the station, the proud Robinson reportedly interrupted when the assistant provost marshal discussed the issue with witnesses without seeking comment from him. Robinson was accused of showing disrespect toward a superior officer and failing to obey a superior officer's command.[22]

Robinson believed he had done nothing wrong, given the regulations that allowed him to sit where he wanted on the bus. Secondly, he was an officer and felt he deserved to be treated as one.

Robinson was arrested and then court-martialed for insubordination. If found guilty, he would be sent to a military prison. It meant little that Robinson had army regulations on his side. To the white bus driver, the white military policemen, the assistant provost marshal, and the army, Robinson was just another uppity black man.

Robinson and others contacted the NAACP, and the *Pittsburgh Courier* and other black newspapers published editorials and articles on his behalf. This might have prevented Robinson, a well-known athlete, from being found guilty, but it did not save him from going on trial and sitting in a courtroom with shackles on his hands and legs.[23]

And yet, as he faced trial and sat in the courtroom, he remained confident that things would work out because of the deep faith in God that his mother had instilled in him. God would take care of him, Mallie had told him since he was a boy. Rachel remembered that her mother-in-law's faith had left a deep impression on Jackie. According to Rachel, Mallie told her son, "You are a child of God, made in God's image. Because God is there, nothing can go wrong with you. You can allow yourself to take risks because you just know that the Lord will not allow you to sink so far that you can't swim."

That spiritual lesson mattered to Robinson during his court-martial. As Rachel recalled, "An ordeal like the court-martial was a sign to Jack that God was testing him. And Jack just knew he would respond well, he would come through, because he was a child of God. His faith in God was not very articulate, but it was real, and it did not allow for much doubt."

The white witnesses who testified against him appeared incredulous that Robinson would be offended by being called a "nigger." In his testimony, Robinson recalled that his grandmother, Mallie's mother, who had been born a slave, told him that a "nigger" was "a low, uncouth person." Robinson said he objected to being called one by the MP. "I am a negro," Robinson said, "but not a nigger."

At the end of the four-hour trial, Robinson's defense counsel insisted that he was innocent of all charges. The case was, Robinson recalled, "simply a situation in which a few individuals sought to vent their bigotry on a Negro they considered 'uppity' because he had the audacity to seek to exercise rights that belonged to him as an American and as a soldier."

Robinson was acquitted of all charges, and the court-martial made him more determined than ever to confront racial discrimination. By the time Robinson was acquitted in August, the 761st Tank Battalion had left for Europe, where they distinguished themselves and suffered heavy casualties in the Battle of the Bulge. The court-martial had been a dehumanizing experience for Robinson. But it saved him from going to Europe. It also made it possible for him to be playing in the Negro leagues when Rickey was looking for someone to confront segregation in baseball.

In late November, Robinson, almost twenty-six years old, was discharged from the army and wondering what he would do next. "Prodigiously gifted as an athlete, with a fierce will to succeed, he was yet without a vocation or a profession or a skill that could be marketed easily in a nation divided by race and indifferent or hostile to its black citizens and their dreams," Rampersad wrote. "Robinson was still drifting, drifting still largely at the mercy of fate and the whims and wishes of whites, even as he continued to nurture the faith that he yet might be destined by God for something great."

Robinson then wrote to Thomas Y. Baird, owner of the Kansas City Monarchs, asking if he could play for the American Negro League team. Baird offered him $400 a month, if he could make the team. He told Robinson to report to spring training with the Monarchs in Houston, Texas, in April.

At the beginning of 1945, Robinson was living in Texas, working for Karl Downs, who had left Pasadena to become president of Samuel Huston College in Austin, a black school affiliated with the Methodist Church. The college was struggling to enroll enough students to stay in business. But Downs was able to raise money for the school with help from a local congressman, Lyndon Johnson, a segregationist who believed in the vitality of black colleges, in part no doubt to keep colleges segregated. "The college was a ghost," a newspaper later reported, "and it was Downs's duty to give this dead institution life and meaning in the community."

To help accomplish this objective, Downs hired Robinson, the heralded college athlete. "Bringing Jackie Robinson to campus was vintage Karl Downs," one of Downs's friends said. "It was the same spirit that led him to put in a visiting artists program that brought in all sorts of celebrated musicians, and that in turn made some very influential local whites take note of our little college. Nothing like that ever happened before Karl came."

Downs hired Robinson to teach physical education at the college. Robinson introduced the first physical education program in the school's history and coached the school's basketball team. The experience was a highly positive one for Robinson, and he left with some reluctance to join the Kansas City Monarchs for spring training.

Robinson had a national reputation as an athlete as he departed for the Monarchs, but he had not played baseball since his junior year at UCLA, when he hit .097. Nevertheless, in his first year of professional baseball, he was fortunate enough to become part of one of the most storied teams in the Negro leagues. The Monarchs roster included Leroy "Satchel" Paige, Hilton Smith, "Double Duty" Ratcliffe, and manager John "Buck" O'Neil.

Black sportswriters covered the Negro leagues, but they also simultaneously called for the end of the color line in white professional baseball. These sportswriters probably knew that if the color line was broken in white baseball, it would sound a death knell for black baseball because many of its best players would leave for white baseball.[24]

Sportswriters Wendell Smith, Sam Lacy, Joe Bostic, and others campaigned for the integration of baseball for several years, but the white baseball establishment ignored them. In April, Bostic, the sports editor of the *People's Voice*, which was published in Harlem, refused to be ignored any longer. He showed up at the Brooklyn Dodgers' spring training camp in Bear Mountain, New York, demanding a tryout for two aging Negro leaguers, Terris McDuffie and Dave "Showboat" Thomas.

Branch Rickey, Brooklyn's team president, was livid about the confrontation because it was done publicly. Rickey also did not like that Bostic was accompanied by Nat Low, a sportswriter with the Communist newspaper *The Daily Worker*. Rickey hated surprises, and he hated communism more. If Rickey allowed the tryout, Bostic and the Communists would make names for themselves. If he rejected it, he would be criticized as an obstructionist. Both players were given try-outs, but neither was young enough nor talented enough for Rickey to be interested.[25]

Bostic was not alone in his efforts. Isadore Muchnick, a Jewish councilman in Boston, told the city's major-league teams, the Red Sox and the Braves, that if they did not engage in a good-faith effort to consider black players, he would revoke the teams' Sunday permits, prohibiting them from playing. When Wendell Smith learned that Muchnick was putting pressure on the Boston teams, he volunteered to bring black prospects to Boston. Smith selected established Negro leaguers Sam Jethroe and Marvin Williams for the tryout. He also handpicked Jackie Robinson, who had not yet played a game in black baseball.[26]

The Red Sox ignored Muchnick, Smith, and the ballplayers when they showed up in Boston. Smith said that he and the players would remain in the city until the team gave the players the tryout they were promised. "We consider ourselves pioneers," Robinson told Smith. "Even if they don't accept us, we are at least making the way easier for those who follow. We want to help make that day a reality."[27]

On April 12, the Red Sox allowed the players into Fenway Park. The team, however, made it clear that while it could be pressured into giving a tryout, nothing could force them to sign black players. A white Boston sportswriter who sat in the bleachers said that he heard someone, perhaps owner Tom Yawkey, holler: "Get those niggers off the field!"[28]

High school pitchers threw batting practice to Jethroe, Williams, and Robinson. Wendell Smith called it demeaning.[29] Robinson agreed. "It would be difficult to call it a tryout because they had these kids throwing," he said. "I sort of laughed within myself at what I felt was the uselessness of the venture. I didn't feel anything would come of it." None of the ballplayers heard from the Red Sox, and Robinson returned to the Monarchs, angry and more discouraged than ever about blacks playing in the major leagues anytime soon.[30]

Robinson was aware that his teammates had played baseball much longer than he had and sought them out for advice on how to adapt his game to the faster tempo of the Negro leagues. " 'Look, I'm here to learn. I know I don't play the brand of baseball you guys play. But help me, I'm here to learn," he told Sammie Haynes. Once, on a crowded bus, he impressed his teammates by sitting on the stairwell. "This is my seat," he said, "I'm a rookie."[31]

Robinson, however, was quickly disenchanted with the business of black baseball. He was used to the discipline and structure of college sports. He found himself trying to adjust to schedules and rosters that were subject to change, sometimes on a daily basis. Teams traveled by bus, often playing two or more games in a day, and the Jim Crow conditions made finding a place to sleep or eat problematic.

"There was no hotel in many of the places we played. Sometimes there was a hotel for blacks, which had no eating facilities. No one even thought of trying to get accommodations in white hotels," Robinson remembered. "Some of the crummy eating joints would not serve us at all. You could never sit down to a relaxed hot meal. You were lucky if they magnanimously permitted you to carry out some greasy hamburgers in a paper bag with a container of coffee. You were really living when you were able to get a plate of cold cuts."[32]

Robinson, who did not smoke or drink, hated the carousing lifestyle of the Negro leagues, and much to the amazement or perhaps consternation of his teammates, refused the alcohol and accommodating women on the road. "His sense of self was tightly wound around core values of dignity and self-esteem, and he believed in God and the Bible," Rampersad wrote about Robinson. "Absurdly or not, he drew a line in the dirt between himself and sin, and tried not to cross it."[33]

Robinson's teammates, including Sammie Haynes, who often roomed with Robinson, grew tired of Robinson extolling the virtues of Rachel Isum. "Well," Haynes said, "have you been to bed with the woman?" Robinson replied he had not. Haynes was astounded. "Are you going to marry somebody you haven't been to bed with? Are you crazy?" Robinson held his ground. "Sammie, this is the lady for me. I don't have to go to bed with her." Haynes then responded, "Man, this thing's crazy. You're crazy."[34]

Robinson, given his unimpressive statistics at UCLA, responded well to the Negro leagues, hitting .345 with the Monarchs and making the East-West all-star game. But he was distant to his fellow players, and his temper flared with teammates, opponents, and umpires. "It was hard to anticipate seeing any black player crack the major leagues, and with Jack's temper being the way it was, it didn't seem likely that a major league team would be willing to take a chance with him," said Quincy Trouppe, who played in the Negro leagues against Robinson.[35]

Most of the Negro leaguers accepted segregation. Robinson did not, whether in baseball or in anything else, and he would tell his team-mates that it would not be long before blacks were accepted into the major leagues.[36] Even before Robinson played his first game with the Monarchs, Wendell Smith and Sam Lacy agreed that Robinson had the qualities to play in the major leagues.[37] He was a devout Christian who would be unlikely to waste his opportunity on alcohol or risky behavior. He was educated, and his self-respect was readily apparent.

Branch Rickey, the archly conservative owner of the Brooklyn Dodgers, was on the move at this point, quietly searching to sign black players. He contacted Wendell Smith and asked him to provide updates on Robinson's performance with the Monarchs. Smith and Rickey exchanged telegrams, referring to Robinson as "the young man from the West." Rickey was told of Robinson's temper and expressed that concern to Smith. "I didn't want to tell Mr. Rickey, 'Yes, he's tough to get along with.' A lot of us knew that." Smith told Robinson that Rickey was scouting him for a new Negro league team. He told Robinson to "watch himself."[38]

By August 1945, Robinson was sick of the Negro leagues and decided he would not play again after the season ended. He would return to California, marry Rachel, and perhaps find a job as a high school coach.

But on August 24, as Robinson was sitting out a game in Chicago with a sore shoulder, a white man introduced himself as Clyde Sukeforth. He said he was there on behalf of Branch Rickey of the Brooklyn Dodgers, and that Rickey was starting a team, the Brooklyn Brown Dodgers, in a new black league. Robinson and Sukeforth talked more after the game. He told Robinson that Rickey wanted a meeting with him.

On August 28, Sukeforth met Robinson outside of Rickey's office in Brooklyn. History was about to change.[39]

PART TWO

A Boundary-Breaking Faith

4

"I Have Kept My Promise"

Branch Rickey and the Push for Integration

Wesley Branch Rickey was born December 20, 1881, in rural Stock-dale in Scioto County in southeastern Ohio, not far from the Ohio River. Religion played a part in his name, as it played a part in seemingly everything in his life. His parents, Jacob Franklin Rickey and the former Emily Brown, named their son Wesley after the founder of Methodism. John Wesley preached that it was the practice of Methodism to serve the poor and the less fortunate. Emily Rickey taught her son Wesley's words: "Having, first, gained all you can, and secondly, saved all you can, then give all you can."[1]

Rickey's middle name came from Isaiah 11:1 in the Hebrew Scriptures: "A shoot shall come out from the stump of Jesse, and a branch shall grow out of his roots." Rickey biographer Lee Lowenfish suggests that the name also might have come from John 15:2 in the New Testament: "He removes every branch in me that bears no fruit. Every branch that bears fruit he prunes to make it bear more fruit." When Rickey was a teenager, he began using his middle name because he liked it and because it distinguished him from a cousin named Wesley.[2]

The Rickeys believed that God would take care of their family. If that was true, God did it just barely. Frank Rickey was a vegetable farmer who toiled long hours on unforgiving soil, often making just enough money to pay his bills and feed his growing family. Frank—unlike his wife, who came to her faith naturally—long struggled with religion. He was raised a Baptist but converted to Methodism because

51

he found being a Baptist as unforgiving as the soil he farmed. Frank reminded his family that they owed what they had to God. "The Lord is the head of this house," he said before meals.[3]

Branch Rickey owed his spiritual guidance, however, to his mother. Before Branch could read, Emily taught him story after story from Scripture. As Rickey grew into boyhood, the Bible stories continued, reinforcing, as Lowenfish put it, "the belief that there was a right way and a wrong way to live." Emily had an abiding faith that her son was capable of achieving great things, for himself but also for his community and for God.[4]

This required that God come first. Rickey, in deference to God, did not attend baseball games on Sundays, whether as a player, manager, general manager, or team president. Rickey said he was brought up a Methodist and taught that Sunday belonged to the Lord.

In 1930, the *St. Louis Globe-Democrat* quoted Rickey as saying he did not have any objections to Sunday baseball himself. "But my good mother had," he said, "and she made me promise when I first became a professional player that I would never play on Sunday. I have kept my promise."[5] Lowenfish doubted the veracity of the quote. "Regardless of what Rickey may have told the *Globe-Democrat* in 1930 or what that writer put down," he said, "I don't think Emily Rickey ever told him outright not to work on Sunday. He thought it was a way of honoring her religious spirit."[6]

Rickey embraced faith at an early age and never let go of it, and because of the intensity of that faith, he stood out from his classmates in school and then at Ohio Wesleyan, a Methodist university that required attendance at chapel. Many of his classmates went unwillingly to chapel, but "it thrilled Rickey," his biographer Murray Polner wrote. Whenever Rickey found himself in stressful circumstances, whether as a child or an adult, he turned to the Bible.[7]

Frank and Emily Rickey were not formally educated themselves but saw to it that their children were. The education of all the Rickey children began with the Bible. Frank bought several volumes of books at a fire sale and brought them home to his family. The collection included a book of illustrated drawings by a French artist, Gustave Doré, a lay Christian preacher. "Dore's graphic representations of biblical struggles and his depictions of stormy and heavenly skies," Lowenfish wrote, "would remain permanently imbedded in Branch Rickey's consciousness."[8]

Unlike Jackie Robinson's father, who left his son with nothing but a name, Rickey's father helped make his son into the man he became. Rickey did not stray from his father's faith or his love of country, politics, and sports. He inherited his father's hard work, patriotism, Republicanism, and athleticism. But Branch would not be a farmer like his father. "He could sit down on a hoe faster than anyone I ever knew," his mother remembered with a smile.[9]

By the time Rickey was a teenager, his family had moved several miles away to Lucasville. Rickey, a good student and a good athlete, wanted to go to college but lacked the money. He taught school for two years before leaving to attend Ohio Wesleyan. At college, Rickey found himself an outsider, a "hayseed," as Lowenfish describes him, wearing ill-fitting clothes and carrying a straw suitcase in one hand and his catching equipment in the other. If this made him self-conscious, he gave himself little time to think about it. He took a full load of classes, worked several jobs to pay his tuition and room and board, and played sports.[10]

Rickey was a catcher on the baseball team and a fullback on the football team. Charles "Tommy" Thomas also played baseball and football. Rickey had no contact with blacks in Scioto County and yet immediately befriended Thomas. Thomas said he faced little outward prejudice from classmates and teammates—in part, he added, because of Rickey. "From the first day I entered Ohio Wesleyan, Branch Rickey took special interest in my welfare," Thomas said.[11]

After his sophomore year, Rickey played semiprofessional baseball during the summer. When school officials learned this, they asked Rickey if it was true. Rickey admitted it was. This made him ineligible to play intercollegiate athletics. The Ohio Wesleyan president, impressed by Rickey's honesty, hired him to be the school's baseball coach.[12] Rickey had no better player than Thomas, who played catcher, first base, and outfield. Thomas, who was the only black player on the team, was apparently treated well by his teammates and students. But he often faced hostility from opposing teams and their fans.

When Ohio Wesleyan played the University of Kentucky at Lexington during the spring of 1903, some of the Kentucky players and fans began chanting, "Get that nigger off the field!" Rickey, who was then twenty-one, reportedly ran across the field to the Kentucky dugout and shouted at the opposing coach, "We won't play without him!" When it appeared that there might not be a game, some of the spectators began cheering, "We want Thomas! We want Thomas!" The game was then played without incident.[13]

During a road trip to the University of Notre Dame that spring, something happened that left a burning impression in Rickey's consciousness. All the Ohio Wesleyan players got in line to register at a hotel's front desk. When it was Thomas's turn, the clerk pulled the registration book away. "We do not register Negroes here," he snapped. Rickey told the clerk that the team was the guest of the University of Notre Dame and that Thomas was the best player on the team. The clerk did not budge.

Rickey asked to see the hotel manager. While he waited, he sent his equipment manager to find another housing option for Thomas. "I later realized that in many cases a Negro could stay in a white hotel if he were a servant traveling with a white man," Rickey said, "and that so long as this relationship of master and servant was obvious, then it was perfectly all right with whites who otherwise would object to a Negro's staying in the hotel."[14]

Rickey asked the hotel manager if Thomas could sleep on a cot in his room. The manager agreed. Once in the room, Rickey saw Thomas rubbing his skin, tearfully saying, "Black skin. Black skin. If only I could make them white."[15]

Lowenfish said that while Rickey knew little of racial discrimination himself, he "instinctively empathized with Thomas's pain of rejection." Rickey tried to console Thomas by telling him that there would be a time when there would be racial equality. He gave Thomas a pep talk. "Come on, Tommy, snap out of it! We'll lick this one day," he said. "But we can't if you feel sorry for yourself."[16]

When Rickey signed Robinson in 1945, he told the Associated Press he had given a lot of thought to racial discrimination since his days coaching baseball at Ohio Wesleyan.[17] Rickey said the incident made a powerful impression on him. But he rarely, if ever, mentioned Thomas to reporters in the four decades since witnessing the ballplayer trying to rub off his black skin.

Rickey recounted the Thomas story often in the days, months, and years after he signed Robinson. Writer Mark Harris, who later wrote the baseball novels *The Southpaw* and *Bang the Drum Slowly*, included the Thomas anecdote in a story he wrote about Rickey and Robinson in September 1947.[18] Arthur Mann, a former sportswriter who later worked for Rickey, quoted the baseball executive, who, remembering the 1903 incident, said, "I never felt so helpless in my life."[19] In his biography of Rickey, David Lipman added the following detail after Rickey saw Thomas crying. "What if they won't let me play?" a tearful Thomas said. "They'll either let you play or we all go home," Rickey replied.[20]

In 1968, A. S. "Doc" Young wrote in *Ebony* magazine that Rickey said he was profoundly moved by the racism he saw directed against Thomas. "From Charlie Thomas," Young said, "Rickey learned about the terrible degradation of racial prejudice, and that one's race, or color of skin, had nothing whatsoever to do with one's ability."[21] In his biography of Jackie Robinson, Arnold Rampersad said the Thomas account was comparable to a story from the life of Abraham Lincoln. "The story begged comparison to another, lodged in American lore," Rampersad said, "about Abe Lincoln going down the Mississippi and seeing slavery, and vowing to see it end one day. Indeed, a portrait of Lincoln hung in Rickey's office."[22]

Jules Tygiel, author of *Baseball's Great Experiment*, which examines the integration of baseball, doubted the role the Thomas incident supposedly had in Rickey's decision to sign Robinson. "The Charlie Thomas story, though based in fact, is vintage Rickey," Tygiel wrote. "The allegory is almost biblical and the sermonlike quality of the tale invites skepticism. Many people place little stock in the episode as the primary rationale for his actions. Even if one accepts the Charlie Thomas story at face value, it does not fully explain why the Dodger president chose to challenge the color barrier four decades later."[23]

Did Rickey embellish the Thomas story to provide a spiritual context to explain why he signed Robinson when he had previously remained silent about the color line? Lowenfish said that Rickey's interest in integrating the national pastime was sincere. While Rickey may have exaggerated the details for dramatic effect, "there is no doubt that the incident occurred," Lowenfish said, and Charlie Thomas confirmed the story.[24]

Rickey graduated from Ohio Wesleyan in 1904, but he remained in touch with Thomas for the rest of his life. The friendship between a prominent white man who spent much of his adult life in St. Louis and Brooklyn, and a black man who spent much of his adult life working as a dentist in Albuquerque, New Mexico, was rare, if not remarkable, given the racial climate of the first half of the century. While living in New Mexico, Thomas traveled to St. Louis and saw Rickey on occasion. He remembered visiting Rickey and hoping to see a Cardinals game, but the two were unable to sit together in the segregated stadium.

"I called Rickey and he invited me down to his office at Sportsman's Park. We talked about old times, but we didn't go to the ball game together that afternoon. You see, Negroes weren't permitted in the lower grandstand at the time. Rick said, 'Tommy, some day, we'll have that changed.'"[25]

When Rickey signed Robinson, the breaking of baseball's color barrier was a personal, spiritual, and business decision. Rickey's friendship with Thomas might have shaped the baseball executive's belief that blacks should have the same opportunities as whites. And, as with just about everything in Rickey's life, he felt that God's hand also was present. Several months after signing Robinson, Rickey told *Life* magazine writer Tim Cohane, "I cannot face my God much longer knowing that His black creatures are held separate and distinct from His white creatures in the game that has given me all I can call my own."[26]

As for the business side, Rickey was a Christian, but he also was a competitor and a capitalist. He wanted to win the National League pennant, and he thought Robinson could help him do so. If the Dodgers succeeded on the field, this meant an increase in attendance at Ebbets Field, and as team president, Rickey stood to profit. Cohane wrote that if Brooklyn won the pennant, it would satisfy the spiritual man in Rickey almost as much as the clicking turnstiles would satisfy the businessman in him.[27] Rickey's faith and life were so intertwined that it is impossible to see where one ended and the other began. Rickey believed that God guided the details of his life, not only the signing of Robinson, but also having the parents he had, attending Ohio Wesleyan, and even the hymn-singing in his Methodist church. One of his favorite hymns included a message of radical inclusion:

> There's a wideness in God's mercy,
> Like the wideness of the sea;
> There's a kindness in His justice,
> Which is more than liberty.[28]

Upon graduation from Ohio Wesleyan in 1904, Rickey played professional baseball in Dallas, where he played well enough to be signed by a major-league team, the Cincinnati Reds. After one game he gave his chest protector to another catcher and said that he would not be playing the next day—a Sunday. The team's manager, Joe Kelley, overheard the exchange and told Rickey that if he did not play the next day, he would be dropped from the team. Unmoved, Rickey drove a hundred miles to Lucasville to attend church with his family.

When Rickey returned to Cincinnati the next day, he went to the office of the team's owner to argue the case of why he should not be released. Owner Garry Herrmann told Rickey to return to the team. Kelley, however, refused to play him and Herrmann did not intervene. The Reds, wanting a catcher who could play every game, released Rickey.[29]

Rickey's refusal to play baseball on Sunday made him a curiosity. A reporter asked him what he thought about mixing baseball and religion. "Why shouldn't they mix well? I try to be both a consistent ballplayer and a consistent Christian. If I fail, it isn't the fault of the game or the religion, is it?"[30]

In the fall of 1904, Rickey found a job at Allegheny College in Meadville, Pennsylvania, where he taught English and history courses, coached the football and baseball teams, and lectured regularly at the Young Men's Christian Association (YMCA).[31] Throughout his life, Rickey was called on to give speeches and to contribute to fund-raising campaigns at local and national YMCA events.[32] "Years of working with young men has taught me the fundamental need of the YMCA, Boy Scouts, and other young agencies," Rickey once wrote in a telegram on behalf of the YMCA.[33]

In early 1905, Rickey signed a contract with Chicago White Sox owner Charles Comiskey, who, according to Rickey, agreed that he did not have to play on Sundays. If Comiskey did agree, he changed his mind; he traded Rickey to another major-league team, the St. Louis Browns.[34]

When Rickey went to spring training with the Browns in 1906, he was engaged to Jane Moulton, whom he had met in Lucasville. On June 1, the couple was married during an off day.

The St. Louis Browns, like the Cincinnati Reds before them, wanted a catcher who could play every day. They traded Rickey to the New York Highlanders, who later changed their name to the Yankees. Rickey began the 1907 season with a sore throwing arm. The Washington Senators took full advantage of the injured catcher and set a major-league record by stealing twelve bases in a game. It became clear to the Highlanders, and probably to Rickey, that he lacked the ability—even with a healthy throwing arm—to be a catcher in the major leagues.

When the 1907 season ended, so did Rickey's major-league playing career. He returned to Ohio Wesleyan, where he coached football, basketball, and baseball, served as athletic director, took night law classes at nearby Ohio State University, and taught Sunday Bible school classes. When spring came, he became involved in Republican Party politics, supporting William Howard Taft, a fellow Ohioan, for president. He also campaigned on behalf of the Anti-Saloon League, which wanted local governments to be able to restrict or prohibit the selling or drinking of alcohol.

The seemingly indefatigable Rickey, however, began to feel the strain of trying to be everywhere and do everything. He was diagnosed with tuberculosis, an often-fatal disease known as consumption because of how the disease consumed the lungs and then spread throughout the body. When the 1909 school year ended, Rickey went to a sanatorium in the Adirondack Mountains to rest and recover. Jane accompanied him. He learned that the illness had not spread beyond his lungs. But to recover, he needed to have total rest for several weeks and sleep outside to breathe in as much fresh air as possible.

By late summer he received news that he had been accepted into the University of Michigan's law school. Rickey became aware that there was a price to be paid for working too hard, and once law school began, he slowed down the pace of his life, though hardly enough for anyone to tell the difference. While taking twenty hours a semester, he also coached the baseball team. Rickey understood he could not continue working so hard without risking a relapse of tuberculosis. During the following summer, Branch and Jane went west to relax in the fresh air of the Rocky Mountains. He received his law degree in June 1911, and the Rickeys spent the summer in the Rockies, as they would again in 1912.

While in Idaho, Rickey was contacted by the St. Louis Browns, who asked him to serve as the team's business manager. The Rickeys moved to St. Louis and joined Grace Methodist Church. Rickey contributed so much time and money that a fellowship hall was eventually named for him. "You have played such a big part in the life of this church through the years," the Rev. Wesley Hager told Rickey. "You are so greatly beloved by this congregation, and you have made such a large contribution to a Christian Society through your leadership in the world of organized baseball."[35]

Rickey stayed in St. Louis for the next three decades. He started in the Browns' front office and then became the team's manager—except on Sundays, when he was replaced by Jimmy Austin. Rickey earned more distinction for his refusal to work on Sundays than for the team's success on the field.

The *Sporting News* published the following ditty poking fun at him:

> Branch Rickey is a funny cuss,
> Though cussin he forbids;
> His rules have started quite a fuss
> Among his Brownie kids.
> When Sunday comes, he leaves his team
> Completely in the lurch,
> And Jimmy Austin rules supreme
> While Branch bikes off to church.[36]

In 1919 Rickey moved across town to the St. Louis Cardinals, where, as general manager, he established the franchise as the best in the National League. He did so by creating baseball's farm system, or minor leagues, by signing scores of promising ballplayers and putting them on teams in the St. Louis organization, thus keeping them from signing with another team. Rickey made a percentage of profits from selling players to other organizations.[37]

Rickey was criticized for the low salaries he paid players and for running a farm system—or "chain gang," as it was derisively called—that kept players under his control. His critics, including baseball commissioner Kenesaw Mountain Landis, criticized Rickey for preaching the virtues of Christianity but acting like a tightfisted tyrant. Landis described Rickey as a "hypocritical Protestant bastard wrapped in those minister's robes."[38]

But others, like Jackie Robinson, found only sincerity and inspiration in Rickey's proclamations of faith. "Others have insinuated that he is not sincere because he speaks so frequently and so fabulously about the fatherhood of God and the brotherhood of men," Robinson said years later. "That is the way of human beings who are too small to speak, live and think big. They laugh and sneer at others who are not ashamed of having faith."[39]

To Robinson, Rickey's faith was like his mother Mallie's. Robinson said that their examples strengthened his own sense of faith. "As I said before, I am not one of the big people in terms of faith," he said. "But I would have to be pretty stupid, very unintelligent and, certainly, ungrateful not to have some of the faith of my mother and Mr. Rickey rub off on me."[40]

In early February 1938, Rickey was invited to be one of several hundred delegates at a Methodist conference that coincided with the 200th anniversary of John Wesley's "strange warming of the heart" experience on Aldersgate Street in London. Rickey played a significant role in the conference by contributing to the writing of a document that called on America's youth to prepare to fight the spread of German totalitarianism in Europe. "To do this," the document said, "we must develop spiritual techniques for tapping sources of power." This, he said, included Bible readings, fellowship groups, and the regular practice of spirituality.[41] The thousand or so attendees included Karl Downs, the young minister of Scott Methodist Church in Pasadena. Before both were mentors to Jackie Robinson, both were disciples of John Wesley. Before Wesley's epiphany on Aldersgate Street, he had traveled to Georgia in the American colonies as a missionary and left with a loathing for slavery.

Baseball's color line—like the color line in American society—had stood firm since the late 1800s. It was unlikely to be relaxed while Landis was commissioner. Like Rickey, Landis grew up in the rural Midwest, was self-educated, and had a keen interest in the law. Landis was a federal judge before becoming commissioner after the 1919 Black Sox scandal. Rickey and Landis also supported the party of Abraham Lincoln—the Republican Party. Landis opposed the rise of the Ku Klux Klan in his home state of Indiana.[42] This did not, however, mean he supported racial equality in either society or in baseball. Landis's attitudes on race represented those of most white Americans and the baseball establishment. As commissioner, he saw to it that no team signed black players.[43]

Landis considered himself the absolute ruler of all things baseball, and few challenged his authority. Rickey was one who did. Landis did not hesitate to remind Rickey that he, and not Rickey, was commissioner. Landis believed Rickey's control over so many minor-league teams was not in the best interests of baseball or its players. Rickey disagreed. He said that his farm system taught players the right methods of playing baseball and gave them moral training that made them better players and athletes. "Rickey genuinely saw himself as a great paternalist," Lowenfish said, "who was providing a priceless opportunity for the eager, hungry, talented young player."[44]

As commissioner, Landis had the authority to do whatever he saw fit to protect the game. In May 1938, he ruled that the St. Louis organization, by owning multiple teams in a single league, and by operating teams in secret, was in violation of baseball's best interests. He ordered the organization to release dozens of players.[45] Rickey told St. Louis owner Sam Breadon to challenge Landis's ruling in court, but Breadon refused. This angered Rickey, and his relationship with the owner never recovered.

During 1941, the United States prepared for what appeared to be the inevitability of American involvement in the war. Breadon knew that he would lose many of his best players to the armed forces, and fewer spectators would therefore patronize Sportsman's Park. He needed to cut expenses. Breadon did not renew Rickey's contract when it expired at the end of 1942.[46] In his last season with the Cardinals, the team defeated the New York Yankees to win the World Series.

Rickey served for nearly a quarter-century as president of the St. Louis Cardinals, and he apparently had the freedom to sign whomever he wanted and promote them to the big leagues. If seeing a sobbing Charlie Thomas had made such an impression on him, why did he not do something about the color line during his time with St. Louis? Rickey's freedom, such as it was, stopped short of signing a black player for a team that played its games in a former slave state in a segregated stadium, Sportsman's Park, owned by a man, Sam Breadon, whose attitudes on race matched those of most of the players on his payroll, the sportswriters who covered the team, the spectators who attended the games, and organized baseball itself.[47]

It is impossible to know if Rickey would have signed black players in the 1920s or 1930s if he had a chance. There is some evidence that he was thinking about integration long before he signed Robinson. In 1939, Art Rust Jr., who would later write a book about racism in baseball, *Get That Nigger Off the Field*, was a black boy growing up near the Polo Grounds, where the New York Giants played their home games. When Rust and his friends tried to get players' autographs after games, ballplayers often responded with racist slurs.[48]

St. Louis Cardinals outfielder Enos Slaughter, who, several years later, viciously spiked Jackie Robinson, called Rust "a little nigger" when he asked for the ballplayer's autograph. Rust remembered thinking to himself, "With all those crackers, ain't no way a black guy's gonna play ball in the majors." But Rust's opinion softened because of a brief conversation he had with Rickey, who put his arm around him and told him blacks would one day be in the big leagues.[49]

Lowenfish said that Rickey's interest in integration did not suddenly come to him in the mid-1940s. "There was a genuine Wesleyan

Methodist conscience at work," he said. Rickey, according to Lowenfish, often said, "The Negro has never been really free in this country.
Legally free since the Civil War yes, but not politically or socially free,
and never morally free."[50]

Shortly after the 1942 season ended, the Brooklyn Dodgers signed
Rickey to be their vice president and general manager. Rickey likely
knew that if there was any city where baseball could be integrated,
it was probably New York City. It had three of the sixteen teams in
the major leagues. New York also had a growing number of voices
demanding the end of baseball's color line. The Rev. Raymond Cam-
pion, the white rector of the largely black St. Peter Claver's Catholic
Church in Brooklyn, said, "It is utterly wrong, unfair, un-American,
un-Democratic, un-Christian to deny a Negro the opportunity to earn
a decent living because of the dark shade of his skin."[51]

Rickey first raised the issue of signing black players during a meeting with George V. McLaughlin, president of the bank that owned the
Brooklyn Dodgers, in early 1943. "I don't see why not," McLaughlin
told Rickey, while also warning him to be aware of the consequences
involved. If Rickey signed a black player, McLaughlin said, he could
not do it to change society or the effort would fail. And, he added, the
ballplayer could not be perceived as temperamental or uppity, or the
effort would fail.[52]

McLaughlin's green light was more like a yellow light. Rickey,
whom Lowenfish called "the cautious revolutionary," moved slowly
and secretly, telling few people about his plan. "As usual," Lowenfish
said, "the persuasive executive was able to enlist a wide variety of people
in his important cause, making sure, however, that he kept secret his
main motive: breaking the color line in the major leagues."[53] Rickey
believed that what he was doing was both right and righteous, and that
history would prove it so. "Rickey saw a chance to intervene in the
moral history of the nation, as Lincoln had done," Arnold Rampersad
wrote. "Aware of the dangers, he moved cautiously. However, he also
saw history on his side."[54]

Rickey contacted friends and associates who told him about black
players in Latin America and in the Negro leagues.[55] Rickey himself
attended Negro league games, including its all-star game, the annual
East-West Classic.[56] Rickey told no one in baseball, not because he
thought somebody else would integrate baseball before him, but
because he did not want Landis or one of the owners maneuvering to
stop him. Rickey believed he was the only baseball executive interested

in signing blacks. If so, he could sign the top black players before the color line was broken.

Commissioner Landis's death on November 25, 1944, removed one obstacle to Rickey's strategy. Another obstacle disappeared on March 13, 1945, when the New York legislature approved the Ives-Quinn Act, which banned discrimination in hiring and created a commission to investigate complaints.

Supporting these efforts were Communists and other social progressives who had been calling for blacks in baseball for nearly a decade. Like-minded politicians added their own voices. Politicians on the New York City Council passed resolutions calling on the city's teams, the Yankees, Giants, and Dodgers, to sign blacks. Congressman Vito Marcantonio of New York introduced a resolution into Congress that authorized the Commerce Department to investigate racial discrimination in Major League Baseball.

Rickey paid particularly close attention to Ives-Quinn. When he read that Governor Thomas Dewey had signed it into law in March, he told his wife, "They can't stop me now."[57] The law would go into effect in July. Rickey felt confident he now had both the moral and legal authority to sign black players, but, trusting his instincts and remembering what George McLaughlin had told him, he did not want to appear to be forcing the issue on baseball.

Rickey then sought out those who could influence how fans would respond to blacks on the Brooklyn team. Shortly after the passage of Ives-Quinn, Rickey met Red Barber, the Brooklyn Dodgers' radio announcer, for lunch at a restaurant in New York City. Rickey said that he was going to share a secret with the announcer that only a few other people knew. But before he did that, he told Barber the story about Charlie Thomas. "That was forty-one years ago," Rickey said after finishing. "And for these forty-one years, I have heard that fine young man crying, 'It's my skin . . . If I could just pull it off . . . It's my skin.'"[58]

Rickey then told Barber why he wanted to talk to him: he wanted to end the color line in baseball and was looking for the right player to do so. "I don't know who he is or where he is," Rickey said to the stunned Barber, "but he is coming."[59]

When Barber, who had grown up in the city of Sanford in rural Florida, went home after the meeting, he told his wife he was going to quit because he had been taught from boyhood that whites and blacks were not equal and should not be treated as such. He did not think he could work for the Dodgers if they had a black player. Barber's wife told him to not make a decision until the next day. Barber then prayed about his decision. He remembered a sentence from the Book of Common Prayer that says, "and hast opened the eyes of the mind to behold things invisible and unseen."

When Barber woke up the next morning, he told himself he was not a player on the Dodgers but the announcer. He decided he would not quit. He told himself he would describe what the black player, whoever he was, did on the field no differently than how he would describe the other players.[60]

It was at this point that Rickey contacted sportswriter Wendell Smith and asked him to come to his office in Brooklyn. Rickey wanted to know more about Robinson and other talented black players. Initially, Rickey did not tell Smith why he was interested.[61]

In early May, Rickey announced that he was interested in owning a team in a new black league, the United States League (USL). Rickey found himself criticized by major-league owners, who profited from renting their ballparks to teams in the established Negro leagues and, therefore, saw the Brooklyn executive as competition. Black sportswriters and team owners also ridiculed Rickey for acting as another "plantation overseer," as Lee Lowenfish put it. The USL failed as a league but succeeded as a diversionary ploy, allowing Rickey and his scouts to observe black players without drawing attention to their motives.[62] Rickey revealed his plan to integrate baseball only to those he felt had to know, and if he did tell someone, he insisted on a vow of secrecy, as he did with Barber and Robinson.

New York mayor Fiorello La Guardia was sympathetic to the cause. Two years earlier, he had created the Mayor's Committee on Unity to study the causes of racial discrimination in the city. He formed this committee after police shot and killed a black soldier who had intervened in the arrest of a black woman in Harlem—a shooting that provoked hundreds of blacks, angry at their living conditions, to begin looting businesses owned by white, predominantly Jewish, merchants.[63]

In 1945, La Guardia was under pressure from the political left to end baseball's color line. La Guardia, who wanted to secure his record on civil rights, created the Mayor's Committee to Integrate Baseball, which included a number of influential social progressives.[64] The mayor asked Rickey to join and he accepted, although, as a political conservative, he was skeptical of the committee because it included so many Communists and social progressives.[65]

Rickey then began meeting with the executive director of the Mayor's Committee on Unity, Daniel Dodson, a New York University sociologist. The two men bonded quickly. Dodson, like Rickey, had grown up poor. The two men also were both Methodists. Rickey trusted Dodson. Once Rickey determined that he was not a communist, he brought him into his confidence, revealing his intentions to sign black players.[66]

In early October—less than two months after Rickey and Robinson had secretly met in Rickey's office on Montague Street—Dodson learned that La Guardia was going to announce the steps his office was taking toward integrating baseball. Rickey asked Dodson if the mayor could postpone his announcement. Rickey did not want it to appear that he was being pressured into signing black players. La Guardia agreed.

Rickey took the time to arrange for the public introduction of Jackie Robinson, and on October 23, Robinson sat in a press conference in Montreal to announce that the city's minor-league baseball team, the Royals, had signed him to a contract.

It was a moment for history.

Hector Racine, the team's president, told sportswriters that blacks had earned their right to play baseball by fighting in World War II. When reporters asked Robinson how he felt, he described himself as "a guinea pig in baseball's great experiment." Robinson added, in a column in the *Pittsburgh Courier*: "I will not forget that I am representing a whole race of people who are pulling for me."[67]

Ludlow Werner, editor of the *New York Age*, wrote that many Americans were hoping he would fail. Robinson "would be haunted by the expectations of his race," Werner said. "Unlike white players, he can never afford any off day or off night. His private life will be watched, too, because white America will judge the Negro race by everything he does. And Lord help him with his fellow Negroes if he should fail them."[68]

Racine said that Robinson was not guaranteed a spot on Montreal's team. He would have to earn that spot like everyone else at spring training in Daytona Beach, Florida, deep in the Deep South. Black baseball fan Jimmie Odoms, interviewed for the *New York Herald Tribune*, said that Robinson would have to face the ugliness that came his way, beginning at spring training in Florida. "This boy Robinson's got to take it," Odoms said. "I hate to think what he got to take. They'll find plenty of ways to give it to him during spring training. And he's got to take it. Otherwise, it don't make no sense sending him."[69]

Rickey hired a new manager for Montreal, Clay Hopper, a Mississippian, who appeared to be a problematic choice, given the circumstances. When Rickey told Hopper, who had managed in the Brooklyn organization for a few years, that the Royals would have at least one black player, the manager told his boss that he did not think he could manage an integrated team. "Please don't do this to me," Hopper pleaded. "I'm white and I've lived in Mississippi all my life. If you're going to do this, you're going to force me to move my family out of Mississippi."[70]

Rickey told Hopper that if he wanted to manage the organization's top minor-league team, he would have to accept Robinson. "You manage this fellow the way I want him managed, and you figure out the way I want him managed." Rickey believed that if Hopper, with his Deep South beliefs, accepted Robinson, so too, perhaps, would the rest of the team.[71]

Rickey found himself under immense pressure. He knew that everything he had done thus far was only preliminary work. The cigar-chomping executive, who rarely exercised, was nearing sixty-four, and once again pushing himself without regard to either his age or his history of working himself to collapse. He spent much of the second half of 1945 trying to buy 25 percent of the Brooklyn organization. This left him heavily in debt and physically exhausted. During the fall he began experiencing dizziness. One day he collapsed on a street in Brooklyn and rested briefly on a cot in a haberdasher's shop. Once he felt better, he resumed his schedule without consulting a doctor.[72]

In December, Rickey attended the annual meeting of major-league executives to discuss trades and rule changes. He suffered a serious dizzy spell and checked into a hospital. He then had another attack on the train back to New York. Rickey spent the next several weeks in a hospital bed recovering from Ménière's disease, an inner-ear disorder that causes vertigo.[73] Doctors warned him that he needed to live a more peaceful life or risk worsening the condition. Rickey, however, ignored the advice.[74]

From his hospital bed, he worked hard to identify all the things that needed to be addressed before Robinson left for spring training. Rickey hired Wendell Smith to find accommodations for Robinson in Florida and then to accompany Robinson during spring training.[75] He also signed a second black player, pitcher Johnny Wright, so Robinson would not have to face history by himself. In a letter to Smith, Rickey asked him to watch over the ballplayers "because much harm could come if either of those boys were to do or say something or other out of turn."[76]

Rickey recovered in time to go to Florida before spring training. Months before, Rickey had found a Florida city for spring training that was relatively progressive on race relations. Daytona Beach was home to a black college, Bethune-Cookman, whose president, Mary McLeod Bethune, had been an adviser to First Lady Eleanor Roosevelt. The city had a black middle class and a black political presence. It also had a baseball field in the city's black section. Rickey had even flown to Daytona Beach to convince city officials that the Montreal Royals and Robinson would obey the city's segregation laws.[77]

After arriving, however, Rickey learned that the city lacked the facilities to accommodate the hundreds of ballplayers who had been invited to try out for the organization. Rickey then moved his minor-league teams forty miles southwest to Sanford, where Red Barber had grown up. Barber recommended Sanford and Rickey trusted Barber. But Sanford was more representative of the Deep South, where segregation laws were enforced by strict and often violent means.[78]

Shortly after the press conference in Montreal, Robinson left on a barnstorming tour of Venezuela with a team of Negro League all-stars. When he returned from Venezuela, he went to New York City, where Rachel, having graduated from the UCLA nursing program, was working at a hospital. Jackie visited Rickey in another hospital.[79] After a few days in New York, Jackie and Rachel took a train across the country to Pasadena. The long journey gave them long-needed time together. The Robinson's engagement had been stressful because they had been apart so much. "But we remained steadfast despite temptations and the turmoil around us," Rachel said.[80]

Jackie and Rachel were married on February 10 at the Independence Church of Christ in Los Angeles. The Rev. Karl Downs came from Austin, Texas, to officiate the ceremony. The church was packed with family and friends. After the reception, the newly married couple spent the night at the Clark Hotel.[81] Once inside the hotel room, they could, if only temporarily, close the door on the rest of the world. "All my fears and doubts vanished," Rachel remembered.[82]

5

"God Has Been Good to Us Today"

Integrating the Minors

Jackie and Rachel Robinson waited in a Los Angeles airport during the early evening of Thursday, February 28, 1946, to board a plane that would take them first to New Orleans, Louisiana, and then to Daytona Beach, Florida, where he would begin his tryout with the Montreal Royals. In a short time, the Robinsons, who had been married for less than three weeks, would leave behind their relatively comfortable world in Pasadena for an unpredictable and perhaps unforgiving one.

Several friends and family members, including Jackie's mother, Mallie, accompanied them to the airport to say good-bye. Mallie handed Jackie and Rachel a shoe box.

"What's this?" Jackie asked.

"It's full of fried chicken and hard-boiled eggs," Mallie said.

"Aw, mamma, you shouldn't have brought this," he protested. "They serve food on the plane."

"I just thought something might happen," she responded, "and I didn't want you starving to death and getting to the baseball camp too weak to hit."

Mallie's experiences as a black woman in Georgia taught her the importance of being self-sufficient.

"God bless the child who got's his own," she said.

Jackie and Rachel abhorred the stereotype of blacks that her food represented—restricted from dining cars, carrying shoe boxes of food, and having picnics on trains. They were of a generation, or so they believed, where blacks flew on planes with whites and ate in the same restaurants as whites.

Rachel had never been in the South, and given what she had heard and read, had no interest in ever going. She wore a dyed, three-quarter ermine coat, which was a wedding gift from Jackie. She also wore a matching black hat and carried a brown alligator-skin handbag that he had bought her a few months earlier when he was playing baseball in Venezuela. Rachel knew a fur coat was inappropriate for the warm weather in the Deep South. It was "my certificate of respectability," she said. "I thought that when I wore it everyone would know that I belonged on the plane, or wherever I happened to be."[1]

This was wishful thinking. No fur coat could change racial attitudes or protect her from bigotry. There had been marginal progress in civil rights during the New Deal and World War II, but racial equality remained an unfulfilled promise.

In the months after the end of the war, there was an escalation of violence against black Americans. In most, perhaps all, cases, the blacks who were beaten, jailed, or murdered posed no real threat to the institution of Jim Crow. This was not the case with Jackie Robinson. He was on his way to confront baseball's color line in the Jim Crow South. Never had so much been riding on an athlete, and no state was more dangerous for blacks than Florida.[2]

A few months earlier, near Tallahassee, Jesse Payne, a black teenager, had been arrested and charged with attacking the five-year-old niece of a Florida sheriff. A white mob dragged Payne from the unguarded jail one night, shot him dead, and left his body on a highway.[3]

Robinson might not have heard of Jesse Payne but, as a black American, he was not naive to racial violence. As he and Rachel headed to Florida, he fully realized he was putting their lives in jeopardy. Rachel, too, knew how segregationists maintained their laws and traditions through violence and, like Branch Rickey, she was worried how Jackie would respond. "I knew how quickly Jack's temper could flare up in the face of a racial insult," she said. If that happened, she did not know if they might be "harmed, or killed" or if Rickey would end the tryout.[4]

As Jackie sat in the airplane, perhaps his thoughts returned to the discussion he had had six months earlier with Rickey. He remembered the promise he had made to Rickey. Robinson knew the time would come when he would have to "turn the other cheek."

Robinson was expected to be at spring training on March 1. He believed he could make it to the training camp by leaving on February

28. If he flew through the night, he could arrive at the Montreal spring training camp the next afternoon. He did not foresee the difficulties ahead. It took Jackie and Rachel almost two full days to get to Daytona Beach.

The Robinsons landed in New Orleans in the early hours of the morning for what was supposed to be a four-hour layover. But, as they waited for their flight, they learned they had been bumped. When Rachel went to use the bathroom, she saw signs for "White Women" and "Colored Women." Proud and indignant, she went into the "white women's" restroom. "I re-emerged my self-esteem momentarily restored and joined Jack," she said.[5]

When the Robinsons tried to enter an airport restaurant, they were told blacks could order food but they were not allowed to eat in the restaurant. They walked away without ordering anything. After a few hours of waiting, they decided to find a hotel room and wait there until receiving word of their flight. A cab driver took them to a nearby hotel, but when he learned it was restricted to whites, he drove them to a black hotel. The room had an awful smell. "I was almost nauseated. It was a dirty, dreadful place," Rachel remembered.[6]

The exhausted Robinsons sat on the side of the bed and opened the shoe box Mallie had given them. "As we quietly ate, I could feel humiliation and a sense of powerlessness overpowering me," Rachel said. "More importantly, I appreciated Mallie's wisdom as never before."[7] Twelve hours passed before the Robinsons boarded another plane to Pensacola in the Florida panhandle. They were scheduled to continue to Daytona Beach after refueling. A flight attendant asked the Robinsons to exit the airplane. Once they were on the tarmac, they were told that the plane was headed into bad weather and needed additional fuel. To counter the weight of the fuel, three passengers had to be removed—the Robinsons and a Mexican.[8] As the Robinsons listened to the implausible explanation, Jackie saw three white passengers boarding the plane.[9] He could feel the rage building in his stomach. But before he lost his temper, he remembered Rickey's warning that he had to choke back his anger.[10]

The Robinsons decided they could not wait for another plane that may or may not have a seat for them. They decided to take a Greyhound bus. When they boarded the bus, it was early in the morning. They sat in comfortable seats near the front of the bus and went to sleep, hoping they would sleep most of the way.[11] When white passengers boarded the bus at the next stop, the driver woke up the Robinsons and, calling Jackie "boy," ordered him to the back of the bus. Jackie, who had once been court-martialed for refusing to go to the back of a bus, obeyed the driver. "We had agreed that I had no right to lose my temper and jeopardize the chances of all the blacks who would follow me if I could break down the barriers," he later said. "So we moved."[12]

It took more than eight hours to cross the state from Pensacola to Jacksonville, where they waited inside the segregated section of a bus station for another bus that would take them the rest of the way to Daytona Beach.

The Robinsons arrived in Daytona Beach at 3:00 p.m. on March 2. The trip from Los Angeles had taken them more than forty hours. Wendell Smith and Billy Rowe of the *Courier* were waiting for the Robinsons and greeted them with smiles. But Jackie was in no mood for niceties.

"Well, I finally made it," he snapped. "But I never want to take another trip like this one again."

Rowe drove the Robinsons to the home of Joe Harris, who was known as the black mayor of Daytona Beach, and his wife, Duff, in the segregated part of Daytona Beach.[13] Robinson said little until Rachel went to bed. He then expressed his fury, repeating indignity after indignity he had endured, from being bumped from planes to being turned away at the airport restaurant to having to sit in the back of a bus—and being called a boy.

"This man had become a 'boy,'" Rowe remembered.[14]

Robinson told Smith and Rowe he wanted to return to California or maybe to the Negro leagues. Robinson did not like black baseball, but at least he was treated the same as everyone else. Smith and Rowe told him he could not quit, not for himself and not for all the black people who depended on him. They said he had to endure certain indignities so other blacks could have opportunities that were now closed to them. "We talked all night. That calmed him down," Rowe said. "We tried to tell him what the whole thing meant, that it was something he had to do."[15]

On Monday, March 4, Rowe drove Robinson and Johnny Wright, the other black prospect signed by Rickey, to Sanford, about forty miles southwest of Daytona Beach. Practice had already started when Robinson and Wright arrived. When they walked toward the field, dozens of ballplayers stopped what they were doing and stared at the two black prospects.[16]

When practice was over, Robinson met Hopper, the Mississippian who worked as a cotton broker in the off-season. If Hopper was still unhappy about having to manage Robinson, he hid it from the ball-player, shaking Robinson's hand.[17]

Rickey did not have the promises in Sanford that he had in Daytona Beach. Sanford was in rural Florida and had a Ku Klux Klan presence. After the second day of practice, a white man approached the house in the segregated neighborhood where Robinson was staying. Smith and Rowe were sitting on the front porch, and Robinson was inside the house. The stranger told the sportswriters that he had come from a meeting of dozens of townspeople. If Robinson did not leave town by sundown, the man said, the ballplayer's life would be in danger. Smith called Rickey, who told them to return to Daytona Beach with Robinson and Wright. Once safely back in Daytona Beach, Jackie was reunited at the Harrises with Rachel, who had not gone to Sanford.[18]

The Sanford experience left Robinson shaken, and again he talked about quitting. Those doubts only increased during the first weeks of spring training.[19] Robinson had rarely had reason to doubt his athletic ability. From the time he was a boy, he was usually the best athlete in any sport he played. Not this time. He was a twenty-seven-year-old rookie who had played relatively little organized baseball. He had played shortstop for the Kansas City Monarchs the year before, but he was aware of criticism that his arm was too weak for the position.

Robinson tried to impress Hopper and the Montreal coaches by throwing the ball as hard as he could on every throw at Kelly Field in Daytona Beach. His arm began hurting, and by the time he returned to the Harrises' he could barely lift it. He could not throw the ball the next day at practice. Rachel massaged his arm after every practice, but there was little one could do for a sore arm except hope that it healed on its own.[20]

Rickey moved Robinson to first base, where a strong throwing arm was not necessary. But a change in his position brought its own frustrations. He worked hard to adapt to first base, a position he had never played, but he had trouble making the adjustment, dropping easy throws, bobbling grounders, and struggling with his footwork. Rickey and his coaches, including Montreal's reluctant manager Clay Hopper, provided Robinson with unceasing encouragement.[21] When Robinson's arm felt better, he was moved to second base, where he appeared far more comfortable.

Rickey's confidence in Hopper was temporarily shaken during one practice when Robinson made a terrific play on a ground ball.

"Have you ever seen a human being make a play like that?" Rickey said to Hopper.

Hopper replied, "Mr. Rickey, do you really think a nigra is a human being?"[22]

Rickey ignored him but quietly wondered if Hopper could rise to the challenge of managing Robinson.[23] Robinson later said that he was treated fairly by Hopper.[24]

Rickey also worried about Robinson's emotional state.

He recognized that Robinson's speed was its own offensive weapon. He worked with him on his baserunning, yelling encouragement: "Be more daring! Take a bigger lead."[25]

Rickey, though, knew that before Robinson could steal a base, he had to get on base, and Robinson continued to struggle with his hitting. The pressure made things worse. He knew that with every swing his shoulders were carrying the hopes of millions of blacks. He constantly heard the cheers of black fans. "I could hear them shouting in the stands," Robinson told Wendell Smith, "and I wanted to produce so much that I was tense and over-anxious. I found myself swinging hard enough to break my back. I started swinging at bad balls and doing a lot of things I wouldn't have done under ordinary circumstances. I wanted to get a hit for them because they were pulling so hard for me."[26]

Robinson felt his world closing in. He remembered the goldfish bowl in Rickey's office. He did not seek out friendship among the Montreal players—and none sought him out. He spent most of his daytime with Smith, Rowe, and Wright. But he spent every minute of every evening with Rachel. The Harrises gave them a room but not much else. The Robinsons ate most meals in nearby black diners. They tried to escape by going to the movies, but there was only one black theater and it showed only one movie. "Night after night we would go to the same old Negro theater, seeing the same old movies over and over," Rachel said. "And day after day I would go out to the ballpark."[27]

In the quiet of their room, Jackie poured out his pain and frustration. This put pressure on the marriage; but instead of straining the marriage, it strengthened it. The two of them became one. Jackie began to refer to himself not as "I" but as "we." As Rachel explained later, "We began to see ourselves in terms of a social and historical problem, to know that the issue wasn't simply about baseball but life and death, freedom and bondage, for an awful lot of people."[28] The newly married couple shared everything, or just about everything. Rachel learned she was pregnant but decided not to tell Jackie just yet. She felt he was under enough pressure.[29]

Robinson continued to say his prayers before he went to sleep. Others prayed for him. Ed Charles, who would later play in the big leagues, was a thirteen-year-old during the spring training of 1946, living in the same neighborhood as Kelly Field, where the Montreal team practiced. After school he would walk to the field and watch Robinson. "I was just a kid, and I was awed by it all, and I prayed for him," Charles said. "I would say, 'Please, God, let him show the whites what we can do and that we can excel like they can.'"[30]

Robinson was scheduled to play his first game on March 17 at City Island Ball Park in downtown Daytona Beach. As blacks sat in church that morning, they thought about and prayed for Robinson, and ministers gave sermons about him. When church was over, blacks who attended a downtown church walked to the ballpark. Mothers and fathers grasped the hands of small children, others clutched the arms of the frail and elderly, and young boys hurried excitedly ahead of their families. The segregated bleachers would be inadequate for all the black spectators that day. But there also were not enough seats for all the whites.[31]

What happened in Daytona Beach repeated itself in Montreal and in Brooklyn and in other cities where Robinson played. He learned that ministers, priests, and rabbis told their parishioners about what Jackie Robinson meant to the cause of racial equality, compassion, and democracy, and urged them to go see him play and, whether they went or not, to pray for him.

"I know how wonderful it felt on a number of occasions, when a Negro minister approached me at the ball club and said, 'You know, I cut my sermon short today so the people could get out of church early and get to the ball park to root for you,'" Robinson said. "My minister friends tell me that when the average minister cuts down his sermon, he is making one of the great sacrifices known to men." He credited black ministers for his success. "I owe so much to the Negro ministers, and it is a debt I never intend to forget."[32]

Robinson's thoughts turned to his faith on the morning of March 17 as he wondered what lay ahead for him. He did not know if he would be allowed to play that afternoon. No black had ever played during a spring training game in Florida. History was against him, and so were the Jim Crow laws. Then there was the question of what would happen if he were allowed to play. Robinson could not help but think about all the things that could go wrong. His life could be in danger. What might spectators yell at him, throw at him—or worse?[33]

Robinson had no choice but to trust Rickey and hope he would make things work. It was a Sunday game, and Rickey, making no exception to his rule about attending baseball games on the Sabbath, would not be at the ballpark. But Rickey, knowing that playing Robinson would violate Daytona Beach's segregation ordinance, pressured city officials to allow the game. He was not interested in changing the city's laws, he told officials, only in giving a black ballplayer an opportunity to play professional baseball.

Rickey won the argument, initially because of his persuasive skills but then because officials saw the crowds of whites and blacks walking toward City Island Ball Park. The crowd of four thousand spectators was the largest ever to see a game at the ballpark. A thousand blacks jammed into the segregated section down the first-base line.[34]

Robinson was nervous when he came up to bat in the second inning. He heard the tremendous ovation from the black spectators, then braced for the jeers from the white spectators. "This is where you're going to get it," he told himself. He heard some scattered boos but nothing like he expected. "They're giving you a chance," one drawling Southern voice said, "now come on and do something about it!"[35]

Robinson went hitless in the game, but he felt satisfied with how he played—and relieved by the response of the white fans. "I knew, of course, that everyone wasn't pulling for me to make good, but I was sure now that the whole world wasn't lined up against me," he said. "When I went to sleep, the applause was still ringing in my ears."[36]

Robinson would play several other games that spring in front of good crowds at City Island Ball Park. There were no incidents on the field or in the bleachers. Daytona Beach was the only city in Florida that allowed Robinson to play in a game. When the Montreal team arrived for a game in Jacksonville, it found the stadium padlocked. DeLand canceled a game because it said the park's lights were not working, even though the game was to be played in the early afternoon. When the Montreal team returned for a game in Sanford, the town's police chief escorted Jackie off the field.[37]

Robinson's hitting improved steadily as spring training progressed. By the end of the spring, both Robinson and Wright had demonstrated that they were good enough to make the Montreal team.

When the team left Daytona Beach on a train to travel north to begin their regular season, Ed Charles and several black children ran after the train until it disappeared from sight. "And when we finally couldn't hear it any longer, we ran some more and finally stopped and put our ears to the tracks so we could feel the vibrations of the train carrying Jackie Robinson," Charles said. "We wanted to be a part of him as long as we could."[38]

The train took them to Jersey City, New Jersey, where Montreal began their regular season before a sellout crowd. In his first plate appearance, Robinson grounded out weakly to the shortstop. When he batted again in the third inning, there were two runners on base and none out. The Jersey City infield prepared for a bunt. Robinson swung away and sent the ball over the left-field fence for a home run. He had hits in his next three appearances. When the game was over, he had four hits, four runs scored, and two stolen bases.[39]

After the game, spectators swarmed onto the field to congratulate him.

"You've had quite a day, little man," Rachel told him after the game.

"God has been good to us today," he responded.[40]

In his column, Wendell Smith quoted Robinson as modestly attributing his performance to some "very special prayers" he recited before the game.[41]

William Nunn of the *Pittsburgh Courier* began his column by writing that Robinson's heroics that day were possible because of Branch Rickey's act of faith when he signed the ballplayer several months earlier. Robinson, Nunn added, responded with his own strong faith. "A man whose faith in God and democracy caused him to defy baseball's infamous 'unwritten law,' teamed up with a 27-year-old athlete who also had faith in God and the democratic way of life," Nunn said. He drove home his point by quoting Robert Browning, who wrote, "God's in His Heaven—All's right with the world."[42]

The beginning of Robinson's season sharply contrasted with that of Johnny Wright, who struggled in his first two appearances and was released and returned to the Negro leagues.

Robinson, an intensely private man, did not like being on center stage in the drama that unfolded around him, and yet he faced the difficult circumstances without succumbing to fear or self-doubt or anger. Few athletes in his position could have done what he did; with so much at stake, he did not just endure but appeared to thrive. He accepted the responsibility that came with being the first black player in Major League Baseball. Unlike other ballplayers, he could not walk off the field, put on his street clothes, and become someone else until the next game. He was always Jackie Robinson—the symbol of racial equality. People made demands on his time. He found it difficult to say no.

In late May he accepted an invitation to chair the New York State Organizing Committee of the United Negro and Allied Veterans. The committee included such black civil rights figures as New York City councilman Benjamin Davis Jr. and Congressman Adam Clayton Powell Jr., who was pastor of the Abyssinian Baptist Church in Harlem. He joined Davis and Powell on June 9 at Abyssinian Church to talk about "the burning problems of discrimination" that faced black war veterans.[43]

Montreal became a sanctuary for the Robinsons after the horrid weeks in Florida. They were treated with kindness and hospitality in Montreal. The Robinsons sublet a furnished apartment from a woman who insisted they use her own linen and kitchen plates and utensils. "We were still shaking from the experience we had before going to Canada," Rachel said. "When we got to Montreal, it was like coming out of a nightmare. The atmosphere in Montreal was so positive, we felt it was a good omen for Jack to play well."[44]

By early June, Robinson led the league in batting average. Fans cheered loudly for Robinson at the team's ballpark, Delorimier Downs. The Montreal fans responded with love. Jackie expressed his appreciation to the people in Montreal. "I owe more to Canadians than they'll ever know," he said.[45]

Montreal saw Robinson as a baseball player. In much of the United States, however, whether in the International League in 1946 or in the National League, Robinson was a black man. "Canadians regarded me as a United States citizen who happened to have a colored skin," Robinson said. "Some of my fellow Americans, especially in Baltimore, regarded me as an obscenity, a savage little above the level of a jungle beast, and told me so in vile language."[46]

Life on the road for Robinson could be brutal, particularly in cities with southern sensibilities, like Baltimore, Maryland, but things were nearly as bad in Syracuse in upstate New York. A Syracuse player threw a black bat from the opposing dugout as Robinson waited on the on-deck circle. One former Syracuse player remembered how his teammates tried to take to the field in blackface but were stopped by their manager. Robinson once stood in the batter's box, waiting to hit, as venomous insults poured down on him from the Syracuse dugout and bleachers. "I don't feel sorry for you," the catcher said from his crouch behind Robinson. "You can go to hell."[47]

Things were different in Buffalo, New York, where business leaders, labor unions, churches, other organizations, and what one journalist called "the biggest crowd" in the ballpark's history honored Robinson as a hero. Lester Granger, head of the National Urban League, wrote that he was pleased to read the enthusiastic response to Robinson in the Buffalo newspapers and to hear a positive news commentator on the radio. After the game in Buffalo, Robinson was walking to his hotel when he was stopped by an elderly white man who recognized him and offered him a religious plaque. The man explained that the plaque had always brought him good fortune and he wanted Robinson to have it "as a testimonial of good will from innumerable and anonymous well-wishers," Granger said.[48]

Robinson vindicated Rickey's faith in him with every hit, stolen base, and defensive gem. Rickey wanted to see how Robinson did in the minor leagues before promoting him to the major leagues. But perhaps just as important, he wanted to see if the ballplayer had the mental toughness to withstand racial slurs and physical abuse from opposing fans and players before subjecting him to the larger crowds in the major leagues.

Robinson remained steadfast in his promise to Rickey—as pitchers threw repeatedly at his head, as base runners slid into him with their cleats high, and as vulgarities were directed at him from opposing players in their dugouts and spectators in the bleachers. Rickey, who was in Brooklyn, could do only so much. He relied on manager Clay Hopper and general manager Mel Jones to see to it that Robinson turned the other cheek. Hopper reminded Robinson to ignore the temptation to retaliate against players or argue with umpires. Jones said Robinson came into his office, restraining his anger. "Nobody knows what I'm going through," Robinson said.[49]

International League president Frank Shaughnessy asked Rickey to keep Robinson in Montreal when the team went to Baltimore for a series in late April because, he said, of the strong possibility of "rioting and bloodshed" that could "wreck organized baseball in the city." Rickey dismissed Shaughnessy's concerns as exaggerated. They were not.[50]

The weather on the first night was frigid, keeping the crowd small. Rachel, who traveled to Baltimore for the game, heard enough from the fans to leave her trembling. When Jackie walked onto the field, a man sitting behind her yelled, "Here comes that nigger son of a bitch! Let's give it to him now!"

Rachel feared for her husband's safety and wept uncontrollably in her hotel room after the game. She wondered if it was time for Jackie to quit white baseball.[51]

Temperatures warmed up the next day for a doubleheader. More than twenty-five thousand fans attended the game, and the bigots in the stands fed off one another. Robinson, who was injured, struggled in the first game and then sat out the second. The second game ended with a fight between Montreal and Baltimore players at home plate. Baltimore fans stormed onto the field and then, learning that Robinson had left the field, headed for the Montreal dressing room.

The mob waited outside the dressing room until 1:00 a.m., screaming at Robinson. "Come out here Robinson, you son of a bitch. We know you're there. We're gonna get you," Johnny "Spider" Jorgenson, a Montreal player, remembered. Jorgenson and two other Montreal players, Tom Tatum and Marvin Rackley, remained with Robinson until the crowd left and then, unable to find a cab, escorted Robinson to his hotel on a city bus.[52]

Robinson had made little impression during the first series in Baltimore, but in his return to the city, he hit a home run and two singles and stole home, leading the Royals to a 10–9, ten-inning win.

"Anger, which can powerfully inhibit athletic ability, did not make Jack less effective as a player but seemed to intensify his concentration and propel him to greater feats," Arnold Rampersad wrote. "Rage and hurt did not drive him to the usual, often destructive therapies—alcohol, tobacco, sexual adventuring."[53]

Robinson depended on Rachel, who quietly listened as he raged against the abuses or retreated into silence. She continued to hide her own struggles from her husband. During her fifth month of pregnancy, her temperature mysteriously rose as high as 103 degrees and then dropped to normal, only to rise again. "I never told Jack about the fever," she said. "I had to make the sacrifice, because I had begun to think that I was married to a man with a destiny, someone who had been chosen for a great task, and I couldn't let him down."[54]

Smith wrote nothing about Robinson's fragile psychological condition during the 1946 season. But during the next spring, he wrote that Robinson had been on the verge of a nervous breakdown during his season with Montreal. Robinson went to a doctor, who recommended that he take some time away from the ballpark and rest. He asked Hopper for several days off. The manager gave him five days. But the Royals were in the middle of a pennant race, and when they lost a few games in a row, Hopper told Robinson he needed him back with the team.[55]

Montreal won one hundred games, more than any other team in the International League. Robinson led the league with a .349 batting average and 113 runs scored. He finished second in the league with forty stolen bases and led the league in fielding percentage.

Montreal finished the season by playing the Louisville Colonels of the American Association in the Little World Series. Robinson faced another hostile crowd in Kentucky. This time, the exhausted Robinson slumped. The worse he played, he remembered, "the more vicious the howling mob became."[56] Fortunately, for Robinson and the Royals, the series returned to Montreal, where, as usual, he had the crowd behind him. Montreal defeated Louisville behind the heroics of Robinson, who hit .400 for the series, was the star of the fifth game, and scored the final run in Montreal's 2–0 win in the decisive sixth game.

During the celebration inside the dressing room, a smiling Clay Hopper warmly shook Robinson's hand and said, "You're a great ballplayer and a fine gentleman. It's been wonderful having you on the team."[57]

Robinson's success vindicated Rickey and redeemed Hopper, who told Rickey he should sign Robinson the next year for the Dodgers.

After showering and putting on his street clothes after the postgame celebration, Robinson left the dressing room. A crowd of French Canadian fans ran to him, hugged him, kissed him, and then carried him on their shoulders, singing, "*Il a gagné ses épaulettes*" (He has earned his stripes).

Robinson finally broke away from the crowd and ran for a cab, and the crowd chased after him.

"It was probably the only day in history," Sam Maltin wrote in the *Pittsburgh Courier*, "that a black man ran from a white mob with love instead of lynching on its mind."[58]

Robinson's season in triple-A had been an unqualified success. Rickey had asked Robinson not merely to succeed on the field but to do so under conditions no ballplayer had ever faced, and he had.

Wendell Smith knew that Robinson was in emotional, psychological, and physical pain. Robinson understood what was required of him and did it. As Smith wrote, "He had to say to himself, 'Although I want to rise up and fight back and challenge my tormentors, I can't. Even if I am right, someone will try to prove that I am wrong.'" Robinson knew he was representing millions of blacks. "I am their representative and I can't afford to let them down," he said, according to Smith. "I'll just have to stick it out and do the very best I can."[59]

If Robinson had not succeeded as he did during his year in Montreal, it is doubtful he would have started the 1947 season with

Brooklyn. Without Montreal, there may never have been a Brooklyn for Robinson.

"So Montreal became a crucible for Jackie," George Mitrovich later wrote in a column in the *Montreal Gazette*, "to see if he could 'turn the other cheek,' as Rickey asked him to do in the spirit of Jesus—and evidence that character before Brooklyn."[60]

Six weeks after Robinson and the Montreal Royals completed their championship season, Rachel gave birth to a healthy Jackie Jr. on November 18.

During the off-season, Robinson and Rickey looked ahead to the 1947 season. Rickey believed that Robinson's chances for success required that he play well, of course. But the Brooklyn executive also felt that the success of Robinson—and other black players who came after him—depended on how spectators responded to the ballplayer. "The only thing we had to fear was the ignorant whites in the South and the ignorant blacks in the North," Rickey said.[61]

There was not much Rickey could do to control bigots in cities like Baltimore and Louisville, but there was something he thought he could do to temper the emotions of black spectators. In February 1947, a month before spring training, Rickey organized a meeting of thirty-three black religious and community leaders at the YMCA in Brooklyn to emphasize that black spectators had to restrain themselves in both their applause for the ballplayer and their response to those bigots in the stadium who yelled abuse at him. If they fought force with force, Rickey said, it would jeopardize integration and vindicate the bigots who claimed that segregation was necessary to prevent race riots.[62]

When spring training came in 1947, Rickey wanted to avoid the Jim Crow laws of the previous year in Florida. He moved his organization from Florida to Havana, Cuba, where there was no legal segregation. But Rickey, Robinson learned, decided to segregate his black players from his white players. There would be no private home for Robinson, as there was in Daytona Beach, however. Montreal's four black players—Robinson, catcher Roy Campanella, and pitchers Don Newcombe and Roy Partlow—were assigned a shabby downtown hotel for blacks near Havana's slum district.[63] "It was a place," Newcombe said, "only a cockroach could love."[64]

This was the first spring training for Campanella, Newcombe, and Partlow, and they had little choice but to accept the conditions. Robinson, however, was livid. He became angrier when he learned that

Rickey was responsible. But he began to calm down when Rickey explained that he did not want the mixing of blacks and whites to provoke a racial incident that might jeopardize everything he was trying to do—when they were, as Rickey put it, "on the threshold of success."[65]

"I reluctantly accepted the explanation," Robinson said.[66]

The accommodations made Robinson sick, the anger made him sicker, and the greasy food in the filthy segregated restaurant made him even sicker. His stomach hurt so badly he had trouble bending over.[67]

Robinson then learned that if he were going to make the Dodgers, it would not be at second base, where the team had the veteran Eddie Stanky. It would be at first base, where the Dodgers, like the Royals a year earlier, had no established player. Once again, Rickey told Clay Hopper to put Robinson at first, and Robinson worked hard at the position.[68]

Rickey knew that if Robinson were to make the Brooklyn roster, he could not just be good enough to make the team. He had to be so good that nobody could doubt whether he belonged, especially his teammates, many of whom did not want a black man in the dugout with them. To do that, Rickey told the ballplayer to run with abandon in games against Brooklyn. "I want you to run wild," Rickey told Robinson before one of the games with the Dodgers, "to steal the pants off them, to be the most conspicuous player on the field."[69]

There were no other major-league teams practicing in Cuba or anywhere else in the Caribbean. This meant that Montreal played a number of games against Brooklyn, as they had the previous year in Florida. Rickey told Robinson the games against Brooklyn were critical not only because he was playing against prospective teammates but also because he would be playing in front of New York City sportswriters. "The stories the newspapermen send back to Brooklyn and New York newspapers will help create demand on the part of the fans that you be brought up to the majors," Rickey told him.[70]

Robinson, once again, rose to the challenge and hit and fielded well, until the stomach pains forced him to sit out. Rickey had hoped that the Brooklyn team would see Robinson as a player who could make them better. But this did not happen—at least not immediately.

A number of Brooklyn players were concerned that Rickey would promote Robinson. A petition was reportedly circulated to keep Robinson off the team. When Rickey learned about the petition, he immediately told Brooklyn manager Leo Durocher, who woke up the team in the middle of the night and directed an obscenity-laced tirade at the players.

"I'm the manager of this team, and I say he plays!" Durocher said.[71]

Durocher's tirade ended the mutiny. Rickey met alone with the players who signed the petition and made it clear he would trade them before he would trade Robinson.

Sportswriters, perhaps knowing about the dissension, questioned whether Rickey would sign Robinson for the Dodgers. Rickey remained noncommittal about whether Robinson would be with the Dodgers or Montreal when the season began. "Only Rickey knows and he ain't talking," Arthur Daley wrote in the *New York Times*. Rickey should not sign Robinson, Daley added, if he "wants to keep peace in his baseball family."[72]

Rickey, in keeping with his cautious nature, made no guarantees to Robinson or anyone else that the ballplayer would start the season with Brooklyn. Robinson, for his part, told reporters that if he were not good enough to play for Brooklyn, he would return to Montreal, where he had the support of his teammates and the team's fans. "Last year I saw more democracy in Montreal than in any city I have ever been in," Robinson said in the *Pittsburgh Courier* on March 22. "They inspired me and, along with the faith I had in God, who was on my side right from opening day of the season, I had a wonderful year."[73]

On April 5, Robinson acknowledged in the *Pittsburgh Courier* that he had read in newspapers that there would be trouble if he were promoted to the major leagues. He said he wanted to play for the Dodgers and wondered why the color of his skin should prevent him from doing that. He also admitted that he sometimes got tired of being the "guinea pig," and that he wanted to walk away from baseball. But something, he said, urged him to continue.

If he succeeded in the major leagues, Robinson said, then perhaps he could change how whites thought about whether blacks should be in the big leagues. If he could do that, he would make it easier for the next black who wanted to play baseball or who wanted to find a job, go to school, or live as he wanted, free of racial discrimination. "I want to prove that God alone has the right to judge a person," he said, "and that He is the one who decides people's fates."[74]

Discussions about whether Robinson would be signed were temporarily put aside when baseball commissioner A. B. "Happy" Chandler suspended Durocher for, among other things, having an affair with a married woman, actress Laraine Day. The Catholic Youth Organization threatened to boycott baseball if something was not done to punish the Brooklyn manager for his moral failings.[75] Rickey lost his manager, and Robinson lost one of his fiercest supporters.

Nevertheless, on April 10, the day after Durocher's suspension, Rickey released a statement that said the Dodgers had signed Robinson. This solidified Robinson's faith in Rickey. Robinson would be in the lineup for Brooklyn's first game of the season on April 15. No black had played in the major leagues since the 1880s.

Robinson was not naive enough to think that Rickey or his own ability would be enough for him to succeed. So much depended on fate or luck. "His religion had taught him that the line between confidence and Satanic pride is a fine one; and chance—a twisted ankle, a turned knee—might yet intervene to reassert the inscrutable ways of Providence," Arnold Rampersad wrote. "The drama would unfold; he would be both spectator and the man at the plate; God would decide the outcome."[76]

Robinson believed God was on his side, and that the outcome would be divine.

6

"I Get Down on My Knees and Pray"
Integrating Major League Baseball

Jackie Robinson woke up early on the morning of April 15 in the small, cluttered hotel room in Manhattan he was sharing with Rachel and five-month-old Jackie Jr. until they found something more permanent. Diapers were drying on a shower rod, and baby bottles sat in the bathroom sink. Jackie looked at Rachel as he was leaving to go to Ebbets Field to break baseball's color line.

"Just in case you have trouble picking me out," he quipped, "I'll be wearing number forty-two."[1]

Robinson took the subway to Ebbets Field for the early afternoon game. Brooklyn pitcher Ralph Branca was in the clubhouse with one other player, Gene Hermanski, a reserve outfielder, when Robinson entered. Robinson knew that a petition had been circulated among Brooklyn players who did not want him to play on their team, but he did not know who had signed it and who had not. Branca sensed what Robinson was thinking, "Are these guys friends or foes?"

Branca, who grew up in Mount Vernon, New York, often playing with blacks, had no objections to having Robinson as a teammate. Neither did the New Jersey-bred Hermanski. Each shook Robinson's hand and wished him good luck. When other players entered the clubhouse, some welcomed Robinson, others did not. At one point, Branca looked over at Robinson, who was quietly sitting on a stool and staring into his locker. He knew there was a lot at stake for Robinson, and he wanted to say something to Jackie but did not. The twenty-one-year-old Branca, who was beginning what would be his first full year in the major leagues, thought instead about his own circumstances. "Instead of saying a prayer for him," he remembered, "I said one for me."[2]

Branca, who was not pitching that day, was sitting next to Robinson in the dugout moments before he took the field.

"You know, Ralph," he said, "this is a big day for me."

Branca understood what Robinson meant.

"It wasn't a big day just for him," Branca wrote decades later, "but for all African-Americans."[3]

Robinson went hitless in his first game but reached base on an error in the seventh and scored the go-ahead run in Brooklyn's 5–3 win.

When Robinson was in his hotel room that evening, there was a knock on the door. Ward Morehouse, a drama critic for the *New York Sun*, asked for an interview. Robinson invited him in, and Morehouse asked what he thought of his first game.

"I did all my thinking last night. Before I went to bed I thanked God for all that's happened," Robinson said, "and for the good fortune that's come my way."

Robinson admitted that he felt a lot of pressure being the first black in the major leagues. But, he added, he liked challenges. He told Morehouse that he taught Sunday school in the Methodist church in Pasadena, and that he had always requested the rowdier boys for his class. Robinson then picked up his infant son, Jackie Jr., and continued: "I know that a lot of players, particularly the southern boys, won't be able to change their feelings overnight on the matter of playing ball with a negro. I can understand that. I have encountered very little antagonism, however; I really expected a great deal more. I guess it's all up to me."[4]

Robinson got his first major-league hit in the second game, which Brooklyn also won. After the second game at Ebbets Field, Brooklyn played their crosstown rival, the New York Giants, in a two-game series at the Polo Grounds, and then returned to Ebbets Field for three games against the Philadelphia Phillies.

During an off day before the Phillies series, Jackie and Rachel moved into an apartment in Brooklyn. Gil Jonas, who was then a high school student in Brooklyn, interviewed Robinson that day for his school newspaper. Jonas, who was white, did not ask Robinson about racial discrimination. Jonas later recalled that he was aware that there were differences between races, religions, and nationalities, but that he had not yet processed how these differences manifested themselves into racism and racial hatred.

That changed on April 22 when Jonas went to see Robinson play during the first game in the series against the Phillies. The cold weather meant a smaller-than-expected crowd. The ballpark was relatively quiet when Robinson came up to bat for the first time. As Robinson dug into the batter's box, the Philadelphia bench let loose a torrent of abuse "harsher than anything Robinson had heard in his professional baseball career," Jonathan Eig wrote in *Opening Day: The Story of Jackie Robinson's First Season.*[5]

Philadelphia manager Ben Chapman, an Alabaman, was a former major-league outfielder who had been traded from the New York Yankees to the Washington Senators in the 1930s after making Nazi salutes at what he perceived to be Jewish fans at Yankee Stadium. Chapman directed a series of hate-filled, bigoted taunts against Robinson as soon he stepped into the batter's box.

"Hey, why don't you go back to the cotton field where you belong?"

"Hey, snowflake, which one of those white boys' wives are you dating tonight?"

"We don't want you here, nigger!"[6]

It continued every time Robinson came to bat that day.

For a moment or so, Robinson wanted to ignore his promise to Rickey. "To hell with Mr. Rickey's 'noble experiment,'" he later said. "To hell with the image of the patient black freak I was supposed to create. I could throw down my bat, stride over to that Phillies dugout, grab one of those white sons of bitches and smash his teeth in with my despised black fist. Then I could walk away from it all."[7]

But Robinson did not move from the batter's box. He did not look at the Phillies dugout. He remembered his pact with Rickey and honored it. By not responding, Robinson won over many of those in the crowd and perhaps many of his own teammates, some of whom did not want him on their team. Rickey later said that Chapman failed to produce his intended effect. "Chapman did more than anybody to unite the Dodgers," Rickey said. "When he poured out that string of unconscionable abuse, he solidified and unified thirty men. . . . Chapman made Jackie a real member of the Dodgers."[8]

Jonas remembered hearing the obscenities from the Phillies dugout. "I didn't know people could be that cruel," he said. Jonas also said he saw things differently after that game. He observed how Robinson won over some of those white spectators who had screamed abominations at him. "I watched people who were hardhearted or antagonistic, and they changed. It was palpable. It changed so completely, and it changed me over the course of the season."[9]

Jonas's racial sensibilities were forever transformed by what he witnessed that day at Ebbets Field. He paid closer and closer attention to racial discrimination. As an adult, he became the chief fund-raiser for the NAACP and wrote *Freedom's Sword: The NAACP and the Struggle against Racism in America, 1909–1969.*[10]

If Robinson could inspire white boys like Gil Jonas, think of the impact he had on young blacks. Colin Powell, who became a four-star general in the US Army and secretary of state in the George W. Bush administration, was ten years old and living in the Bronx in 1947. He was a New York Giants fan but, like many of his friends, he rooted for Jackie Robinson, even though he played for the Giants' hated rival, the Dodgers. "We said, 'Oh Lord, don't let him strike out,'" Powell remembered. "The greatest fear was that he wouldn't do well, and that would be a mark against all of us."[11]

Robinson succeeded, and in doing so he changed the way that whites saw blacks and, more importantly, how blacks saw themselves. Roger Wilkins, nephew of NAACP leader Roy Wilkins, was fifteen years old in 1947. He said that young blacks like himself saw in Robinson that things which once were impossible were suddenly possible. "This man, in a very personal sense," Wilkins said, "became a permanent part of my spirit and the spirit of a generation of black kids like me because of the way he faced his ordeal."[12] Poet Langston Hughes, who lived in New York City, marveled at what happened that season. "Anyhow, this summer of our Lord 1947, the Dodgers are doing right with Jackie Robinson at first," Hughes said. If Robinson and the Dodgers succeeded, he added, "a hundred years from now history will still be grinning."[13]

Robinson represented hope for some, but for others he touched on darker impulses: anxieties, fears, bigotry. If his teammates did not want to play on the same team with him, it stood to reason that players on other teams did not want to play against him. St. Louis Cardinals' owner Sam Breadon learned of a possible plot among his team's players to go on strike on May 6 rather than play Robinson and the Dodgers. The conspirators hoped that if they succeeded, players on other National League teams would follow, forcing Robinson out of baseball. Breadon took his concerns to National League president Ford Frick, who thought the talk of a strike was just talk.[14]

Stanley Woodward, the veteran sportswriter of the *New York Herald Tribune*, wrote a column about the plot. Woodward praised Robinson, "whose intelligence and degree of education are far beyond that of the average ball player," as one who "has behaved himself in an exemplary manner." Tom Meany, who wrote for the liberal New York City newspaper *P.M.*, criticized the Cardinals and anyone else who would refuse to play against Robinson. "The world, they should learn, is made up of many different races and religions, of Protestants, of Jews, of Catholics, of whites, of yellows, and of blacks," Meany wrote. Walter Winchell, whose syndicated radio program was heard by millions, denounced anyone who opposed Robinson or any other black in baseball.[15]

Frick announced that anyone who refused to play against Robinson would be suspended.[16] The Cardinals took the field against the Dodgers on May 6 without incident. If there was talk of a league-wide boycott against Robinson, it never materialized.

After a good start to the season, Robinson went into a hitting slump. One New York City newspaper headlined a story, "Robinson's Job in Jeopardy."[17] He read the newspapers and knew what people were saying and thinking. He began doubting himself under the unrelenting pressure.

But he hid those doubts from his critics who did not want him in the major leagues. "By checking his temper and remaining stoic, Robinson established an image of strength and courage," Eig wrote. "Still, he would admit at the end of the season that the controversy affected his performance on the field, and he worried that he would survive the taunting only to find himself back in the minors because he couldn't hit."[18]

Robinson believed that he was given a purpose—not just by Rickey but by a higher authority—to confront baseball and history. Other blacks drew on their faith and on Robinson's courage. From that first game when he took the field, black Americans discussed with one another what Robinson did that day and in every game after that. People talked about Robinson in churches, barbershops, taverns, and on the streets, in small towns and in big cities.

In the years before teams used chartered jets, teams often arrived by train late in the evening before a road game. When the Dodgers disembarked, they would inevitably be met, no matter the hour, by crowds—by fathers, most of them African American, with their young sons, who sought, in respectful silence, a glimpse of Jackie Robinson.[19] Railroads made special runs to accommodate black fans who came from distant cities and towns to Brooklyn or other National League ballparks to see Robinson play.[20]

Wendell Smith, who sometimes roomed with Robinson when the ballplayer was not allowed in the hotel with the rest of his team, recognized that Robinson could not go about his life as another ballplayer could. Wherever Robinson went, people wanted to get his autograph, to shake his hand, to wish him well, or to tell him how much they were praying for him. "He seldom has a moment to himself," Smith said.[21]

Robinson broke out of his slump in early May, and from that point on, few questioned whether he had the ability for the big leagues. But his skill did not prevent the recalcitrant from maintaining that he did not belong on a Major League Baseball field.

When the Dodgers took their first trip to Philadelphia, Rickey received a phone call from the team's general manager, Herb Pennock, once a pitching great for the New York Yankees. "You can't bring that nigger here with the rest of the team," Pennock told Rickey. "We're just not ready for that sort of thing yet."[22]

Rickey told him that if the Phillies did not take the field, Brooklyn would win the game on forfeit. Only then did Pennock relent.

In the movie 42, Rickey tells Pennock: "You think God likes baseball, Herb?"

"What?" Pennock responds. "What the hell is that supposed to mean?"

"It means someday you're gonna meet God, and when he inquires as to why you didn't take the field against Robinson in Philadelphia, and you answer that it's because he was a Negro, it may not be a sufficient reply!"

The exchange in the movie, in all likelihood, did not happen.

"Must be a Hollywood concoction," Rickey biographer Lee Lowenfish said.[23]

When the Dodgers arrived at their hotel in Philadelphia, the Benjamin Franklin, the hotel's manager told the team they would not be allowed to stay at the hotel "while you have any Nigras with you."[24]

Bigotry trailed Robinson like a curse. He did not know where or how it would rear itself next. Robinson was, by nature, an introvert, a private man; most of the time he suffered in silence and by himself, on the train, at a restaurant, in the dugout, or in the dressing room. This did not go unnoticed by sportswriters. Jimmy Cannon of the *New York Post* described Robinson as "the loneliest man I have seen in sports."[25]

Robinson was playing well, and so were the Dodgers. Robinson was a big part of that success, and yet his teammates kept their distance, some because they did not want him on their team but others because they did not know what to say to him. For some, it was the first time they had been so close to a black person. Others, those perhaps more sympathetic, had never seen anyone take such a beating, physically and verbally, and simply did not know to respond.

Ralph Branca said he felt guilty for not doing more to express his support. "Shouldn't I do more to help him?" he asked himself. He prayed for a response. After one game on the road, he asked Robinson if he wanted to have dinner. Branca did not think that anyone on the team had yet invited Robinson to dinner after a game.

The dinner conversation was limited to baseball at first, but then the pitcher asked Robinson, "How do you just sit silently and take it?"

Robinson told Branca the story of his first meeting with Rickey two years earlier, when the Dodgers manager had read from Giovanni Papini's *Life of Christ*, and about his promise that he would not fight back.

"Ralph," Robinson said, "many nights I get down on my knees and pray to God for the strength not to fight back."[26]

Robinson's prayer time was intensely private, Rachel Robinson said. She left him alone to pray for strength to deal with the unrelenting pressures of what was demanded of him. When those pressures wore him down, she dealt with his moody silence. Through everything Jackie faced, Rachel stood by him and with him, a towering source of strength who gave him unconditional love.

His teammate Carl Erskine said that Robinson could not have survived the ordeal without Rachel. "Rachel is a story in herself because she stood by Jackie, as the Good Book says, tempered his fire, and affected his life in a positive manner," Erskine said. "The first couple of years in Brooklyn, Jackie told me, took their toll on him, but not on her. She held back the tears—for his sake—and the angst so that they could persevere together. She made Jackie a calmer person and in doing so made him a better player. I don't think he would have lasted without her by his side."[27]

Jackie often brought the day's agony home with him. He sometimes talked about what happened but other times kept it to himself, suffering in silence. There were days when the hatred came to the door in letters from bigots. Rachel turned over the worst of the letters—the ones that threatened to kill Jackie or to kidnap Jackie Jr.—to the police.[28] Other hate mail went to Robinson at Ebbets Field. Some of the letters, Rickey's assistant Harold Parrott said, were "scrawled and scribbled like the smut you see on toilet walls."[29]

Not all the players in the National League were against Robinson, but few outwardly expressed their support either. One of those who did was Hank Greenberg, the first baseman of the Pittsburgh Pirates in 1947. Greenberg, as a Jew, had played his career hearing racial epithets and vile names such as "Christ killer." He, too, had been the subject of pitchers who threw at his head and base runners who ran into him, hoping to cause an injury. "I think Hank was abused more than any other white ballplayer or any ethnic player except Jackie Robinson," said Birdie Tebbetts, who had played against Greenberg.[30]

During a game in Pittsburgh, Robinson, trying to beat out an infield grounder, ran into Greenberg as the big first baseman reached across the baseline for the errant throw. The ball got away from Greenberg, and Robinson advanced to second. Later in the game, Robinson was on first base when Greenberg told him he hoped he had not hurt the ballplayer when the two collided. Robinson said he had not been hurt.

Greenberg then gave Robinson a few encouraging words. "I know it's plenty tough," he said. "You're a good ball player, however, and you'll do all right. Just stay in there and fight back, and always remember to keep your head up."

During the series, Pittsburgh pitcher Fritz Ostermueller, who had once pitched for the Dodgers, threw a pitch that sailed toward Robinson's head. Robinson threw up an arm in self-defense, and the ball hit him in the wrist, leaving him in the dirt, in considerable pain. Robinson's teammates showered Ostermueller with verbal abuse. "Don't forget you guys have to bat, too," the Brooklyn players yelled.[31]

Robinson faced the possibility of a brutal injury every time he stepped across the white lines in the batter's box or crossed a white baseline to take his position in the field. "Players slid into the base Jackie was covering with their spikes high to draw blood," Rachel remembered, "pitchers threw balls at his head, intending to injure him, not just brush him back from the plate; and the bench jockeying crossed the line from insulting repartee to inciting, abusive language intended to provoke rage."[32]

During a June game in Cincinnati, across the Ohio River from the former slave state of Kentucky, Reds pitcher Ewell Blackwell was two outs away from throwing a no-hitter in consecutive games, something that had happened only once in major-league history. Eddie Stanky broke up the no-hitter with a single. An out later, Blackwell threw his first pitch at Robinson's head. Robinson fell to the dirt, then stood up and glared at Blackwell.

"Come on you black . . . ," Blackwell yelled at Robinson, "stand in there and hit."

Robinson then smiled and told Blackwell he was just mad because Stanky broke up his no-hitter. Robinson then got a hit.[33]

Branca saw, as others did, that the best thing Robinson could do to silence his critics was to play well. Robinson's skin color set him apart from everyone else on the field, but so did the way he played baseball. He fought against prejudice by succeeding on the field, with his bat and glove, but also by running the bases with such speed and ferocity that it unnerved pitchers and confounded infielders. "While other men made it a point to avoid danger on the base paths," Jonathan Eig wrote, "Robinson put himself in harm's way every chance he got. His speed and guile broke down the game's natural order and left opponents cursing and hurling their gloves."[34]

Robinson made opponents worse and his teammates better. "Jackie was one of those rare athletes who had the ability to make those of us around him better athletes," Carl Erskine said.[35]

In August 1947, the first-place Dodgers played the second-place Cardinals, the defending National League champions, at Ebbets Field. In the fifth inning, Enos Slaughter, a North Carolinian with the revealing nickname Country, who was believed to be one of the conspirators in the purported plan to strike at the beginning of the season, came down hard on Robinson's ankle with his spikes. The spikes barely missed Robinson's Achilles tendon, risking a season-ending or perhaps career-ending injury. Slaughter denied that he had intentionally tried to hurt Robinson.

But Robinson did not believe him. Neither did Robinson's teammates, sportswriters, and many of those in the crowd, including Douglas Wilder, then sixteen, who had made the trip from Richmond, Virginia, to root for Robinson but also, paradoxically, for the Cardinals, his favorite team. Wilder later said he learned an important lesson as he watched Robinson, writhing in pain, rise to his feet to complete the game. " 'I will show you I can rise over and above,' " Robinson's actions said to Wilder. "It's not a matter of forgiving you for doing it. It's a matter of saying, 'No matter, not withstanding what you did, it doesn't prevent me from being the man I am.' It was a tremendous lesson."

Wilder worked his way through college waiting tables and then became a hero in the Korean War. When he returned from the war, he went to law school and then became the first black to win statewide office in Virginia since Reconstruction. In 1990, he became the state's first black governor.[36]

Perhaps no ballplayer ever left such a profound impact in so many different ways as Robinson. Black parents named their children after him. White business owners integrated their businesses and factories because of him and then wrote him letters expressing their gratitude for opening their eyes to racial discrimination. Black boys imitated him on sandlot fields—and so too did white boys, running pigeon-toed from base to base.

"Jewish families in Brooklyn gathered around their dining-room tables for Passover Seders," Eig says, "and discussed what Moses had in common with a fleet-footed, right-handed hitting infielder with the number 42 on his back."[37] Jews saw in Robinson someone who represented their own struggles to be accepted without prejudice. Some Jews saw Robinson as one of their own. "We called him Jackie Rubinson," said one Jewish man who grew up in Brooklyn.[38]

Robinson also felt a kinship with Jews. As he became more involved in civil rights, he sought out the Anti-Defamation League of B'nai B'rith (ADL). During a meeting with ADL general counsel Arnold Foster, Robinson impressed him by asking questions about the methods and strategies employed by the Jewish organization to fight anti-Semitism. Robinson thought that blacks could benefit from such strategies in their own fight against discrimination.

In September, Karl Downs visited the Robinsons, attending one of Jackie's games at Ebbets Field. Shortly thereafter, he began having chronic stomach pains. Rachel took him to a hospital and urged him to remain in Brooklyn for further tests. A few days later, Downs began feeling better and returned to his job at Samuel Huston College in Austin.[39] Robinson was concerned about his good friend. He owed so much to Downs, who had rescued him from the streets of Pasadena and instilled in him the Christian faith that he relied on so heavily during his season of pain and torment. Robinson knew he never would have achieved what he had if it had not been for Downs and his spiritual guidance.

The same was true of Branch Rickey, who now believed that Robinson could help the team win its first pennant in a quarter century. He was right about this, too. The Dodgers won the National League pennant, and Robinson was a big part of his team's success, hitting .297 and leading the team in several offensive categories, including runs scored and stolen bases with twenty-eight, which led the National League. Brooklyn won the pennant five more times and finished second in the league three times in Robinson's ten years with the team. The *Sporting News*, which had long campaigned against blacks in baseball, named Robinson its rookie of the year.

Robinson's triumph that season did not belong just to Brooklyn; it belonged to all blacks and anyone else who believed in racial equality. "He had revolutionized the image of black Americans in the eyes of many whites. Starting as a token, he had utterly complicated their sense of the nature of black people, how they thought and felt, their dignity and courage in the face of adversity," Arnold Rampersad said. "No black American man had ever shone so brightly for so long as the epitome not only of stoic endurance but also of intelligence, bravery, physical power, and grit. Because baseball was lodged so deeply in the average white man's psyche, Robinson's protracted victory had left an intimate mark there."[40]

The experience exacted a terrible toll on Robinson. Yet, as Dan Burley wrote in the *Amsterdam News*, the ballplayer had not just survived but succeeded. "All season long the first Negro to play in modern big league baseball had endured the insults, name-calling, hate-filled looks of opposing players and had suffered in martyred silence," Burley said. "They had hit him deliberately, as some would have it, with pitched balls; had tried to spike him, to make him lose his nerve and will and thus be automatically thumbed out of the big show. But they failed."[41]

There would be no break in the hostilities during the World Series against the New York Yankees, who directed what Robinson called the worst invective he heard all season from the relative anonymity of their dugout. "They haven't got the guts to come out in the open and call me names," Robinson told Burley. "They are dirty cowards who hide in the darkness of their dugout and make their low, nasty remarks."[42] The Yankees defeated the Dodgers in a seven-game series that ended on October 6.

Once the season ended, Robinson could not retreat into a private world, as most other ballplayers could. He could take a temporary break from being Jackie Robinson the ballplayer, but he could not take a break from being Jackie Robinson, the inspiration for millions of blacks who saw in him the chance for a better life.

The day after the series ended, Robinson received a letter from the Rev. John Curran, priest of the St. Thomas Rectory, one of eight Catholic parishes in Harlem, who told the ballplayer that black America had long waited for someone to integrate baseball. Whoever did so would require uncommon courage, Curran said. "Thank God you have what it took and takes," he wrote. "You must know by now, tho only feebly, what a tremendous boon you have been to our underprivileged youth."

Curran recognized that Robinson represented something far bigger than himself. "You know all too well the difficulties besetting the way of life of the Negro, and we are all so extremely proud of you and your accomplishments in the face of almost insurmountable odds," he wrote. "God spare you many years to your wife and family. May you continue further to inspire our youth to bigger and greater things."[43]

Ministers from different faiths used their sermons to reinforce the faith of those who believed in racial equality and to convince others that integration was not to be feared and that racial equality was in the best interests of the country and all those who believe in religious and democratic principles.

In late February, the Robinsons received word that their friend Karl Downs was dead. On February 26, he underwent an emergency operation by a white doctor at segregated Brackenridge Hospital in Austin. "Complications set in," Robinson later recalled. "Rather than returning his black patient to the operating room or to a recovery room to be closely watched, the doctor in charge let him go to a segregated ward where he died." Robinson said that Downs would have lived if he had either been a white patient in Texas or received care in Brooklyn. Robinson believed that Downs had died "of racism."

If Downs had lived, Robinson said, he would have ranked with some of the great figures of the civil rights movement, including Roy Wilkins, Whitney Young, and Martin Luther King Jr. "He was able to communicate with people of all colors because he was endowed with the ability to inspire confidence," Robinson said. "It was hard to believe that God had taken the life of a man with such a promising future."[44] Robinson's own future on the baseball diamond was about to take a different turn.

When he had first met with Rickey in August 1945, he promised he would respond to his detractors by turning the other cheek. He lived up to that promise. "In observing that trust," Rickey said admiringly, "he has had an almost Christ-like taste of turning the other cheek."[45]

By 1949, Robinson had more than earned the right to be himself. With Rickey's permission, he now refused to back down from umpires, players, sportswriters, and anyone else who insisted that he be deferential or compliant. Robinson was at last his mother's son, reflecting the fiercely strong woman who straightened her back in Georgia, believing that "God wants human beings to work and speak for the freedom and equality which is rightfully theirs, even if they must suffer because they do this."[46]

In doing so, Robinson disappointed and angered many of those who accepted him in the big leagues as long as he was compliant, as long as he was seen and not heard. "I learned that as long as I appeared to ignore insult and injury, I was a martyred hero to a lot of people who had sympathy for the underdog," he said. "But the minute I began to sound off—I became a swell head, wise guy, an 'uppity nigger.'"[47]

During the 1949 season, as Robinson became more assertive on the field, he was asked to rebut the views of another assertive black man, Paul Robeson, who had been one of the great college football players of his day and then earned his law degree at Columbia University before succeeding as a singer, actor, lecturer, and activist. Robeson rejected racial discrimination by becoming a Communist, which made him an enemy of conservative America, particularly during the Red Scare after World War II, when tensions increased between the United States and the Soviet Union. Robeson outraged his critics when he said that blacks would not fight for the United States during a war with the Soviet Union.[48]

The House Committee on Un-American Activities subpoenaed Robinson, who characterized Robeson's remarks as "silly" and criticized communism as godless and antithetical to his own views on politics and religion. "I am a religious man," he said. "Therefore I cherish America where I am free to worship as I please, a privilege which some countries do not give."[49]

Robinson did not denounce Robeson but did present a contrary point of view from a prominent black man. This pleased the committee, communist-hating conservatives, including Rickey, and most Americans. Robinson, however, would later express regret over his appearance before the HUAC committee. He came to believe he had a lot in common with Robeson, once expressing his sadness that in America, "anything progressive is called Communism."[50]

In January 1950, Jackie and Rachel celebrated the birth of their daughter, Sharon. David, their third and final child, was born a little more than two years later. Several weeks after Sharon's birth, Jackie left his family for spring training.

During Robinson's fourth season, he began discussing his faith more openly in interviews. He told the *Brooklyn Eagle* about his dependence on faith and his nightly routine of praying before going to bed. "It's the best way to get close to God," he said, and then added with a smile, "and a hard-hit ground ball."[51] Faith provided Robinson comfort against the ongoing pressures in life and baseball. But Sunday games often prevented him from going to church. He wondered if maybe a chapel could be built inside Ebbets Field, he said, "where the fellows of all religions could go and worship a little while."[52]

When the 1950 season ended, so did Branch Rickey's relationship with the Brooklyn Dodgers. He sold his share of the team for a little more than one million dollars. Rickey was then hired as vice president and general manager of the Pittsburgh Pirates, and he committed the organization to signing black prospects. He also signed Puerto Rican outfielder Roberto Clemente, who would become the first Latin American in the Baseball Hall of Fame. But he could not duplicate the success he had in Brooklyn. When his contract ended, he was not rehired. Rickey returned to the front office of the St. Louis Cardinals in 1962 and served with the organization during the team's World Series championship in 1964.

Rickey's departure from Brooklyn stung Robinson, who had depended on Rickey for so much and reposed his faith so completely in the Brooklyn executive. The relationship between the two men did not end but, according to Rampersad, "seemed to open the way to a deeper understanding." Branch B. Rickey later said that his grandfather thought of Robinson as a second son. "God brought these two men together at this time in our history. If they had not met, I am sure that baseball would have become integrated eventually," Branch B. Rickey said, "but never on the same plane, never in the same way, because of the synergy that existed between them."[53]

Robinson, like Rickey, began publicly demonstrating his faith. He was featured in a national advertisement campaign, "Religion in American Life." In a photo with Rachel and Jackie Jr., Robinson was quoted as saying, "Being without the help of God is something we cannot imagine."[54]

In 1951, Robinson contributed his name to the Committee to Proclaim Liberty, which included dozens of other prominent names, to emphasize religion in the observance of the Fourth of July.[55] A year later, Robinson recorded an essay for Edward R. Murrow's syndicated radio series, *This I Believe*, which he concluded by addressing his Christianity. "And, in the largest sense, I believe that what I did was done for me—that my faith in God sustained me in my fight. And that what was done for me, must and will be done for others."[56]

Robinson became actively involved with other Christian causes. He donated financially to build a parochial school on 141st Street in Harlem.[57] He served on a committee, chaired by former First Lady Eleanor Roosevelt, to raise money to rebuild Concord Baptist Church of Christ in Brooklyn, which had been destroyed by a fire.[58] In 1956, Robinson appeared at a program for youths at a national conference for the Methodist Church in Minneapolis.[59]

Robinson had also long been active as a coach and counselor at the YMCA on 135th Street. Juvenile membership doubled during Robinson's association with the Harlem YMCA, where he served on the board of directors long after he retired from baseball.[60] Robinson, however, preferred spending time with the boys at the YMCA, and whenever he could he went to the neighborhoods near the Y. He also frequented hospitals, sent signed baseballs to sick children, and answered mail from other children.[61]

During spring training in March 1954, Robinson received a letter from a man in Fort Wayne, Indiana, who volunteered at an orphanage. During the course of his volunteer work, the man had met Jimmy, a black boy who kept to himself. When he asked Jimmy what was wrong, the boy said, "I wish I was white." Troubled by this answer, the man asked Robinson if he would send an encouraging word to the boy.

Robinson agreed, and in his letter to Jimmy he wrote that while it was "understandable for a boy your age" to want to be something he was not, he should be proud of being black in spite of the "problems before us." Things were improving for blacks in America, Robinson said, and for this to continue young black children like Jimmy had to remain hopeful and keep their faith in God. "Just remember that because of some handicaps we are better off," he said. "Look in the mirror at yourself and be proud of what God gave you. I, too, felt the pains you must feel, but I never have been ashamed of what God has given me. Good luck to you!"[62]

Robinson became increasingly involved in the issue of civil rights. In late 1953, he became chair of the Commission on Community Organizations of the National Conference of Christians and Jews, an organization that emphasized racial justice in the period preceding what would become the civil rights movement.[63] He also went on an extended tour of towns and cities during the off-season, preaching self-respect and racial tolerance. Louis A. Radelet, the commission's director, praised Robinson's work on the tour in a letter to Rachel and also acknowledged that it took him away from his family. "I know that you had confidence in him and in the fact that the sacrifice you were making was worthwhile," Radelet wrote on February 16, 1954. "I believe that you may feel sure, now that the trip has been concluded, that the benefits were great."[64]

Three months later, the US Supreme Court ruled in *Brown v. Board of Education of Topeka* that the doctrine of "separate but equal" was unconstitutional, affirming the hopes of blacks and liberal whites in a way that few things had since Rickey had signed Robinson nearly a decade earlier. Robinson was responsible in part for what was happening in America, according to those who viewed racial equality with revulsion and fear.

In 1956, Louisiana passed a law prohibiting integration in sports, and Bill Keefe, sports editor of the *New Orleans Times-Picayune*, blamed Robinson for the law because the ballplayer had stirred up racial animosity. "The NAACP can thank Jackie Robinson, persistently insolent and antegonistic [*sic*] trouble-making Negro of the Brooklyn Dodgers," Keefe said. "He has been the most harmful influence the Negro Race has suffered in the attempt to give the Negro nationwide recognition in the sports field."[65]

A white Louisiana priest reminded Keefe that the Irish had long faced discrimination in the United States. Keefe responded to the priest by writing that God knew what he was doing when he created blacks as inferior beings—"the thickness of his skull, his ape-like arms and characteristic odor."[66] Robinson also responded to Keefe, saying that he was not a troublemaker but rather an "American who happens to be an American Negro, one who is proud of that heritage." He asked Keefe if the sportswriter would use the word "insolent" to describe Ted Williams, a white ballplayer who was more demonstrative with his emotions. "Am I insolent, or am I insolent for a Negro (who has courage enough to speak against injustices such as yours and people like you)?"[67]

During the 1956 season, Robinson knew his career was ending: his statistics were down, his playing time was limited, and his body was worn out. Robinson was tired, physically and emotionally, and he was tired of baseball. But while his career was winding down, Robinson was becoming more energized, and more captivated, by his work in the civil rights movement.

Others recognized this in Robinson, and on December 8, 1956, approximately five hundred invited guests gathered at the Roosevelt Hotel in New York City to honor Robinson as he received the NAACP's Spingarn Medal, an annual award "for the highest achievement of an American Negro." Robinson was grateful. "Today marks the high point in my career," he said. "To be honored in this way by the NAACP means more than anything that has happened to me before. That is because the NAACP, to me, represents everything that a man should stand for: for human dignity, for brotherhood, for fair play."[68]

Among the celebrity guests at the swanky luncheon were former medal recipient Thurgood Marshall, television host Ed Sullivan, and heavyweight boxing champion Floyd Patterson. But, for Robinson, one person stood tall above all others—his mother. "The love and devotion of my mother, who sacrificed all her life so that her children could have the things she missed; and the struggle she had trying to keep a poor family going, are things I can never forget," he said. "Her faith in God and her constant advice that I, too, place that same faith in Him, has proven itself time and time again. I am humbly thankful that God gave me such a mother."[69]

While the NAACP honor buoyed Robinson's spirits, the end of his baseball career still loomed large. Complicating matters was his contentious relationship with Brooklyn managers and the front office, particularly Walter O'Malley, who had bought Rickey's share of the Dodgers. Robinson had never warmed up to the new owner, and O'Malley had never warmed up to Robinson. Robinson later suggested that the owner had questioned his integrity.

Five days after Robinson had received the Spingarn award, O'Malley traded him to the Dodgers' crosstown rival, the New York Giants. Brooklyn was stunned. So was Robinson. He took the trade as a vicious insult, and rather than betraying himself and his fans, he simply retired from the game he had transformed.

PART THREE

Fighting for Freedom

7

"Hoeing with God"

An Impatient Faith

After Jackie Robinson retired from baseball in 1956, he became vice president and director of personnel at Chock full o'Nuts, a chain of coffee shops owned by white businessman William Black. The job offered Robinson financial security for the immediate future, and he appreciated his early relationship with Black so much that he described it as nothing less than the work of God. "It is the kind of relationship which developed, in my opinion, not by accident—but all as a part of the mysterious and miraculous way in which God works in the lives of people," he stated.[1] Black had a different sense about the origins of the relationship: "I hired Jackie because a majority of the people who work for me are colored—and I figured they would worship him."[2]

However divinely inspired Robinson thought it to be, the partnership fell apart by 1964. Robinson believed that Black and another colleague, Herb Samuel, had deliberately undermined his authority in personnel-related decisions. But Robinson was always grateful for Black's willingness to let him spend so much of his time doing volunteer work for the National Association for the Advancement of Colored People (NAACP).

In his new role as national chairman of the NAACP's Freedom Fund Campaign in 1956, Robinson traveled the country, speaking in numerous black churches—the vital center of black politics—to inspire activism, raise money, and solicit members. It was a role he relished, and the NAACP audiences thoroughly enjoyed the opportunity to be in the presence of one of their heroes.

Robinson characterized his civil rights work as "hoeing with God," using the gifts of God to grow goodness wherever it was needed. While a lot of people "expect God to do everything for them while they do nothing for themselves," he said, earthly success requires people to commit themselves—their time, energy, and resources—to improving their own lives.

Robinson used the following story to illustrate his spiritual conviction about the importance of human responsibility:

> I have a favorite story about a man who moved to a new farm on which the land was a horrible mess. He worked from dawn until night, tilling the soil and planting the crops. When harvest time came along, one of his neighbors passed by and noticed the mostly tilled soil, the rows of crops.
>
> "The Lord has certainly been good to you," the neighbor said to the farmer.
>
> "Sure has," the farmer answered. Then he added, "But you should have seen this before I started hoeing."
>
> I've always believed that God will help us do anything we want to do which is decent and good. But I like to think he feels that we are doing a little of the hoeing.[3]

For Robinson, hoeing meant much more than merely praying for civil rights. It also meant refusing to wait around for God, religious leaders, or anyone else, for that matter, to undertake the painfully slow process of converting the hearts of civil rights opponents.

Robinson's conviction about the urgent need for earthly justice set him at radical odds with those, such as President Dwight Eisenhower, who called on him and other activists to be patient in the face of racial injustice.

Robinson first met Eisenhower in 1953, when he and the president attended the nationally televised fortieth-anniversary dinner for the Anti-Defamation League of B'nai B'rith in Washington, DC. Immediately after the president delivered the keynote address, he made a beeline to the table where Jackie and Rachel were sitting. Robinson, whose politics, like Branch Rickey's, steered Republican, stood up proudly, and he and the president beamed as they shook hands before the national audience.

Two days later Robinson wrote Eisenhower a heartfelt letter. "My wife and I will always remember our experience that night," he penned. "It is events like this that make certain our faith in democracy is justified."[4]

But Robinson's faith in Eisenhower would plummet in subsequent years, mostly because of the president's slow, quiet, and indirect approach to civil rights. Robinson grew especially disenchanted when Eisenhower remained silent following the January 30, 1956, bombing of the home of the Rev. Martin Luther King Jr. in Montgomery, Alabama.

Like millions of blacks, Robinson admired from afar the Montgomery bus boycott sparked by Rosa Parks's courageous refusal to surrender her bus seat to a white passenger. "The more I read about the Montgomery situation, the more respect I have for the job they are doing," he wrote in a letter to Rachel.[5]

His respect for King in particular, the twenty-six-year-old pastor of Dexter Avenue Baptist Church and the newly elected president of the Montgomery Improvement Association, only deepened after thugs bombed King's house and the homes and churches of other civil rights activists in Montgomery.

King was not at home at the time, but his wife, Coretta, was. She and a visitor were sitting in the front living room when a noise on the porch—she said it sounded like a brick landing with a thud—scared them so much they immediately started for the back room, where baby daughter Yolanda, only seven weeks old, was sleeping peacefully. As Coretta and her friend were rushing down the hallway, a bomb exploded in the front of the house, shattering four windows and causing considerable damage to the porch and the surrounding area. No one was physically harmed.

King, who had been leading a mass meeting of local activists, arrived home about fifteen minutes later to find not only a damaged house and a scared spouse but also a growing crowd of armed and angry African Americans seemingly set on exacting revenge. Standing before the anxious and pulsating crowd, the young minister said, "We believe in law and order. Don't get panicky. Don't do anything panicky at all. Don't get your weapons. He who lives by the sword will perish by the sword. Remember that is what God said. We are not advocating violence. We want to love our enemies. I want you to love our enemies. Be good to them. Love them and let them know you love them. I did not start this boycott. I was asked by you to serve as your spokesman. I want it to be known the length and breadth of this land that if I am stopped this movement will not stop. If I am stopped our work will not stop. For what we are doing is right. What we are doing is just. And God is with us."[6]

King's God—the God revealed and known in Jesus of Nazareth, the Prince of Peace—was consistently nonviolent, even in violent situations, and always present with those who struggled and suffered for earthly justice.

Jackie Robinson was moved, and Alfred Duckett, a mutual friend, arranged for Robinson to meet King shortly after the horrific bombing. "I had been extremely impressed by his calmness in the face of such terrible violence and threats to his family," Jackie recalled. "Godliness, strength, courage, and patience in the face of overwhelming odds were his chief characteristics."[7]

The respect was certainly mutual. In later years, King often acknowledged that Robinson's courageous and nonviolent leadership in shattering the color barrier in Major League Baseball, both while and after Robinson turned the other cheek in the early part of his career, played a major role in inspiring the new wave of civil rights activism, including his own.

Heroes to each other, King and Robinson remained in touch after that initial meeting, and the civil rights leader invited Robinson to speak at a May 1956 rally marking the end of the campaign to rebuild the scorched churches of Montgomery. Busy with NAACP responsibilities, Robinson declined the invitation, but his reply exuded warmth and sympathy. "I have read with mounting concern of the attacks upon our churches in your city," he wrote. "There is no cause more deserving of support than the campaign for funds to rebuild these structures."[8]

Less deserving of support was President Eisenhower. Not long after the Montgomery bombings, Robinson lobbied the administration for a presidential statement condemning racial violence. But none was forthcoming. Eisenhower, whose advisers included the Rev. Billy Graham, the famous white evangelist who often publicly called for a "go slow" approach on racial issues, was simply too reticent on civil rights issues to deliver one.

In September 1957, Eisenhower advised patience when speaking to a group of Rhode Island Republicans about the school integration crisis in Little Rock, Arkansas, and soon after he read the president's comments, Robinson sat down and penned a letter in which he poured out his frustration. "It is easy for those who haven't felt the evils of a society to urge [patience], but for us who as Americans have patiently waited all these years for the rights supposedly guaranteed us under our Constitution, it is not an easy task," Jackie wrote. "Nevertheless, we have done it."[9]

Increasingly impatient, Robinson demanded that Eisenhower use his executive powers to do more than condemn violence in general. "A mere statement that you don't like violence is not enough," he argued. "In my opinion, people the world over would hail you if you made a statement that would clearly put your office behind the efforts for civil rights."[10]

Eisenhower did more than that after Arkansas governor Orval Faubus withdrew the National Guard from Central High School in Little Rock, allowing a white mob to terrorize the African American students integrating the public school for the first time. Eisenhower finally acted, ordering the deployment of the 101st Airborne Division of the US Army to Central High School.

Two days later, Robinson sent Eisenhower a congratulatory note. "I should have known you would do the right thing at the crucial time," he wrote. "May God continue giving you the wisdom to lead us in this struggle."[11]

Robinson was also largely pleased with the Eisenhower administration's leadership in the passage of the 1957 Civil Rights Act in the late fall. But shortly after the president signed the legislation, Robinson protested Attorney General William Rogers's comment that the administration would not seek additional civil rights legislation in 1958.

Four months later, in a keynote speech at the Summit Meeting of Negro Leaders in Washington, DC, the gap between Robinson and the administration widened all the more when Eisenhower declared that there were no "revolutionary cures" for the nation's racial crises and suggested that civil rights activists exercise "patience and forbearance."[12]

But not all was frustrating. In retirement from baseball, Robinson spent more time with Rachel, Jackie Jr., Sharon, and David, and their Stamford, Connecticut, home became a favorite hangout for children in the area, with swimming and ice hockey games. Spring and summer vacations were spent on Montauk Island, and Rachel's brother Chuck and his family would also head to the island for deep-sea fishing.

The Robinsons also made sure to steep their children in North Stamford Congregational Church, just down the block from their home. "We hoped the lessons they heard in our local Congregational church reinforced our spiritual and ethical teachings," Rachel recounted. "Our faith was just that as we had learned to make our way in the world by watching our parents and grandparents and the community at large and by relying on ourselves, so our children would find observation and practice, not didactic discussion, the best teacher."[13]

Robinson publicly shared his own faith-based morality in 1958, when he served as a moderator of *Talk Back*, a television program produced by the Methodist Church and the National Council of Churches. Shown on WOR-TV in New York, *Talk Back* featured a dramatization about a moral problem, followed by a discussion analyzing the moral issue from various perspectives.

In the episode moderated by Robinson, the dramatization focused on a plastics business and two main characters: a clerk whose frequent (and evidently faked) car problems suggest he has little stake in the company and a valuable office manager whose error results in the company losing its biggest client.

Robinson invited the panelists to answer several questions: If someone needs to be fired, why not just go ahead and chop the useless clerk? Why not sacrifice the clerk for the greater good of the company? Isn't the bottom line most important?

Robinson, at the time directing personnel at Chock full o'Nuts, revealed his own bias when he said, "I happen to be with a firm. I know that we sometimes get into problems because I will not fire for one mistake. But I think you have to live with yourself. You must give a person opportunity."[14]

In the fall of 1958, Robinson, never one to shrink from offering opportunities, asked Eisenhower to meet with activists demonstrating in a march for school integration, an issue that the president was not especially interested in pushing.

Jackie had first heard the idea for a march in a September meeting with A. Philip Randolph, the powerful black leader of the Brotherhood of Sleeping Car Porters and a visionary civil rights leader who had threatened to stage a massive march on Washington in 1941 if the federal government continued to prevent African Americans from securing jobs in the defense industry. President Roosevelt relented and issued an executive order that effectively opened up the munitions industry to blacks seeking employment.

Randolph, angered by the school crisis in Little Rock, pitched the idea of another march on Washington, this time by youths protesting the ongoing segregation of public schools. Four years earlier, the Supreme Court had ruled against such segregation in *Brown v. Board of Education*, but the justices had refused to establish a deadline for desegregation. Consequently, many school districts across the country, not merely in Little Rock, did little or nothing to desegregate their schools.

With his activist faith in tow, Robinson expressed his vigorous support for the plan, and shortly afterward he became marshal of the march, although the planning details were carried out by Randolph's mentee, Bayard Rustin, a brilliant tactician who would later mastermind the 1963 March on Washington for Jobs and Freedom. Two weeks before the event, Rustin wrote to President Eisenhower, describing the purpose of the march and asking him to welcome some of the youth at the White House to talk with them about the importance of integrating public schools.

The White House was silent. But the marchers were not, and on October 25, 1958, ten thousand excited young people, led by Jackie Robinson, Coretta Scott King, and Harry Belafonte, demonstrated for integrated schools by marching from Constitution Avenue to the Lincoln Memorial. Coretta gave an inspirational speech encouraging the young demonstrators to see the day as part of a worldwide march to freedom, and a racially integrated group of young people then presented a petition, a written statement about the march's purpose, at the White House gate. But, to Robinson's chagrin, a guard denied their request to meet with the president or any other White House official. Nevertheless, the march attracted positive national publicity for their efforts to integrate public schools, and Robinson was generally pleased with the day.

Rustin organized another march to take place the following spring, and on April 18, 1959, approximately twenty-five thousand youths and activists, led once again by Jackie Robinson, took to the streets in Washington, many of them shouting, "Five, six, seven, eight, these United States must integrate!"[15] President Eisenhower was out of town, but he sent the students a message saying that he would never be satisfied as long as racial segregation existed in the nation.

Six days later, the *New York Post* proudly announced that Jackie had just signed a contract to write a nationally syndicated triweekly column. "I believe this is the first time that real national syndication has been attempted for a columnist who happens to be a Negro," James Wechsler, the *Post*'s editor, stated.[16]

Robinson was delighted with the opportunity, especially since the *Post* had agreed that he could write on any subject.

One day after Wechsler announced Robinson's hiring, a mob of whites kidnapped Mack Charles Parker from his cell in the Pearl River

County, Mississippi, courthouse, where he had been waiting for his trial on charges of raping a white woman. The mob shot Parker numerous times before dumping him into the river.

Robinson, who relied on ghostwriter William Branch to put his thoughts on paper, chose to address the Parker lynching in the first column following his introductory one, and he took the opportunity to slam those who, like President Eisenhower and the Rev. Billy Graham, among many others, had called for a "go slow" approach to civil rights. "I can't really express my deep outrage about this terrible incident," Jackie stated. "The lynching of Mack Parker is but the end result of . . . all the weak-kneed 'gradualism' of those entrusted with enforcing and protecting civil rights."[17]

Robinson's frustration deepened the following month, shortly after an all-white jury in Monroe, North Carolina, had acquitted a white man charged with raping an African American woman in front of her children and other witnesses. At the time, Eisenhower stated that he based his hopes for greater civil rights on moral law rather than legislation because he believed that statutory laws had little effect on changing the human heart or eliminating prejudice.

Robinson fumed. "Can the president possibly mean that we must go ahead and allow these people to commit these crimes and merely stand and wait, and hope and pray, that their hearts will change?" he said. "When a man has his foot on your throat, you can worry later about changing his heart. Right now, your main concern is to keep him from choking you, else you may never live to save his soul."[18]

Law and morality were combined in Robinson's thought, and so even as he traveled to churches around the country, demanding that Eisenhower and other public officials take immediate and direct action to combat racial violence and injustice, Robinson continued to advance a theology of personal responsibility among African Americans themselves.

In June 1959, he traveled to Tuskegee, Alabama, home to Booker T. Washington's Tuskegee Institute, and praised local African Americans for building their own economy, including a shopping center, a savings and loan association, a car dealership, and other businesses, after white politicians and business leaders had ignored their vigorous protests of a gerrymandering that had effectively disenfranchised many African American voters.

"It seems to me their story is clearly indicative of the emergence of a new and determined spirit in the South," Robinson stated. "Negroes are getting tired of waiting for someone else to do something about granting them their rights, and are taking the initiative to help themselves. And in so doing, I found the Negro residents of Tuskegee, Ala., had developed new pride, industry and sense of importance in life."[19] He concluded his high praise by encouraging others to embrace and enact the same spiritual slogan adopted by the African Americans of Tuskegee: "God helps those who help themselves."[20]

That was also Jackie Robinson's spiritual slogan.

Robinson's theology of responsibility combined doses of individualism and communalism—as individuals and as a people, African Americans were to be responsible for their own lives—and in his ongoing work with the NAACP, which clearly provided him with a meaningful life purpose, he depicted himself not as a lone ranger but as someone inextricably connected with his oppressed brothers and sisters.

"I have to point out . . . that no Negro really has it 'made' until the most underprivileged Negro in America retains his full rights and dignity as a free and equal human being," Robinson explained in July 1959. "It is the responsibility of us all—Negro or white, privileged or oppressed—to contribute actively toward gaining greater freedom for all."[21]

Because of his early life in the black church, which often spoke of church members as a family, Robinson had an active sense of human interconnectedness.

His fervently held conviction about the vital importance of contributing to freedom was also far from merely a practical or pragmatic point. As a believer, Robinson noted that the responsibility to fight for freedom for all was ultimately grounded in the Bible's admonitions to proclaim liberty and end oppression, and he cited the jubilee passage in Leviticus 25:10–14 to back his point. For Robinson, setting *all* the captives free was the pressing work of the people of God.

That same month, Robinson followed his own biblical advice by siding with American Jews facing religious discrimination from the Arabian-American Oil Company (Aramco). For years, the company had required job applicants to list their religion as a qualification for employment, with the purpose of denying jobs to Jewish men and women, an undeniably discriminatory practice that reflected and abided by King Saud's policies of refusing to allow Jews to enter Saudi Arabia or work for Saudi Arabian companies in the United States.

In response to this discrimination, the American Jewish Congress (AJC) filed suit against the New York State Commission against Discrimination for allowing Aramco to practice religious discrimination in the state, and in July 1959, New York Supreme Court justice Henry Epstein ruled in favor of AJC. In his written decision, Epstein told Aramco to "go elsewhere to serve your Arab master—but not in New York State."[22]

Robinson lauded the ruling, arguing that religious discrimination was similar to racial discrimination in its character and effects. "There seems to be little difference in this case than if a Northern company doing business with the State of Mississippi refused to hire Negroes because Mississippi's Governor objected," he said. Jews in New York were like African Americans in the South; both were captives to prejudice and discrimination practiced and demanded by governing authorities. And, further, it was incumbent upon everyone to help Jews enjoy the religious freedom guaranteed them by law and morality. "There is no question in my mind but that discrimination must be fought by all of us on all fronts—religious or racial, at home or abroad," Robinson stated.[23]

However popular he remained in his postbaseball career, Robinson was not immune to personal experiences with racial prejudice, and in October he found himself face-to-face with discrimination after delivering a speech to seventeen hundred NAACP supporters in Greenville, South Carolina.

Arriving at the airport for his trip back to New York, Jackie and his NAACP colleagues lawfully bypassed the "colored lounge" in favor of the main lounge reserved for whites. As they sat there, according to Robinson, "a disheveled, unshaven man," carrying a gun and dressed in what appeared to be a uniform jacket, approached the party, identified himself as a police officer, and in "halting, seemingly uneducated speech," demanded that they move to the "colored lounge."[24]

The airport manager soon arrived, making the same demand, and as Robinson and his friends stood to protest, the manager summoned another police officer to arrest the party should they sit back down in their seats.

The Robinson party then instructed the officer that the lounge was a federally subsidized facility under the jurisdiction of the Interstate Commerce Commission and that, according to ICC regulations, it was completely lawful for them to sit in the lounge reserved for whites.

According to Robinson, the white officer acted "completely perplexed," and after making a few quick phone calls, simply "quit the scene," allowing Robinson's party to stay in the main waiting room.[25]

As 1959 drew to a close, Jackie and Rachel experienced deep satisfaction and joy while watching their children exchange gifts on Christmas Day. It was the first year that Jackie Jr. had earned his own money for the presents he gave to Sharon and David, and Rachel and Jackie were more than proud of their eldest son.

At least as meaningful for Robinson during the Christmas season was the experience of playing Santa Claus for underprivileged children at an airport terminal in New Jersey. Clad in a long beard and a red suit stuffed with pillows, Robinson did not fool all the children. "Hi, Jackie Robinson—you can't fool me!" shouted one precocious boy. But the many other children simply swarmed around Santa and took their turns to talk personally with the jolly man who might bring them gifts.[26]

The opportunity troubled Robinson as well. "How do you promise a child a present that may never come?" he wondered when he heard requests for bikes, dolls, and trains. He settled on telling the children that he would talk to their parents to see if they had been good and that perhaps their presents would arrive on Christmas Day. "It was a feeling of sadness," Robinson recalled, "but one of great happiness, too, as I watched each child go away with hope dancing in their eyes. . . . And hope, after all is the greatest gift of all at Christmastime."

But Christmas 1959 was not hope-filled everywhere, and it proved more than a troubling period for Jews in Europe and across the world. On Christmas Eve in Cologne, two young German men, members of the far-right German Reich Party, vandalized a synagogue and a nearby Holocaust memorial with swastikas and anti-Semitic slogans. The resulting publicity gave rise to similar anti-Semitic expressions throughout Europe and many other areas populated by Jews.

With the arrival of the New Year, Robinson, a fierce opponent of religious discrimination, could not help but comment on the shocking wave of anti-Semitism. "This revival of Hitlerism, with its swastika smears on the walls of synagogues, Jewish places of business and even private homes, is but another symptom of rabid sickness in our society," he said. "Since every one of us is a member of some vulnerable minority—whether it be by race, religion, national origin, political party, education, occupation, or other differences—none of us is safe once group-hate is unleashed against any other."[27]

Robinson congratulated Eisenhower for publicly condemning the new wave of anti-Semitism. But he also criticized the president for recently expressing doubt about enlisting Congress to pass laws designed to shore up voting rights for blacks in the South. "As I've said before, I submit that Negroes have been patient for nigh unto a hundred years, and now our patience is wearing thin," Robinson said, adding that the time had long passed for Eisenhower to show some "aggressive direction" on racial justice in the United States. "Even a simple, forthright statement of moral principle—such as he unhesitatingly made concerning anti-Semitism—would go a long way to lend needed encouragement to both whites and Negroes who are struggling to live up to both the spirit and the letter of the law."[28]

No such statement came.

In early 1960 Robinson supported the student sit-ins at segregated lunch counters throughout the South. He was impressed when he met some of the young protesters in New York in March. "Their calm but serious determination impressed me no end," he said. "Some of them have been personally assaulted, arrested, manhandled by the police and placed in jail."[29]

Eisenhower was not the only president who attracted Robinson's wrath at this point. So did former president Harry Truman, who, a week after Robinson had met with student protesters, sharply condemned the student sit-ins. "If anybody came to my store and tried to stop business, I'd throw him out," Truman stated. "The Negro should behave himself and show he's a good citizen. Commonsense and goodwill can solve this whole thing."[30]

Robinson, shocked and surprised, characterized Truman's comments as "regrettable but insignificant," and he taunted the former president by saying that if he really meant what he said, he should open his own business and expect to be protested. "And it is exceedingly pathetic," Robinson added, "to hear a former President declare he would resort to violence to oppose children peacefully asking to buy ice cream at a soda fountain."[31]

Robinson contributed money to the sit-ins—his good friend Marian Logan had established an emergency fund for the students—and in April he made time to watch "Anatomy of a Demonstration," a CBS news report on lunch counter sit-ins carried out by trained groups of integrated students in Nashville, Tennessee. Robinson was spellbound by the report and especially impressed by an exchange between a CBS interviewer and the Rev. James Lawson, the Gandhian leader who personally trained the students in nonviolent direct action.

When the interviewer asked Lawson whether African Americans, too, had contributed to the crisis, Lawson replied, "Yes. We have sinned by cooperating with the evils of segregation for as long as we have."[32]

Lawson's answer fit so perfectly with Robinson's own spiritual emphasis on responsibility that he included the quotation verbatim in his newspaper column.

Robinson's theology of responsibility also extolled the spiritual weapon of nonviolence in domestic politics, and he felt a close kinship with the students whom Lawson was training to withstand racist jeers and physical assaults. Watching them try to remain calm and nonviolent in these workshops took Robinson back to the first year he was with the Dodgers, when he and Rickey had agreed that he would not physically or even verbally resist those who wanted to drive him out of Major League Baseball, and Robinson praised the students for their nonviolent resolve.

By this point, Robinson was also thick in the political fray of the 1960 presidential election. As a registered independent, he had refused to back any political party and sought instead to align with the individual candidate who would best advance civil rights for African Americans.

He preferred Democrat Hubert Humphrey in the early part of the race, but the Minnesota senator's failure to gain a solid base of support led Robinson to Republican Richard Nixon.

Unlike many African Americans in 1960, Robinson had an intense dislike for John F. Kennedy and his seeming indifference to the civil rights movement, including his vote to send the 1957 civil rights bill back to committee in a wider attempt to kill the legislation.

Robinson's distaste for Kennedy grew even stronger when the candidate selected Lyndon Johnson, a former segregationist from Texas, as his running mate on the Democratic ticket.

The Kennedy team, particularly former Connecticut governor Chester Bowles, reached out to Robinson, arranging a meeting between him and the senator in Washington, DC, but the effort proved disastrous when Kennedy, according to Robinson's account, avoided all eye contact and conceded he knew very little about the concerns of African Americans.

Robinson also gave a number of reasons for settling on Nixon: the vice president's anticommunism, his willingness to tour Africa, his leading role in engineering passage of the 1957 civil rights legislation, and his pledge to move faster on civil rights than Eisenhower had.

Robinson felt so strongly about the presidential election that he took leave from his position as a columnist with the *Post* in September to campaign full-time for Nixon.

But Robinson also grew impatient while stumping for Nixon, complaining that the campaign managers simply ignored or dismissed opportunities to connect with African American voters, especially those in Harlem.

His greatest frustration occurred in October, when Nixon refused Robinson's personal urging that he telephone Martin Luther King Jr., who was beginning to serve a sentence of four months at Reidsville State Prison in Georgia. While Nixon felt a call would be "grandstanding," Kennedy called Coretta Scott King, and his brother Robert enlisted a local judge to help secure King's release.[33]

Robinson was visibly upset after Nixon refused to call King, and his frustration was so intense that he almost quit the campaign immediately. But he stayed the course, urged on by Branch Rickey himself, and agonized time and again as he watched the African American vote, including Rachel's, swing in wide favor of Kennedy.

Although disappointed with the Democratic victory, Robinson wrote Kennedy a letter of praise one day after the new president appointed Harris Wofford as the White House staff member in charge of civil rights issues. "I thank you for what you have done so far, but it is not how much has been done but how much more there is to do," Robinson wrote. "I would like to be patient, Mr. President, but patience has cost us years in our struggle for human dignity. I will continue to hope and pray for your aggressive leadership but will not refuse to criticize if the feeling persists that Civil Rights is not on the agenda for months to come. May God give you the strength and the energy to accomplish your most difficult task."[34]

Robinson's "hope," as he put it to the president, was yet another part of his Christian faith—an abiding hope that the will of God would indeed flourish on earth, right here and now, if he and others just worked hard enough, long enough, and sacrificially enough, for the cause of civil rights.

In early 1961, Robinson praised Attorney General Robert Kennedy for delivering a major civil rights speech in which he pledged that when confronted with civil rights violations, the Kennedy administration would act swiftly. In his letter, Robinson confessed that he had had "grave doubts about your sincerity," but that the speech had changed his perspective. "I find it a pleasure to be proven wrong," he wrote.[35]

At the beginning of 1962, Robinson began writing a regular column for the *New York Amsterdam News*, the oldest black newspaper in the United States.[36] *New York Post* editor James Wechsler had fired Robinson just before the 1960 presidential election because he believed that Robinson's political partisanship had clouded his ability to be an accurate and fair columnist.

If Robinson was a bit cranky as 1962 began, he soon became exhilarated when he learned that the Baseball Writers Association of America had elected him on the first ballot to the Baseball Hall of Fame in Cooperstown, New York. Robinson had earlier stated that he would never dare "crawl" to the hall, especially if he had to keep his mouth shut to win over writers who had long treated him unfairly, but with the resounding election he found himself relieved and grateful.[37]

Reflecting on the award, which he considered to be the greatest he had ever received, Robinson said, "I just want to say that if this [election] can happen to a guy whose parents were virtual slaves, a guy from a broken home, a guy whose mother worked as a domestic from sun-up to sun-down for a number of years; if this can happen to someone who, in his early years, was a delinquent and who learned that he had to change his life—then it can happen to you kids out there who think that life is against you."[38]

And to a news reporter in his living room, Robinson punctuated his reflections with a sense of gratitude. "And now to end up like this," he said. "You have to thank God for having a mother like I have who taught me right from wrong and for guiding me to my wife."[39]

Just before he was inducted into the Baseball Hall of Fame, Robinson found himself embroiled in a controversy between Jews and black nationalists in Harlem.

During the summer of 1962, Robinson defended the right of Frank Schiffman, the Jewish owner of the Apollo Theater in Harlem, to lease a neighborhood property to white businessman Sol Singer for the purpose of opening a low-cost steakhouse.

Some local blacks, fearing that the proposed business would undermine the success of a more expensive black-owned restaurant in the same general area, had begun to picket the Apollo Theater with signs that described Schiffman as Shylock from Shakespeare's *Merchant of Venice*. Organized by Lewis H. Michaux, a black nationalist and owner of the famous National Memorial African Bookstore in Harlem, and supported by Malcolm X and the Nation of Islam, the demonstrators also did not hesitate to use anti-Semitic epithets when chanting outside the Apollo. One of their sayings was "Black man must stay; Jew must go."[40]

Robinson grew incensed when he noticed that Harlem leaders remained largely silent in the face of these anti-Semitic protests, and he expressed his frustration in his column. "Here we are, a group as persecuted as anyone in the world," he observed. "Yet, we stand passively or turn our heads in the other direction when a handful of Negroes mouth the kind of thing which Hitler popularized in Nazi Germany."[41]

Robinson's work with the NAACP had put him in close touch with a number of progressive Jewish leaders active in the NAACP, and he often spoke at Jewish events across the nation. It was his way of returning some of the support that rabbis and other Jewish leaders had offered him so courageously during his first years with the Dodgers.

"When I think of the Jewish rabbis, it brings my mind to how deeply I have been impressed by the wonderful unity and teamwork of the Jewish people," Robinson stated. "Often, while making appearances for benefits or rallies in which the Jewish people were interested, I would look about me and see the positive evidence of this unity. I would say to myself, 'Gee, if the Negro people ever grew into this kind of togetherness, they'll have half the problem licked.'"[42]

But Robinson's defense of Schiffman earned scathing attacks from black militants sympathetic with the demonstrators. Some launched a "hate Jackie Robinson campaign" and turned their pickets on the Chock full o'Nuts coffee shop in Harlem.[43]

Prominent civil rights leaders, like Roy Wilkins of the NAACP and A. Philip Randolph of the Brotherhood of Sleeping Car Porters, supported Robinson. So too did several black Christian ministers, including the Rev. George Lawrence, pastor of Antioch Baptist Church in Brooklyn, and the Rev. Thomas Kilgore of Manhattan. Lawrence and Kilgore used their pulpits to ask their congregation members to purchase two cans of Chock full o'Nuts coffee every time they needed just one pound.

After the controversy faded, Robinson again turned his attention to President Kennedy, this time faulting him for not intervening in the brewing civil rights crisis in Albany, Georgia, where Martin Luther King Jr. had recently been arrested. Robinson invoked God in his defense of King, suggesting that the lack of action by Kennedy and the rest of the country was virtually godless in character. "It is time for America to take a long look inward," Robinson said. "What has happened in our country—a country which emphasizes that the main difference between us and the Russians is that we are a God-fearing people? What has happened when men are beaten, jailed and intimidated because they turn to God for an answer, because they fall upon their knees to pray?"[44]

Robinson directed his frustration toward Kennedy shortly after approximately one hundred black Christian ministers had marched on the White House in support of King. The ministers had demanded a meeting with the president, but their efforts resulted only in a brief session with an assistant attorney general. Robinson was deeply offended, and he characterized Kennedy's refusal to meet with the ministers as "an insult to the national Negro community."[45]

Perhaps with his memories of the Rev. Karl Downs in mind, Robinson also took the occasion to highlight the important roles of the black Christian minister: "The President seems to be unaware that there is no one closer to the pulse of the Negro than his ministers. From the cradle to the grave, the minister remains in intimate contact with his people. He christens or baptizes our babies, counsels, praises and chastises our youth, conducts our marriages, seeks to help prevent divorces and administers the funerals of our loved ones. In crisis, sickness and in triumph, the minister is a power, an influence and a leader."[46]

Robinson and King remained in close contact.

King's organization, the Southern Christian Leadership Conference, had hosted a tribute dinner for Robinson at the Waldorf Astoria in Manhattan to honor him for his induction into the Baseball Hall of Fame. It was a delightful occasion for Robinson, and although King could not attend because of urgent demands in Albany, Georgia, he asked his assistant, the Rev. Wyatt Tee Walker, to read his tribute speech at the stunning event attended by Branch Rickey, Roy Wilkins, Mallie Robinson, Rachel, and hundreds of others important in Jackie's life.

King also used the speech as text for a widely read column in which he lauded Robinson's entire career while also tending to the recent flare-up with black nationalists. "It needs to be noted that Jackie Robinson speaks not only of the evils which misguided whites heap upon the Negro," King wrote. "He speaks also to the Negro about the evils he heaps upon himself or visits upon others."[47]

The civil rights leader observed that Robinson had "always exercised the honesty, the courage and the conviction to speak out against the forces which would seek to solve the ravaging fear of the black man's dilemma by rubbing upon it the vicious virus of anti-Semitism and religious and racial hatred."[48]

To King, Robinson was a truth-teller, above all else. "Thank God for a Jackie Robinson who can stand his ground and say: 'I have spoken what I believe to be the truth and I cannot retract the truth,'" King wrote, adding that Robinson's passion for truth was a product of his faith. "But here is a man who recognizes that God offers to every mind the choice between truth and repose. Jackie Robinson has chosen truth. The Truth, within himself."[49]

While acknowledging that Robinson's truth-telling had caused a number of critics to question his right to speak out in such a forthright manner—after all, he was a baseball player, not a politician or the head of a civil rights organization—King insisted that Robinson had earned the right because "he underwent trauma and the humiliation and the loneliness which comes with being a pilgrim walking the lonesome byways toward the high road of freedom." It was Robinson's shoulders on which all the present activists stood. "He was a sit-inner before the sit-ins, a freedom rider before the freedom rides," King declared.[50]

King also invited Robinson to travel to Albany at the end of the summer to help rally a group of tired and beaten civil rights workers.

After delivering an inspiring speech before Albany activists in mid-August, Robinson then traveled to the small community of Sasser, Georgia, where he stood before the ashes of Mount Olivet Baptist Church, one of three black churches burned because of its efforts to register African American voters. Robinson could not help but be visibly moved by the sight of the church's minister and his flock. "I watched a strong man, the Rev. F. S. Swaggott, the pastor of the church, weeping as though his heart would break as he looked over the debris and the wreckage of the institution into which he and his people poured their devotion and their dreams," Robinson later recalled.[51]

It was a deeply sad moment, and Robinson, whose heart could be as soft as his resolve was steely, agreed with Walker that something needed to be done to show the world that the fires could not stop the march toward freedom. Robinson suggested the creation of a fund to rebuild the churches, and he pledged $100 on the spot. Later that day, he agreed to King's suggestion that he chair a national committee that would raise all the funds required to rebuild the churches.

But Robinson had to slow down when he faced serious complications of surgery to repair torn cartilage in his knee in early 1963. The unexpected complications, from Robinson's ongoing struggles with diabetes, left him hallucinating and, worse, suspended in that frightening area between life and death.

"All I can say is that I have been a very sick man," Robinson stated at the time.[52]

He took the sobering occasion to reflect on his life through the lens of his faith: "My experience has impressed me tremendously with the realization of how wonderful God has been to me."[53]

Robinson's feelings of gratitude were heightened by his encounters with ailing children who had learned of his presence in the hospital and had requested that he visit their rooms. He obliged, of course, and he came away with a deepening faith, as he explained in his column:

> If I ever start feeling blue, I am going to remember the sixth floor of this hospital where I saw so many young people suffering without complaining.
>
> But, most of all, I'll remember a five-year-old who was so badly burned that I found it difficult to sit and talk with her. Not a complaint came from this child's lips.
>
> It's hard to describe one's feelings when someone in this condition looks down at a leg that is taped from hip to foot and asks, "What happened?"
>
> I do know that as I was wheeled off the floor and spoke with Doug Brown, who had requested that I stop in to visit him, I pledged to be grateful to God for all of his blessings.
>
> I have suffered but witnessing the suffering of an uncomplaining, pain-stricken five-year-old makes you feel the power of God's blessings.[54]

The lengthy hospital stay also forced Robinson to confront his own mortality in terms of his faith. As he stared at the possibility of death, Robinson resisted, saying that he was not quite ready to "steal home," and when a friend asked if he was afraid of dying, he said, "My reply was that I was not afraid—but deeply concerned about the effect it would have on my wife and our young children if I were taken away at this time."[55]

With the welfare of his family foremost in his thoughts, Robinson turned yet again to the Christian virtue of hope. "I like to think that God has a lot of work left for me to do and wants to give me time to do it the best I possibly can," he added.[56]

A decade of life, with all its challenges and promises, still awaited him.

8

"Do You Know What God Did?"

For King, against Malcolm

Jackie Robinson's brush with death did not quiet him. In some ways he seemed even fiercer than before, and not long after he left the hospital, he stood up to one of the most powerful black ministers in the nation, the Rev. Adam Clayton Powell Jr. of Abyssinian Baptist Church in Harlem. Embodying the black church's traditional mixing of church and politics, Powell, a strikingly handsome man with a smooth baritone voice, also represented Harlem in the US House of Representatives.

Always colorful, Powell courted controversy throughout his career, and in a mid-March 1963 rally in Harlem, he called on African Americans to boycott major civil rights organizations that they did not control. It was a clear reference, at the very least, to Jewish leadership on the board of the National Association for the Advancement of Colored People (NAACP).

Jews had played a significant role in the NAACP ever since its founding in 1908 as an organized attempt to counter the horrific practice of lynching and the fallout from a race riot in Springfield, Illinois, the home of the Great Emancipator, Abraham Lincoln. Joel Spingarn, a retired professor from Columbia University, had been a founding member of the NAACP, even serving as chair of the board, and he recruited several leading Jewish men to join him on the newly created board.

While Powell later denied that he had called for a boycott, he continued to insist that African Americans should occupy the primary leadership positions in civil rights organizations.

That separatist message played well in Harlem, where Malcolm X, the Nation of Islam, and other black militants called for the separation of blacks and whites and even the creation of a separate state for blacks. But Robinson, a Christian integrationist, was not pleased, and he decided to pen an open letter in his newspaper column.

In the hard-hitting letter, Robinson defended the NAACP as the nation's "greatest organization working in behalf of all those principles of freedom and human dignity for the black man in America." He described Jewish leaders of the NAACP as having "done a dedicated job and organized more moral and financial support for this cause than any ten Negroes." And he criticized Malcolm X and the Nation of Islam, arguing that "the answer for the Negro is to be found, not in segregation or separation, but by his insistence upon moving into his rightful place."[1]

Robinson's sharply worded letter yielded a torrent of criticism from black militants and followers of Powell and Malcolm X.

If the criticism stung, Robinson did not let on, but he did attend to a critic who had argued that African Americans should "stick together." "I agree," Robinson responded. "I have been pleading for Negro unity for years. But if 'sticking together' means you continue to blindly endorse a man simply because he is black—or green—or white—when you truly feel he has been wrong, you can have that kind of sticking together. One of the most precious assets a man has is his right to speak the truth as he sees it."[2]

In early May, more than one thousand African American children and teenagers joined the Southern Christian Leadership Conference's campaign to desegregate Birmingham, Alabama, one of the most dangerous places for blacks in the United States. Its nickname, Bombingham, was easily deserved.

Marching from Sixteenth Street Baptist Church and through city streets, many of the youths ended up in cramped jail cells. More than a few also suffered physical and emotional injuries because Commissioner of Public Safety Eugene "Bull" Connor, who had shown no patience for the young demonstrators, ordered police and firefighters to unleash German shepherds and turn high-pressure fire hoses on the demonstrators. Newspaper photographs and televised images of police brutality against children and youths peacefully demonstrating for their rights shocked the nation and the wider world.

As impatient as ever, Robinson replied to the violence by sending an urgent telegram to President Kennedy, stating that "the pace at which our country is moving toward total equality for all peoples is miserably slow" and calling for the president to cut off federal aid to Alabama and declare martial law. "The revolution that is taking place in this country cannot be squelched by police dogs or high power hoses," he added.[3]

Martin Luther King Jr. asked Robinson to visit Birmingham, and Robinson announced at a May 7 news conference that he would indeed head to Alabama. "I don't like to be bitten by dogs, because I'm a coward," he stated. "I don't like to go to jail either, because, as I say, I'm a coward. But we've got to show Martin Luther King that we are behind him."[4]

Three days later, not long after a bomb exploded at King's head-quarters at the Gaston Motel, Robinson and heavyweight boxer Floyd Patterson, his good friend, left for Birmingham, where he delivered rousing addresses in two black churches full of cheering crowds. If only for a short time, Robinson and Patterson offered the activists respite from the brutality they would suffer yet again. That night, in a coura-geous act that symbolized the movement's unfailing determination, Robinson and Patterson stayed at the bombed-out Gaston Motel before heading back to New York the following morning.

President Kennedy responded to the Birmingham violence by put-ting on alert federal troops near the city and by delivering a speech, nationally televised on June 11, in which he stated, at the urging of King and others, that racial segregation was a moral issue "as old as the Scriptures and as clear as the American Constitution."[5] Even more significant was the president's pledge of sweeping civil rights legisla-tion that would correct the wrongs that Robinson and other civil rights activists had been attacking.

Robinson was delighted. Although he had been a tough critic at times, he could not help but admire the president's commitment to advancing civil rights through legislation. Robinson wired the president his support. "Thank you for emerging as the most forthright president we have ever had and for providing us with the inspired leadership that we so desperately needed," he wrote. "I am more proud than ever of my American heritage."[6]

Just hours after the president's historic speech, Byron De La Beck-with gunned down Medgar Evers, the top NAACP official in Missis-sippi, in his driveway in Jackson. Robinson, who had gone to Jackson twice at Evers's bidding, wired the president yet again, this time seek-ing federal protection for King as he attended Evers's funeral. "Should harm come to Dr. King to add to the misery which decent Americans of both races experienced with the murder of Mr. Evers, the restraint of many people all over this nation might burst its bonds and bring about a brutal bloody holocaust the like of which this country has not seen," Robinson wrote.[7]

A few months later, supporters of Malcolm X and the Nation of Islam threw eggs at King and the car he was riding in as he arrived for a preaching engagement at Salem Methodist Church in Harlem. A disgusted Robinson blamed the incident on Malcolm, though the minister of the Nation of Islam unequivocally denied any involvement.

Robinson also loudly registered his disappointment with Malcolm's disavowal of nonviolence and his calls for the physical separation of blacks and whites. However, Robinson did acknowledge that Malcolm had a right to disagree with King and conceded that he too had deep misgivings about nonviolence. "Personally, I am not and don't know how I could ever be nonviolent," Robinson observed. "If anyone punches me or otherwise physically assaults me, you can bet your bottom dollar that I will try to give him back as good as he sent."[8]

Turning the other cheek—the nonviolent practice demanded by Jesus—was not part of Robinson's personal repertoire, despite the restraint he practiced during his first years in baseball. If someone attacked him or his family, Robinson would not have thought twice about using physical force in response. Unlike King, who embraced nonviolence as a way of life, Robinson echoed Malcolm's embrace of a self-defensive posture open to the use of physical force. Nevertheless, Robinson sharply critiqued Malcolm's opposition to nonviolence as the main strategy for the civil rights movement, not because Robinson believed that the movement should follow Jesus' nonviolence in any and all circumstances but because he found King's nonviolence to be the most effective strategy for advancing civil rights.

In early July, Robinson traveled to Denver, Colorado, to accept the Churchmanship Award at the Fourth General Synod of the United Church of Christ (UCC), a largely white denomination long known for its liberal theology and politics.

Given by the Christian Social Action Committee, the award described Robinson as a "Christian layman fulfilling your ministry to the world" and honored him for his "Christian commitment of time, energy, and skill in the struggle for social justice."[9]

Members of the synod gave Robinson a standing ovation, and he delivered a stirring speech that opened with a story about an African American boy whose family, like young Jackie's, had moved into a white community that openly demonstrated a frigid attitude toward blacks. When the young boy tried to attend Sunday school at a church across the street from his home, an usher denied him entrance, telling him that the church was for whites only.

"The little boy was terribly disappointed, so disappointed that he sat down on the church step and began to cry," Robinson continued. But then God came along and asked the little boy why he was crying. "I'm crying, because those mean, old people won't let me in their church," the boy replied.

"Ladies and gentlemen," Robinson stated, "do you know what God did? He sat right down at the little boy's side and started to cry too. And do you know why—because that was one church God had been trying to get into for many, many years."[10]

This was Jackie Robinson's God, one who is faithfully present to, and suffers with, the captive, the oppressed, the victims of racial prejudice.

Robinson used the story to prick racist churches. "I think we can honestly say that there are many churches in this nation where God cannot feel welcome because some of His children are not welcome," he said. "For years, as it has been pointed out often in the past, it has been a national shame that 11 a.m. was the most segregated hour in America."[11]

But the primary emphasis of Robinson's talk was that times were changing and that "all over this nation today, the consciences of clergyman and the heads of denominations have been stirred."[12]

Leading the way, Robinson believed, was the United Church of Christ and its public stance against racial injustice. Earlier in the week, the synod had adopted a bold resolution, easily the most liberal passed by any US Christian denomination up to this point, that described the racial crisis in the summer of 1963 as "a sign of God's action in the history of the United States" and implored the church to join in God's work by becoming "radically committed" to the struggle for racial justice in employment practices, housing, education, judicial processes, voting, and access to public accommodations and capital.[13]

Although the Voting Rights Act of 1965 was still two years away, the prophetic resolution also called for the church to help African Americans "register, vote, and run for office without fear of retaliation, either overt or subtle."[14]

Even more striking, though, was the resolution's sense of urgency, its dramatic call for the church "to push for all that is due here and now without heeding those who counsel patience, moderation, and gratitude."

African Americans suffering from the brutalities of racial injustice should not have to wait for the heavens to open and Jesus Christ to appear.[15]

A man of impatient faith, Robinson could not have been more pleased, and he devoted a column to praising the UCC for its "forth-right stance." He described the trip to Denver as "one of the finest experiences I've ever had," and he expressed renewed hope that large groups of white Christians could come together, as groups, not just as individuals, to fight for racial justice here and now.[16]

Robinson observed that he had long been familiar with many examples of individual white Christians and Jews acting heroically in the civil rights movement. "One thinks of a white minister who led a Negro girl to school in Little Rock, the group of rabbis who went to Albany, Georgia, to be jailed, the young Catholic priests who have marched in freedom demonstrations," he stated. And while these individual actions were admirable, Robinson and others felt that they were also insufficient, especially in light of the resources and credibility that groups of believers could offer the civil rights movement. As Robinson put it, "Many of us in the civil rights movement were disturbed at the way large denominations and conferences acted either timidly or not at all on the question of civil rights."[17]

For Robinson, the best model was the one offered by the UCC. "We need more powerful movements and denominations to realize as the United Church of Christ realizes that America has too long stopped payment on the blank check . . . of justice and equality which is the rightful legacy of every American simply by virtue of his birth,."[18]

A month later, Jackie and Rachel took their three children—Jackie Jr., Sharon, and David—to the March on Washington for Jobs and Freedom. "I have never been so proud to be a Negro," Robinson stated when reflecting on that momentous occasion. "I have never been so proud to be an American."[19]

What made him so proud on that day in August was watching masses of blacks and whites come together to demonstrate their full support for the civil rights movement. "One had to be deeply moved as he stood, watching Negroes and whites, marching hand in hand, singing songs for freedom," Robinson said. "What a beautiful picture we marchers gave to the world."[20]

His family's presence made the day especially meaningful. Marching with his son David and explaining to him the meaning of the movement, seeing Rachel marvel as King shared his dream, hearing about Jackie Jr. singing and clapping, and experiencing the care others showed when Sharon fainted because of the heat—all this made the day full of "personal thrills."[21]

But however thrilled he was, Robinson also sounded an ominous note about southern segregationists like Senators Strom Thurmond of South Carolina, John Stennis of Mississippi, and Russell Long of Louisiana, all of whom had made disparaging comments about the march, and the possibility that they might block civil rights legislation.

Less than a month after King shared his dream at the march, four young girls—Addie Mae Collins, Denise McNair, Carole Robertson, and Cynthia Wesley—were murdered when white racists dynamited their home church, Sixteenth Street Baptist Church in Birmingham, during closing prayers at Sunday school.

The bomb shattered stained-glass windows, destroyed the church's basement, crushed nearby cars, and left dozens bloodied and dazed. One stained-glass window, depicting Jesus with a group of children, remained in its frame, but the bomb had blown out the face of Jesus. It was the twenty-first bombing in eight years in Birmingham. None were solved by the local police.

Angry men and women flocked to the church following the explosion, and the Rev. John Cross, the church's pastor, sobbed as he asked everyone to go home. "The Lord is our shepherd," he shouted. "We shall not want."[22]

Robinson had a different reaction. After drawing attention to the song "If I Had a Hammer," Robinson wrote, "If I had been a parent in Birmingham on a Sunday morning which was shattered by a detonation more vicious than any ever released by Hitler in Nazi Germany—and if, in the ruins of that bombing, one of my children had been found, crushed to death, I know what I would have done with that hammer."[23]

Robinson would not have loved his enemies. He would not have put down the sword. He would not have followed the nonviolent Jesus to the cross. "God bless Dr. Martin Luther King," Robinson stated. "But, I'm afraid he would have lost me as a potential disciple of his credo of nonviolence."[24]

Robinson also demanded immediate action from President Kennedy in the wake of the bombing. "When these people start throwing bombs in a church where kids are worshipping their God, it's time for President Kennedy to draw the line."[25]

In effect, Robinson hoped that Kennedy would declare martial law and order federal troops to the city, and he warned of pending violence if the federal government failed to respond to the bombing. "But if you want to see a people inflamed, just let the goons and punks keep messing around with our children," he said. "There's a line the most docile human beings draw—and this is it!"[26]

A little more than two months later, Lee Harvey Oswald assassinated President Kennedy in Dallas, Texas.

"A noble man is gone," Robinson stated shortly after the assassination. He conceded that he had sharply criticized the president, but he also hastened to add his positive assessment that Kennedy "had emerged as the chief executive who has done more for the civil rights cause than any other president."[27]

With the violent year of 1963 behind him, Robinson began a three-year term as president of the United Church Men, a division of the National Council of Churches (NCC). The NCC, a broad coalition of Protestant and Orthodox churches, leaned left on civil rights issues.

At the beginning of the Montgomery bus boycott, the NCC had characterized segregation as a violation of love and telegrammed its support to Martin Luther King Jr. The NCC had also criticized President Eisenhower for remaining silent as racial violence exploded in the South. And like Robinson, the council had thrown its support behind King's subsequent campaigns, the student-led sit-ins, the March on Washington, and various calls for civil rights legislation. The NCC was Robinson's kind of organization, and he hoped he could steep it even more deeply in the civil rights movement.

Directly below *Jet* magazine's announcement of Robinson's election as president of the United Church Men was a brief report on the Nation of Islam's rejection of white applicants. When asked about the rejection, the Nation of Islam's leader, the Honorable Elijah Muhammad, had stated, "There have been hundreds who asked about joining. But I told them . . . since Abraham, Moses and Jesus couldn't teach you, there's nothing we can do either." Whites were altogether hopeless unless they experienced a new identity. "No prophet can reform them," Muhammad added. "They must have a rebirth; be grafted into the black man."[28]

The contrast between the integrationist Robinson and the separatist Elijah Muhammad, each driven by his particular faith, could not have been clearer.

In early March, Rachel saw Jackie Jr. walking down one of the main streets of Stamford. It had been a tough year for him. He was disappointed to be back at Stamford High School, and his frustration was compounded by a lack of communication between him and his father. Jackie and Rachel had sought to help him, as well as Sharon and David, by joining Jack and Jill, a social organization that brought together black families, and becoming active at North Stamford Congregational Church, but nothing seemed to reach Jackie Jr. as he withdrew from his parents and others.

But when Rachel saw her son, he appeared positive and upbeat. He was on his way to enlist in the army.

Rachel implored him to consider other options, but Jackie Jr. enlisted on March 30. His father, according to Rachel, "accepted this momentous change largely in silence, which was not surprising, given what his relationship with his son had become."[29]

In mid-April, Robinson turned his attention once again to inner-city violence when approximately seventy-five African American youths were involved in vandalism at a fruit-and-vegetable stand in Harlem. The minor event exploded into what became known as the Fruit Riot when the New York Police Department used brutal tactics against the vandals.

When he learned of the riot, Robinson publicly expressed his burning hope that he could have a "heart-to-heart, man-to-man" talk with the youths so he might tell them that they were harming the freedom struggle, their community, their families and friends, and their own lives. He would also emphasize "that you don't win like this," that you cannot achieve your freedom and civil rights by lashing out in violence. He hoped his reticence on nonviolence as a principle would make his argument more convincing to the youths. "I would say that there is a better way and, frankly, I don't happen to be one of the turn-the-other-cheek advocates, despite my deep admiration for Dr. King," Robinson explained. "Personally, I am afraid I have not learned to return hatred with love."[30]

It was yet another public confession that Robinson was not altogether enamored of teachings in the New Testament, both Jesus' admonition to turn the other cheek and the apostle Paul's counsel about responding to evil with nobility and goodness. Nevertheless, however wary of Jesus' and Paul's teachings Robinson personally was at times, he remained firmly convinced that nonviolent direct action was the most practical and effective strategy for gaining civil rights in the United States.

This conviction was challenged yet again when Robinson was guest of honor at a banquet held during the NAACP's 55th annual convention. The relaxing dinner was well under way when a crazed white man, waving a swastika, jumped onto the dais and shouted words about "sending all the niggers back to Africa." Robinson's response to the threatening spectacle was predictable, given his earlier comments. "I will be very honest with you," he stated when reflecting on the event. "I am not nonviolent in such circumstances."[31]

As he watched the racist, Robinson felt himself growing angry. "Not only was my anger rising," he recalled, "but I found that I was rising with every intention of letting this unexpected visitor have a good swift jab in the head."[32]

But the younger attendees got to the racist before Robinson did, and they were forcefully nonviolent in their handling of the racist. "They didn't hit him," Robinson recalled. "They didn't maul him. They surrounded him, they took hold of him and hustled him out of the room."[33]

At the same time Robinson renounced nonviolence as a viable option for himself, he still refused to give any quarter to Malcolm X, even after he left the Nation of Islam, converted to Sunni Islam, and went on a pilgrimage to Mecca, where he recounted his moving experience in a letter that detailed a shift in religious perspective. Malcolm founded and led the Organization of Afro-American Unity, with hopes of entering the political arena and even cooperating with other civil rights leaders, something that Elijah Muhammad had never allowed him to do.

But Robinson would have none of Malcolm's conversion. "Yesterday, he owed 'all in my life' to the Honorable Elijah Muhammad," Robinson stated. "Today the Honorable Elijah is not so honorable in Malcolm's book. Yesterday, he vigorously denied that Muslims teach hatred. Today, he tells the white press that he became disenchanted with the Muslims because 'they teach hate.' Yesterday, to Malcolm, all white folks were devils. Today, after seeing some startling vision during his travels, Mr. X has decided that some white folks are all right. What does this man really think?" He even dared to call Malcolm "the fair-haired boy of the white press" and ridiculed his new organization as likely to amount to nothing.[34]

But Robinson was not opposed to all converts. One who captured his close attention in 1964 was the fast-talking boxer Cassius Clay, who, after defeating Sonny Liston in February for the title of heavyweight champion, announced that, with encouragement and help from Malcolm X, he had converted to the Nation of Islam and that his new name was Muhammad Ali.

In explaining his religion to the media, Ali observed that "Islam" means "peace," and that while people often branded the Nation of

Islam as a hate group, that was simply untrue. "All they want to do is live in peace with the world," Ali said. "They don't hate anybody." Ali also stated that Islam had given him "inner peace" and that it was responsible for his defeat of Liston. "God was with me—I couldn't have done it without God."[35]

Robinson, a huge boxing fan, responded to Ali's conversion to Islam. "Clay has just as much a right to ally himself with the Muslim religion as anyone else has to be a Protestant or a Catholic," he argued. He also took on those who denied that the Nation of Islam was a real religion, saying that "one of the basic American principles involves the right of each individual to embrace a philosophy and call it his religion."[36]

He added another significant point about Ali, one that reached way back to the spiritual lessons of self-worth he had learned from his mother, Mallie, and his minister, the Rev. Karl Downs: "[Clay] has spread the message that more of us need to know: 'I am the greatest,' he says. I am not advocating that Negroes think they are greater than anyone else. But I want them to know that they are just as great as other human beings. If we can learn to believe in ourselves one iota of the way Clay does, we'll be in great shape."[37]

Robinson was also accepting of another dramatic conversion in 1964. While he had earlier derided Lyndon Baines Johnson as a segregationist, by the summer of 1964 he depicted the new president as bold and courageous in advancing civil rights.

But Jackie did not offer the same openness and generosity to Senator Barry Goldwater of Arizona, comparing the Republican nominee for the presidency with the much-reviled segregationist governor of Alabama, George Wallace. "In my opinion he is a bigot, an advocate of white supremacy and more dangerous than Governor Wallace," Robinson said.[38]

Robinson had publicly detailed his disaffection for the changing flavor of the GOP during the summer of 1963, drawing connections between the Nation of Islam and the Republican Party in an article he wrote for the *Saturday Evening Post*. "It seems to me that there is a striking parallel between the thinking of the Black Muslims and of the growing number of conservative Republicans who support Sen. Barry Goldwater," he had argued. "Both groups feel they can reach their goals by traveling the road of racial separation."[39]

To back his point, Robinson referred to Southern business leaders and politicians who had begun to make progressive statements on civil rights. He also offered churches as evidence. "The leading religious denominations are making statements and raising funds and executing policy designed to expose the hypocrisy of acknowledging the fatherhood of God on Sunday and denying the brotherhood of man on Monday."[40]

Robinson ended up fleeing the Republicans during the summer of 1964. Hubert Humphrey, the Democratic candidate for vice president, assured Robinson that Johnson was indeed sincere in his conversion to racial justice and civil rights, and Jackie, after lauding Governor Nelson Rockefeller of New York as the best presidential candidate and traveling with him to the Republican National Convention, threw his final support to the Johnson-Humphrey ticket, even helping to chair the Republicans for Johnson committee.

In the early fall of 1964, Robinson traveled to Philadelphia to speak to a cause near and dear to his heart: economic advancement for African Americans.

Robinson took great delight when he learned of black clergy members in Philadelphia who were establishing the Organization of Industrialization Center (OIC), a systematic and cooperative effort to train African Americans for jobs in skilled and semiskilled jobs in industry. The Rev. Leon Sullivan, a graduate of Union Theological Seminary in New York City and pastor of Zion Baptist Church in Philadelphia, was the driving force behind the emerging organization. Sullivan was the dynamic embodiment of Robinson's vision of the good minister: socially conscious, focused on community needs, and intent on building economic programs designed to help blacks help themselves.

With donations from community members and others, Sullivan converted a dilapidated jail into the first OIC training center and schooled its students in job and life skills. Undergirded by a theology of personal responsibility, the OIC quickly became a success, training and placing thousands of African Americans in local companies.

Robinson could not have been more pleased than he was to offer his support to OIC, and he delivered an inspiring speech to hundreds of its students in October. Reflecting later on what he called "one of the most wholesome evenings I have spent in some time," he stated: "I don't know whether I inspired any of the hundreds of trainees who were present. I do know that I was inspired by the eagerness of these people, inspired by their recognition of the fact that it is one thing to cry out, to picket, to demonstrate for equality and it is equally important to qualify for the 'breaks' when they come to us."[41]

But Sullivan, "a minister's minister," was the one who most inspired Jackie that evening because of his theology of self-help, his concern for economic justice, his community focus, his hope-filled action, his sensitivity to injustice. For Robinson, Sullivan was "a mover and shaker of men who gets things going not for personal greed, gain or glory—but to fulfill his mission as a man of God and the one who points the way."[42]

The fall brought other good news to Robinson: the defeat of Barry Goldwater and the election of Lyndon Johnson as president of the United States. Robinson had campaigned vigorously for the Texan convert to racial justice, and he breathed a sigh of relief when Johnson handily beat the Arizona senator. After the election, Robinson shrewdly claimed that the Republican Party should have learned from the results that racism would not grant them access to the White House.

But, as 1964 came to a close, Robinson's prophetic wrath erupted when FBI director J. Edgar Hoover publicly condemned Martin Luther King Jr. as "the most notorious liar in the country."[43] Hoover did not give the public any evidence to back his claim, but he no doubt had in mind evidence he had gathered from FBI wiretaps, authorized by Attorney General Robert Kennedy, in King's home, office, and hotel rooms.

Robinson launched a counterattack against Hoover.

"Mr. Hoover's absurd accusation that Dr. King is a 'notorious liar' is evidence that the boss of the FBI is a much disturbed man," Robinson said. Rather than assaulting King's integrity, Hoover "ought to go down on his knees to bless Martin King." Had it not been for King's insistence on nonviolence in the civil rights movement, "we might have had a most terrible holocaust of racial violence."[44]

The year ended with the happy return of Jackie Jr. Home on leave from the army, he left his parents with the impression that he had matured. "Jackie has grown a great deal," Jack wrote in a letter to David and Caroline Wallerstein. "He seems to be developing into a real man and I am certain his Army stint will be a blessing."[45] But the army, and the coming year, would prove to be far different for Jackie Jr. and his family.

9

"The Good Lord Has Showered Blessings on Me and This Country"

From Freedom National Bank to Vietnam

January 4, 1965, was a festive day in Harlem. It marked the official dedication of Freedom National Bank on 125th Street, and Alex Quaison-Sackey, the first black president of the United Nations General Assembly, cut the ceremonial ribbon stretching across the bank's front doors. Colorful flags decorated the renovated facade, and among the many notables in attendance was the bank's smartly dressed chairman of the board: Jackie Robinson.

Robinson's leadership of the bank reflected his long-held belief that African Americans would not achieve first-class citizenship until they entered the mainstream of economic society and enjoyed the material advantages that capitalism had long been reserved for whites. He was a capitalist at heart and believed that the material fruits of hard work, the type he enjoyed in his own life, were evidence of God's blessings.

In describing Freedom National, Robinson stated, "It is the only bank in Harlem which is interracially owned and operated. It is also the only bank in Harlem which is controlled mainly by Negroes."[1]

An early proposal and rationale for the bank had noted that Harlem suffered from a deficiency of banking options, and that its residents were "underrepresented in the formation of policies that prominently affect the economic life of the community."[2] It was thus easy for white-controlled banks in Harlem to discriminate against African Americans seeking affordable loans and reasonable mortgage rates, among other things. Underrepresented in local financial institutions,

Harlem residents were financially stuck, barely on the fringes of the US economy.

Robinson hoped that Freedom National Bank would change that, and that African Americans across the country would follow Harlem's lead. His dream of economic integration, as it came to expression in Freedom National, was part and parcel of his spiritual conviction that God helps those who help themselves.

Although the bank demanded countless hours of Robinson's time, he remained active in politics and continued to strengthen his ties to Governor Nelson Rockefeller of New York.

In early 1965 Robinson traveled to Phoenix, Arizona, to address the closing session of a Republican conference on poverty. He took the occasion to sketch progressive goals for the Republican Party and cheer for the governor of New York. In a later letter to Rockefeller, Jackie wrote that his time in Phoenix reinforced his belief that liberal Republicans needed to rally around Rockefeller's desire to widen the base of the party. "We must let minority people in America know that they are needed in order that the two party system—and therefore the political health of our nation—may be preserved," Robinson said.

A day later, Jackie and Rachel went to Washington for a lavish White House dinner honoring Vice President Hubert Humphrey and others. President Johnson had not yet warmed up to Robinson, but that did not stop the president from dancing with Rachel. Two days later, Robinson sent the president a letter of deep appreciation. "Words cannot express the gratitude my wife and I felt for one of the most enjoyable evenings of our lives," he wrote. "My wife is still floating on cloud nine because she had the honor of dancing with the President of the United States."

As always, Robinson also felt the need to send along his own assessment of the president. "Your inspired leadership more than justifies the confidence we all have in you," he stated. "May God give you continued good health and wisdom—in my humble opinion, no American in public office has grown as you have. No President could have affected the progress in our drive for human dignity as you have."

The conversion of the Texan had apparently held, especially given his leadership in passing the Civil Rights Act of 1964, and Robinson was supportive, at least until Bloody Sunday.

Violence exploded in Selma, Alabama, on Sunday, March 7, 1965, when John Lewis, chair of the Student Nonviolent Coordinating Committee, and Hosea Williams, a staff member of the Southern Christian

Leadership Conference, led six hundred marchers in a protest for voting rights. The march also commemorated the February 26 murder of Jimmie Lee Jackson, who had been shot while helping to protect his family at a civil rights rally.

With Lewis and Williams at the front, the Selma marchers were able to advance only six blocks before state and local law officers, positioned at the Edmund Pettus Bridge on US Route 80, used billy clubs and tear gas to force them, now bloodied, screaming, and gasping for air, back into downtown Selma.

Robinson grew livid as he watched the carnage on television at his home in Stamford, and he wired Johnson a telegram on March 9. "Important you take immediate action in Alabama," he wrote. "One more day of savage treatment by legalized hatchet men could lead to open warfare by aroused Negroes. America cannot afford this in 1965."

Six hundred marchers showed up at the White House that day to demand that the Johnson administration send federal troops to Selma to protect the activists from further violence and to arrest the perpetrators of Bloody Sunday. Vice President Hubert Humphrey met with the marchers, and although he was sympathetic, he did not satisfy their urgent demands. When Robinson learned of this failure, he fired off a letter to the vice president, beginning with an uncustomary greeting of "Sir."

Johnson, too, was concerned about the potential for more violence, and he ordered federal troops to protect the marchers as they finally made the fifty-four-mile trek from Selma to Montgomery, where Martin Luther King Jr., buoyed by the swelling interracial crowd of thousands, gave a riveting speech on voting rights. "Our God is marching on!" he declared in front of the state capitol.[3]

Johnson, appearing before a joint session of Congress on March 15, proposed voting legislation, saying, "But even if we pass this bill, the battle will not be over. What happened in Selma is part of a far larger movement which reaches into every section and State of America. It is the effort of Negroes to secure for themselves the full blessings of American life. Their cause must be our cause too. Because it's not just Negroes, but really it's all of us, who must overcome the crippling legacy of bigotry and injustice. And we shall overcome."[4]

Robinson breathed a sigh of relief.

He enjoyed another breather of sorts later in the month when Roone Arledge, head of ABC-TV Sports, called a press conference to announce that Robinson would provide commentary for Major League Baseball games televised in the East during the upcoming season.

Four years earlier, Robinson had told his friend Caroline Wallerstein that he had felt disconnected from Major League Baseball: "I can't get worked up at all over the game. I believe it's primarily because I feel the people connected with the game are such little people. It's bad to say all, and I know there are some very good people connected; however, a bad experience spoils it all."[5]

Robinson was still stinging from his troubling experiences with Dodgers owner Walter O'Malley.

Nevertheless, Robinson had often commented on baseball in his newspaper columns, and Rachel later told biographer Arnold Rampersad that, while Jackie did not go to the ballpark before the ABC gig, he loved watching it on television and would even jump out of his seat and yell at the players and managers during a game.

Robinson was certainly excited about, and thankful for, the opportunity to provide commentary for ABC-TV in 1965. "If it hadn't been for sports, I doubt I would have accomplished much in life," he said at the end of March. "Maybe God would have given me some other ability. I don't know. I do know what athletics have meant to me. It's nice to be able to repay debts, and I have paid mine, but it's good to be back in sports."[6]

In early summer, Robinson took his family to yet another event honoring his contributions to baseball and US history. The Los Angeles County Board of Supervisors had proclaimed June 16, 1965, as Jackie Robinson Day, and part of the festivities were held at Dodger Stadium. The driving force behind the proclamation was Jackie's childhood friend and Los Angeles County supervisor Walter Dorn, who had arranged not only for a local park to be named after Robinson but also for the Dodgers to honor him at a pregame event.

The involvement of the Dodgers was significant because Robinson and O'Malley had been estranged since Jackie's departure from baseball. Rachel had long encouraged her husband to make amends with O'Malley, and Jackie felt a similar pull during a cordial conversation with Kay O'Malley, Walter's spouse, on the night before his 1962 induction into the Baseball Hall of Fame.

Robinson sent O'Malley a letter indicating his willingness to discuss their past problems during an upcoming trip to Los Angeles, and while the proposed meeting did not take place, O'Malley later approved of Jackie Robinson Day at Dodger Stadium.

Robinson was grateful for the owner's cooperation, even if the two did not meet during the event, and a few weeks after the celebration he wrote to O'Malley. "Thanks for helping to make the Jackie Robinson Day a big success, at least for my family," he wrote. "I am told everyone considered the day a success; much of it was due to your cooperation." The owner of the Dodgers replied shortly thereafter, saying, "It was thoughtful of you to write me and I do appreciate it."[7] The simple exchange of letters was far from pregnant with words of sorrow and forgiveness, but it indicated at least some level of reconciliation between the two men.

Back in his adopted hometown of Stamford, a shocking event occurred, much to Jackie's dismay, in the summer of 1965: two thousand residents turned out for a meeting of the John Birch Society. Established in 1958, the society used appeals to God and Christian Scripture to oppose both communism and the civil rights movement. Like others on the far right, John Birchers claimed that atheistic communists were founding members of the civil rights movement and that they continued to control the movement, with a desire to disrupt and take over the country.

Since its founding, the society had spread rapidly, and Robinson had recently learned that the organization was opening offices in Washington, DC, and even in Los Angeles, which had just experienced a race-related riot in the Watts area.

"We cannot afford any more riots," Jackie wrote to Vice President Humphrey, suggesting that the growth of the society would result in an explosion of violence from frustrated African Americans.[8]

In his reply, the vice president stated not only that he shared Robinson's concern about the far right but also that he was pleased to be able to point to President Johnson's June 2 announcement of a future White House conference titled "To Fulfill These Rights," which would seek to help "the American Negro fulfill the rights which, after the long time of injustice, he is finally about to secure."[9]

Robinson was displeased that the administration would not respond more urgently to the danger posed by the John Birch Society. As impatient as he had been with Eisenhower, Jackie demanded presidential action now.

But that did not happen.

By now the president was busily plotting the war in Vietnam, a quickly escalating war that visited the Robinson home in the fall of 1965 in a way that Jackie and Rachel had often feared since they had learned, in June, that the army had shipped their eldest child to Vietnam. "The transfer evoked my worst fears," Rachel recalled. "We prayed endlessly for his safety."[10]

On November 19, Jackie Jr. and his platoon came under fierce assault, leaving him wounded in the shoulder. Two friends who were next to him also came under heavy fire, and while Jackie managed to drag one of them out of the heat of battle, neither of those injured men survived. Still suffering from his shrapnel wounds, Jackie returned to active duty about a week after the ambush, a decision that did nothing to calm his parents' fears or quiet their prayers.

Less than a month later, the Robinsons experienced more troubling times when they learned that Branch Rickey had died at the age of eighty-six after suffering a heart attack while speaking at his induction into the Missouri Sports Hall of Fame on November 13.

"Now I'm going to tell you a story from the Bible about spiritual courage," Rickey said just before collapsing and falling into a coma from which he never recovered. He died a few weeks later.[11]

The Rev. Ralph Sockman of Christ Church in Manhattan, one of the country's most prominent Protestant ministers, delivered the eulogy at Grace Methodist Church in St. Louis.

Sockman, who had been friends with Rickey since he was an undergraduate student at Ohio Wesleyan, told his audience that while he did not know what, in particular, Rickey was going to say about spiritual courage, the baseball executive certainly demonstrated courage in his career by confronting and changing racism in baseball and society. "He was adventurous enough to explore new trails," Sockman said, "and he was brotherly enough to bring others along with him."[12]

Jackie and Rachel attended the funeral, as did Major League Baseball commissioner William Eckert and National League president Warren Giles. Jackie was disappointed that only two other African American baseball players were in the pews.

Robinson gave his own eulogy for Rickey in a column for the Associated Negro Press. "With the passing of Branch Rickey, I feel it can be truly said that God has called one of the greatest men of our time," he wrote. Robinson drew some attention to their years together with the Dodgers, but he focused primarily on their postbaseball relationship. "It is that relationship which makes me feel almost as if I had lost my own father. For, Branch Rickey, even after I was no longer in the sports spotlight, treated me like a son."[13]

Robinson recalled how proud Rickey seemed when the two stood close to each other during Jackie's induction into the Baseball Hall of Fame, and he remembered Rickey visiting him in the hospital when he had the surgery that left him struggling for his life. "Very few people know it, but I faced the possibility of death at that time," he said. "Branch Rickey was sick himself. But he traveled to New York just to come to see me. He talked with me and treated me like a son. That's the way I feel now—like a father is gone."[14]

For all Rickey accomplished in baseball, he found his greatest glory by signing Jackie Robinson. He often spoke about how he had been motivated to do so by his Christian principles. He believed that progress toward real racial equality would come slowly but that the time would come when Americans would look back and see what had been achieved. "All of us will soon look back upon this day with wonder and incredulity," Rickey said, "for we shall surely face the brotherhood of man as surely as we recognize the common brotherhood of God."[15]

Robinson's faith had been shaped by Branch Rickey, the Rev. Karl Downs, and his mother, Mallie, and now only his mother survived. But Robinson, as he always did, persevered.

By the end of the year he was delivering a speech that touched on the Vietnam War. "My son was wounded in Vietnam," he told a crowd in Washington, DC. "He suffered shrapnel wounds, but the two boys on either side of him were killed. I sometimes wonder why my boy is fighting in Vietnam when right here I see . . ." Unfortunately, the reporter who covered the speech could not hear the rest of the sentence; the crowd's cheers drowned out Jackie's voice.[16]

Although Robinson had struck a chord on Vietnam, the main purpose of his comments was to address home rule in the District of Columbia, an effort to gain full representation in the US Congress. As one whose theology centered on self-help, Jackie embraced the cause with enthusiasm. "You'll get it if you really want it and show that you want it," he told the rally. "You must unite; you must go out and fight for it. You must sacrifice a little more, and let the people know how you feel. God helps those who get out and help themselves."[17] The crowd roared its approval.

In early 1966, Robinson turned his attention once again to politics, this time by writing a pointed letter criticizing his favorite politician, Nelson Rockefeller, for having no blacks on his staff. Rockefeller responded by hiring Robinson as a special assistant for community affairs, a full-time position paid out of the governor's own wallet.

Robinson's interest in racial equality took him far from New York, though, and in January he traveled to North Carolina A&T College in Greensboro, home to the four students who had birthed the sit-in movement in 1960. Robinson awarded the young activists a special plaque of commendation from Freedom National Bank.

He later used his column to praise the students and lambaste the "tremendous opposition" that came not only from whites but also from "'let's not push too hard' Negroes and from Negroes who feared the possibility of stirring up the wrath of the white community and from others who were afraid that violence would result."[18]

In mid-February, Robinson again took on the issue of bigotry within the African American community. He had in mind a black Congress of Racial Equality (CORE) leader in Westchester County who had declared during a recent public meeting, attended by a number of local Jews, that Hitler had not killed enough Jewish people. The CORE leader later apologized, but Robinson declared that apologies at this point were "inadequate," and that the man should be forced out of his office. "Bigotry has no color," he said. "There are black bigots as well as white bigots."[19]

At the same time, Robinson also scolded James Farmer, the head of CORE, for apparently diminishing the gravity of the staffer's remark. Robinson was dumbfounded. "This man did not attack the Jews, he attacked God," he said. "He attacked man, the Son of God, he attacked you and me."[20]

There was one social issue prominent at this time that Robinson said little about—women's rights.

Demands for equality for women were pervasive in US society and culture in the early to mid-1960s. In 1963, Betty Friedan had penned *The Feminine Mystique*, an early feminist manifesto, and in 1965 feminists had successfully demanded that the Civil Rights Act of 1964 include a provision prohibiting sex discrimination in employment, a provision that became part of Title VII of the act. And when the Equal Employment Opportunity Commission, formed in 1965 to implement Title VII, failed to take sufficient steps to curb discrimination against women in employment, feminists erupted in frustration at a June 1966 conference on women and employment. Gathering in Friedan's hotel room, fifteen to twenty women talked about the urgent need for their own political organization. During the enlivening conversation, Friedan wrote the acronym "NOW" on a paper napkin, giving a name, the National Organization for Women, to a new organization focused on ending discrimination against women and advancing their rights and equality.

Less than one month before Friedan wrote on her napkin, Robinson had devoted a column to society's treatment of women. He began by lamenting the times he had witnessed men grabbing taxis that women had been waiting for, lunging for subway seats that left women standing, or manhandling women with "unbelievable roughness" during the subway rush hour. "Maybe I am a little square," Robinson stated. "I grew up in a home where we loved and respected our mother and a home in which we were taught that due deference must be given to the ladies." Jackie also referred to Rachel, his "partner and helper," saying that he shuddered "to think of how I would feel or react if someone showed open disrespect to her."[21]

Robinson pointed to the strong women of the civil rights movement, too, although without naming any of them. "Let us face it: Negro women have been the backbone of our freedom movement," he declared. "They have carried more than their share of load." African American women had certainly carried more than their share during his own efforts to advance freedom. "For myself, I know that I never would have been able to make it without the support, devotion, and love of my Rachel," he stated. "To my mother I owe the realization at an early age that no one individual is better than another."[22]

But Robinson chose not to focus on women's rights in this column. Instead, his main suggestion was that men should begin to demonstrate gratitude to women by showing them respect in everyday matters like offering them seats on public transportation and not shoving them during rush hour. It was the type of chivalrous stance that typically led to loud groans and vigorous protests within the feminist community. Feminists wanted rights, not seats, but Robinson remained silent on those demands.

That might not have come as a surprise to Rachel, who recalled that Jackie was not too pleased when she first told him, in 1958, when their youngest child, David, was in school full-time, that she wanted to work outside the home. As she recalled it, "Mallie, his mother, had been overworked, and since his youth he had savored the thought that he would be the sole supporter of his family."[23] Rachel understood she would be disappointing Jackie, but she applied to New York University's Graduate School of Nursing.

Jackie conceded because he knew he could not stop her. After she was accepted into the program, he showed his support for her by waiting for her in a Chuck full o'Nuts shop while she finished her classes for the day. Rachel deeply appreciated his thoughtfulness, and they grew closer as they rode home together.

Rachel graduated in 1959 and happily took her first job with the Albert Einstein College of Medicine Department of Social and

Community Psychiatry, where she helped to create the first day hospital for acutely ill psychiatric patients. In 1960, she took a long-lasting position as director of a psychiatric nursing program at Yale, where she also served as an assistant professor of nursing. She felt some guilt about being absent from home so much, but her own mother, Zellee Isum, who lived with the Robinsons, helped considerably around the house while Jackie continued to offer his own quiet support in the years ahead.

He did not remain quiet, though, when Ronald Reagan was elected governor of California in the same month that NOW came into being. "If I read Reagan correctly, he is another Goldwater—with what the kids call 'smarts,'" Robinson stated.[24]

There was worse news in the summer of 1966, though: the eruption of violence in cities across the country.

Robinson had addressed the possibility of a violent summer in the prior spring, and in doing so he drew directly from Martin Luther King Jr., who had long embraced a comprehensive view of societal violence, one far larger than that which focused narrowly on violent uprisings in inner-city ghettos during the summer months.

In King's view, the governing authorities simply ignored "the daily violence done to human beings who live under inhuman, intolerable circumstances from day to day: the slums, the rat-infested apartments, the rejections of ghetto-living, the poor schools, indifferent teachers and education officials, the doors slammed in employment and personnel offices." These conditions comprised "a violence for all seasons," and one that political leaders should address if they wanted to avoid violence in the summer.[25]

Robinson agreed with King.

"How shall we profit by winning a war in Vietnam if we lose the war for decency at home?" Robinson asked.[26] The time had come for a year-round effort to make the Johnson administration's dream of the Great Society come alive for all the poor, black and white.

But politicians on both sides of the aisle largely failed to implement plans for the Great Society, and another long, hot summer was in full boil in 1966.

As the summer riots continued across the country, Robinson rightly acknowledged that the Old Guard of the civil rights movement held "no power of persuasion over these youngsters."[27] The frustrated ghettos looked up to Malcolm X, who had been assassinated in 1965; Stokely Carmichael, the forceful new chairman of the Student Nonviolent

Coordinating Committee (SNCC); and others who were now shouting for "black power."

Although the phrase "black power" had appeared as the title of a 1954 book by Richard Wright, the Rev. Adam Clayton Powell Jr. popularized the term, even claiming to coin it, in 1965 and 1966. One of the first times he used the phrase was in a March 1965 talk in which he "urged black people to mobilize their political, economic, financial, and educational power to build their communities into neighborhoods of excellence."[28]

Powell popularized the term even more when he used it in a series of sermons he later delivered and especially in a baccalaureate address he gave at Howard University on May 29, 1966. As Powell himself recalled his comments, "I urged my people to pursue excellence and to purpose our lives to the fulfillment of divine-souled human rights instead of narrow-souled civil rights. I declared on that day: 'To demand these God-given rights is to seek black power, audacious power—the power to build black institutions of splendid achievement.'"

Stokely Carmichael was in the Howard audience, listening intently and appreciatively. Less than a month later Carmichael would carry the phrase "black power" deep into the state of Mississippi.

On June 1, 1966, James Meredith, who had gained national fame when he attempted to matriculate at the University of Mississippi in 1961 and then became the school's first black student in 1962, began a one-man march through Mississippi. His purpose was to draw attention to voting rights and to encourage blacks to register to vote.

Meredith was shot on the second day of his march, and Martin Luther King Jr. and Carmichael decided to complete the trek on the wounded Meredith's behalf. King and Carmichael debated the future of the civil rights movement as they marched together, and at a rally in Greenwood, Mississippi, Carmichael sought to steer the nonviolent movement in a different direction by encouraging the crowd to shout out its support for black power. As the crowd repeated the phrase in reply to Carmichael's urging, their anger seemed to mount to a degree not felt in prior marches led by King.

Shortly after the Greenwood rally, SNCC, under Carmichael's leadership, called for an all-black civil rights struggle that would be open to employing force to accomplish its goals. This appeal resulted in a drop in membership and funds for SNCC, and it also served to fracture the movement. On one side were the Old Guard leaders who favored achieving integration through nonviolence: King, A. Philip

Randolph, Roy Wilkins, and Whitney Young. On the other were those who embraced racial separatism and the threat of violence to achieve their ends: Carmichael and all the other young militants of the emerging black power movement.

Robinson belonged to the Old Guard, and in the fall of 1966 he demonstrated his fierce opposition to Carmichael by enthusiastically applauding a new sermon by Powell titled "Black Power: A Form of Godly Power." It was one of the rare times when Robinson lauded the Harlem congressman.

Clad in his minister's robe at Abyssinian Baptist, Powell used his sermon to plot a middle course between King and black power advocates who embraced racial separatism and the use of violence.

"First of all, black power is not anti-white," Powell preached. "Black power incorporates everybody who wishes to work together, vote together and worship together."

The minister fittingly turned to Scripture as his moral authority for opposing separatism as a final goal. "If white people can accept black leadership in any given political, business or educational situation—which is, in a sense a kind of black power—then I, Adam Clayton Powell, welcome them, because, as Paul said: 'There is neither Jew nor Greek, there is neither bond nor free, there is neither male nor female: for ye are all one in Christ Jesus.'"

Separatism as an end goal was wrong, Powell said, because faithful followers of Jesus were ultimately bound together by the inclusive identity of the one they followed.

Powell also forcefully criticized black power advocates who believed in the use of "any means necessary" in the fight for racial justice. "Black power is a constructive approach to the new life of freedom for black people in the Great Society," he explained. "Violence must play no part in its fulfillment." Using "any means necessary" was destructive, not constructive. "Instead of 'Burn, baby, burn,' we should be shouting, 'Learn, baby, learn' and 'Earn, baby, earn,'" Powell preached, to the delight of his rapt congregation. "Instead of lighting up the sky with Molotov cocktails, we should be brightening the skies with the stars of millions of registered voters," he continued. "Instead of throwing fire bombs, we should fire up our energies to build more black-owned businesses in our communities." Powell backed his call for nonviolence by drawing from Jesus' demand that his disciples put away their swords.

But having excluded racial separatism and violence as ingredients of black power, Powell also made sure to separate black power from the civil rights movement led by King. "We have indulged ourselves in the past five years in a magnificent exercise of near futility with our marches, our sit-ins, our demonstrations, our picketing and now our rebellions," he argued, still to the pleasure of his congregation.

Powell also implored his listeners to stop expecting that civil rights legislation would be the answer to their problems and to start practicing self-help. "Black people themselves must exercise a massive responsibility for their fate. Black people themselves must assume control and direction for their destiny."

With this call for self-help, Powell then defined "black power" as he understood it. "Black power is, *first and foremost*, Godly power," a power that ultimately embraces equality of and unity among the races. "Without the hand of God in man's hand, there can be no coming together of black and white in this world. Unless man is committed to the belief that all of mankind are his brothers, then he labors in vain and hypocritically in the vineyards of equality."

Black power is also "black pride," a "belief in self and in the dignity of the black man's soul." It's also "black initiative" and "black productivity—the increase of black jobs for black men and women, the contribution of black people to the gross national product, the beautification of black neighborhoods, and the expansion of black businesses." And, finally, black power is "black responsibility—the recognition by black people that they must demand and have a proportionate share of the responsibilities of running the communities, the cities and the states in which they live."

Robinson could barely contain his excitement about Powell's sermon, calling it nothing less than "a blessing."[29]

Although he could not accept the minister's dismissal of the significance of the civil rights movement and governmental action, Robinson did agree that the time had come to move beyond marches and to begin exercising black power exactly as Powell, not Carmichael, had described it.

"There is real strength among us," Robinson added. "I salute Adam Powell for his latest version and suggest when we use our ballot and our dollars wisely, we are exercising black power without having to define it."[30]

Robinson also added that he liked Powell's understanding of black power as "our sincere faith and trust in God."[31]

Black power, for Robinson, was spiritual in its core.

In early 1967, Robinson defended heavyweight boxing champion Muhammad Ali, who found himself ridiculed by the white press for his name change, his faith, and his brashness.

Robinson hearkened back to his own experiences in Major League Baseball. "I know what he is going through," he said. "For, during my own career in sports, I came to learn that there are many writers who like tame Negroes who 'stay in their place.' " The place for Ali was not prostrate before the public, according to Jackie. "Of course, by backing up his words with deeds, Clay or Ali has clearly demonstrated where his 'place' is—right up there at the top."[32]

Robinson even defended Ali following his conviction for refusing to submit to the draft during the Vietnam War. "It is in the light of my consciousness as a Muslim minister and my own personal convictions that I take my stand in rejecting the call to be inducted into the armed services," Ali explained.[33]

When someone asked him why he did not just leave the country, he added: "You serious? I got to stay right here and lead my people to the right man—Elijah Muhammad."[34]

Ali interpreted the war through the lens of his faith, seeing it as yet another assault by "the white man" on people of color. "You want me to do what the white man says and go fight a war against some people I don't know nothing about—get some freedom for some other people when my own people can't get theirs here?" he asked. No, he would never do that, no matter how much criticism came his way, no matter how many fines he would have to pay, no matter how much time he would have to serve in jail. "Allah okays the adversary to try us," Ali stated. "That's how he sees if you're a true believer."[35]

Robinson considered Ali a true believer. "In my view, the deposed champion has demonstrated that he is fighting for a principle. While I cannot agree with it, I respect him sincerely."[36]

Robinson disagreed with Ali's religious interpretation of the war as well as the broader opposition to the war by Black Muslims, but he applauded Ali's willingness to accept the penalties resulting from his refusal to be drafted. "He fully understood the penalty and price he would have to pay for taking his stand. He was willing and prepared to make the challenge out of his deeply rooted convictions. And he is ready to accept the consequences. This is his heroism—and I believe it to be genuine."[37]

Robinson was libertarian in the sense that he strongly believed that US citizens were free to believe whatever they wanted to about God and faith, even if those beliefs flew in the face of his own religious convictions, and he was careful not to call on Ali to leave the Black Muslims.

One month after Ali announced his refusal to be inducted into the armed forces, Robinson also opposed, though for different reasons, demands that Governor George Romney of Michigan, a racially progressive Republican, leave the Church of Jesus Christ of Latter-day Saints because of its racially restrictive practices.

At this point, the Mormon Church allowed blacks to become members but prohibited them from attaining the status of lay ministers, a barrier that prevented them from exercising any management or leadership roles in the church. The Mormons maintained this restriction because of their religious conviction that blackness was a divine curse that began when Noah punished one of his sons for seeing his father naked.

Romney disagreed with the consignment of blacks to second-class membership, and he publicly called on the church to change its practices. But that did not satisfy everyone, and African American clergymen and politicians in his home state demanded that he either resign from the church or forgo his run for the Republican nomination for the US presidency.

Robinson disagreed with those demands, citing the governor's strong record on civil rights, as well as the "courage and personal conviction" he demonstrated when criticizing Mormon practices before a group of Mormons.[38]

Less than a month later, Martin Luther King Jr. walked into Riverside Church in Manhattan and, to Robinson's disappointment, publicly took the side of anti–Vietnam War activists. More than three thousand people, gathered together by a religious group called Clergy and Laity Concerned about Vietnam, gave King a standing ovation as he rose to share his own concerns about the war.

Speaking in somber tones, King wasted no time in depicting the war as an enemy of the American poor, who saw money move from the War on Poverty to the war in southeast Asia; as an enemy of young black men, who were serving in combat in massively disproportionate numbers; as an enemy of Vietnamese peasants, whose cries for land reform were met with US bombs that destroyed their land and their lives; and as an enemy of disciples of Jesus, who were called to love their enemies.

The Baptist preacher said that he had to break his silence about the war partly because of his "commitment to the ministry of Jesus Christ." His antiwar stance was simply part and parcel of his identity as a Christian minister. "To me the relationship of this ministry to the making of peace is so obvious that I sometimes marvel at those who ask me why I am speaking against the war," King stated. "Have they forgotten that my ministry is in obedience to the one who loved his enemies so fully that he died for them? What then can I say to the 'Vietcong' or to Castro or to Mao as a faithful minister to this one? Can I threaten them with death or must I not share with them my life?"[39]

King emphasized spiritual themes, claiming that his calling, his vocation, was not to be a good citizen whose loyalties were bound to a nation, even the United States, but rather to be "a son of the living God," a God concerned especially for the suffering, the helpless, and the outcast.[40]

Called by God to speak for all the victims of war, King decried the US government as "the greatest purveyor of violence in the world," encouraged draftable men to become conscientious objectors, and suggested that the government extricate itself from Vietnam by, among other things, ending all bombing and declaring a unilateral cease-fire. He also called on all nations to join a worldwide fellowship of neighborly concern for all, to practice "an all-embracing and unconditional love for all men."[41]

Robinson resisted his friend's admonitions, and he did so by using his newspaper column to send King an open letter addressed to "Dear Martin."[42]

Robinson criticized King for being "unfair" in placing all blame for the conflict on the United States alone. "Why is it, Martin, that you seem to ignore the blood which is upon their [Vietcong's] hands and to speak only of the 'guilt' of the United States?"[43]

As he criticized King, Robinson lauded President Johnson's efforts to establish peace talks with the Vietcong. "I am firmly convinced that President Johnson wants an end to this war as much as anyone else," Jackie wrote.[44]

Robinson was concerned that King's stance on Vietnam would negatively affect Johnson's support for the civil rights movement, and he expressed this concern in an April 18 letter to the president: "While I am certain your faith has been shaken by demonstrations against the Viet Nam war, I hope the actions of any one individual does not make you feel as Vice President Humphrey does, that Dr. King's stand will hurt the Civil Rights movement."[45]

Missing from Robinson's critique was any commentary on King's Christian beliefs.

Nowhere did Robinson address King's spiritual conviction that Americans and Vietnamese together were children of God, that sons and daughters of God had a special obligation to side with the oppressed (including Vietnamese peasants), that followers of Jesus must not kill those he gave his life for (anyone and everyone), and that those who believe in the Bible should love not only their friends and family but also their enemies. Robinson ignored all these points, once again allowing his patriotic convictions to trump spiritual convictions about the Prince of Peace and his demand that his followers put up the sword.

But King did not give up on Robinson. Although King did not take his friend up on his invitation to reply in writing, King picked up the phone and called his longtime friend in the quiet of an evening.

As Jackie recounted it, "Before the rich, deep voice identified the caller, I knew that he was my dear friend, Dr. Martin Luther King Jr." The civil rights leader had called so that his friend would better understand his convictions and motivations. The two talked about the critical points Jackie had raised in his letter, as well as related matters, and while Robinson found his friend to be "brilliant" in his replies, he did not find them compelling enough to change "all the opinions" he had of King's position.[46]

Robinson recounted the conversation in his newspaper column, and rather than detailing their points and counterpoints, he decided simply to make his readers understand that his opinion of King as sincere and courageous had not changed. "He is still my leader—a man to whose defense I would come at any time he might need me. That is a personal commitment and a public pledge."[47]

But he also set forth another reason for standing by King even as he disagreed with him: "If ever a man was placed on this earth by divine force, to help solve the doubts and ease the hearts and dispel the fears of mortal man, I believe that man is Dr. King."[48]

However divinely inspired King might have been, Robinson continued to oppose his position on Vietnam. He expressed concern about those demanding that President Johnson cease bombing raids in the war-torn country. "I am convinced we must deal from a position of strength," he said. "I have found this to be good policy in athletics and I think it is probably the best policy in war."[49]

A "position of strength" meant the continuation of bombing, especially those raids that provided cover for US soldiers. "Should we cease to bomb the enemy's bridges, to destroy and cut off their ammunition bases, we would be extending them an open invitation to commit a wholesale carnage of which our own fighting men would become the helpless victims."[50]

As the long, hot summer of 1967 came to a close, Robinson felt the need to speak more on inner-city riots, warning of the possibility that violence might erupt not only in summers to come but also at times like Thanksgiving, Christmas, and New Year's Day.

Unlike conservative Christians who saw the root of riots in unchristian hearts, Robinson identified something else as causal. "Riots begin with the hopelessness which lives in the hearts of people who, from childhood, expect to live in a rundown house, to be raised by one parent, to be denied proper recreation, to attend an inferior school, to experience police brutality, to be turned down when seeking a decent job," he said.[51]

The cause of riots was not unconverted hearts in need of Jesus but hopeless hearts ignited by dreadful living conditions, and this meant that the solution to rioting was not fire-and-brimstone preaching but a collective effort by leaders in politics, business, and civil society to improve the quality of life for those poised to explode.

In a sermon he later preached in New Rochelle, New York, Robinson added a spiritual framework to this point, hearkening back to his illustration about the farmer who hoed the land God had given him. "I think we need to think less in terms of 'helping' the Negro and more in terms of making sure he has the tools with which to give God a little help by helping himself," Robinson preached.[52] The proper response to the riots was to give African Americans the God-given tools they need to help themselves: quality schools, housing, and jobs.

At this point, Robinson also took special aim at H. Rap Brown, the new leader of the Student Nonviolent Coordinating Committee, for having recently told a crowd of fifteen hundred supporters in Jackie's old neighborhood in Queens that the summer riots were "dress rehearsals for revolution."[53] Brown had encouraged his followers to attend a nearby courtroom to show support for seventeen African Americans, some of them members of the Revolutionary Action Movement (RAM), who had been indicted for plotting to murder African American leaders they considered too moderate, including Roy Wilkins of the National Association for the Advancement of Colored People (NAACP) and Whitney Young of the Urban League.

Robinson blasted Brown, calling him "a sensationalist, dangerous, irresponsible agitator who has a talent for getting fires ignited and getting himself safely out of the way, leaving those he agitated to face the music."[54]

Hate mail poured into Robinson's office following his vocal opposition to Brown and his supporters, and one piece even included a jack-of-spades playing card with the word "Ram" written on it. Robinson said that while he was uncertain whether the card really came from the Revolutionary Action Movement, he would never allow such a threat to deter him from speaking his mind. "I don't seek to be anyone's martyr or hero, but telling it like I think it is—that's the only way I know how to be me."[55]

Underlying this conviction, once again, was his gratitude to God and his sense of human interconnectedness. "The Good Lord has showered blessings on me and this country and its people, black and white, have been good to me," Jackie reiterated. "But no matter how rich or famous I might become, no matter what luxuries or special privileges I might achieve, no matter how many powerful friends I might make, I would never be the man I want to be until my humblest brother, black and white, becomes the man he wants to be. So I must be involved in our fight for freedom."

In his fight for freedom, Robinson hoped that the president would not halt the War on Poverty. Although he touted self-reliance in financial matters, Robinson was also convinced that the nation's poor, whatever the color of their skin, desperately needed federal assistance in their efforts to escape poverty and that the government had a basic obligation to implement constructive antipoverty programs like many of those found in the War on Poverty.

But as 1967 drew to a close, Robinson also emphasized his conviction that governmental assistance was not sufficient and that Christian churches must become a more forceful presence in the fight against poverty and racial injustice.

The racial segregation so pervasive throughout Christian churches, he said, betrayed the fundamental spiritual conviction that "if God is truly Father to us all, then this truly makes us all brothers." If Christians started to act as if they were all members of the one family of God, he said, the church could become "the most powerful force for racial decency in the nation."[56]

10

"I Guess the Good Lord Has a Job for Me"

Heading Home

On March 5, 1968, Robinson learned the awful news that Jackie Jr. had been arrested for possession of drugs. When the police stopped him for questioning in a seedy area of Stamford around 2:15 a.m., Jackie Jr. had fled, but the officers apprehended him about a block away, finding not only marijuana in his possession but also heroin and a .22 revolver.

Jackie Jr. had returned home from Vietnam in June 1967, addicted to drugs, unwilling to start a career, and still anxious to move out from the long shadow his father had cast. Telling his parents he needed to find his own way, he bolted from the family home and headed to the drug-infested sections of Stamford.

At the time of his arrest, Jackie and Rachel did not know where their eldest child had been living. The prior Saturday, Robinson had left a message at a pool hall that Jackie Jr. frequented, asking his son to call him, but that effort, too, had failed.

Rachel and Sharon, both in tears, accompanied Robinson to the Stamford police station, where he posted $5,000 in bail to secure the release of their son and brother. Before leaving, Jackie walked over to a group of waiting reporters and spoke openly of his pained feelings.

Rachel recalled how her white-haired husband, just forty-nine, looked at that moment: "His stance was dignified, but his head was slightly bowed . . . heavy, it seemed."[1] The *New York Times* reported that Robinson "stared despondently at the floor" as he spoke.[2]

161

"I guess I had more of an effect on other people's kids than I had on my own," Robinson lamented. "My problem was my inability to spend more time at home. I guess I thought my family was secure, that at least we wouldn't have anything to worry about, so I went running around everywhere else."[3]

While he held himself responsible, Robinson suggested that God, too, had played a hand in the potentially transformative moment. "God is testing me," he said.[4]

Rachel stood by silently, but in the days ahead she was the one to arrange for Jackie Jr. to receive treatment at Yale New Haven Hospital, a positive move that left the family feeling hopeful.

But more disappointment entered Robinson's life a short time later, when Nelson Rockefeller announced that he would not be a candidate for the Republican nomination for the presidency. Robinson believed strongly in providence and was convinced that it was Rockefeller's destiny to become the Republican Party's nominee for president and to win the 1968 presidential election.

"I believe that each man is placed upon this earth with a destiny to fulfill," Robinson told the governor. "I feel strongly that you were meant to lead in world councils, in national affairs and domestic problems, and within a political party which was born slanted towards freedom, but which in recent times has turned its back on its own heritage."[5]

After Rockefeller made his announcement, Robinson wrote him a letter full of disappointment and frustration. "I am hurt because Negroes desperately need the kind of positive relationship your dedication can bring," he said. "I am confused because I now must search for a candidate and the choice is difficult."[6]

The days grew even bleaker, far bleaker, for Robinson and the world, a little more than a week later, when James Earl Ray assassinated Martin Luther King Jr. as he stood alone on the balcony at the Lorraine Motel in Memphis, Tennessee. King had traveled to the city to help sanitation workers protest for better working conditions, and on the night before his death, he sought to instill a sense of hope within the weary workers and their supporters. "I've been to the *mountaintop!*" King preached. "I may not get there with you. But I want you to know tonight that *we* as a *people* will *get* to the *Promised Land!*"[7]

Robinson was crushed by the news of King's murder, and he and Rachel joined Rockefeller on his private plane for the trip to King's funeral at Ebenezer Baptist Church in Atlanta.

Morehouse College president Benjamin E. Mays delivered the eulogy. In a tape recording played during the funeral, King himself spoke of how he wanted others to remember him in death: "I'd like somebody to mention that day that Martin Luther King, Jr. tried to give his life serving others."[8]

Robinson turned to his faith, even while modestly stating he was not a "deeply religious man," when trying to make sense of the assassination of his friend. "I do not pretend that I have begun to reach the mountaintop which God showed the man who, in my view, was the greatest leader of the Twentieth Century," he stated. "But I have been able to come to regard his death as perhaps one of those great mysteries with which the Almighty moves—his wonders to perform."[9]

With these words, Robinson echoed the first refrain of William Cowper's "Light Shining Out of Darkness," a popular Christian hymn: "God moves in a mysterious way, His wonders to perform; He plants his footsteps in the sea, and rides upon the storm."[10]

But Robinson's faith was also the type that liked answers, a sure and certain footing, and so he also tried to explain King's death in concrete terms. He did so by returning to a sermon King had preached on the Sunday following the bombing of his home in January 1957.

In that sermon, King put a series of questions before his congregation: "Where is God in the midst of falling bombs?"[11] Is God totally detached from the horrific event? Is God merely contemplating the pain and suffering from above? Is God a loving Father concerned for his children?

In answering these questions, King delivered a small theological treatise, claiming that although the will of God causes goodness, it is also "permissive" in relation to evil. God allows evil to exist so that humans can be truly free in the exercise of their own free wills. God also works to achieve something good out of the evil chosen by people. "And so God never causes evil," King preached. "But sometimes he permits evil to exist in order to carry out his creative and redemptive work."[12]

King's biblical text for the day was the Genesis story of Joseph, and he used the narrative to explain that although God did not directly harm Joseph, God did indeed allow Joseph's brothers to plot his murder. And after they had left him for dead, God helped Joseph escape to Egypt, become politically powerful, and achieve so much wealth that he could eventually save his own murderous brothers from famine.

In summing up King's sermon, Robinson added: "Dr. King said that perhaps this is what God had done in Montgomery; allowed some bombs to fall, allowed some property to be destroyed so that the white community could feel the necessity for reconciliation within the black community."[13]

Robinson agreed. And not only did he join King in believing that God had allowed whites to dynamite black homes and churches so that God could help bring about racial healing in Montgomery. Robinson also suggested that God had allowed the murder of King in order to bring about racial reconciliation in the United States.

"Perhaps this will happen today in America," Robinson claimed. "Perhaps, after the raging emotions quiet down; perhaps, after the streets of our cities are no longer haunted by angry black people seeking revenge."[14]

Crushed, Robinson remained hopeful, buoyed by faith in a God who can find a way out of no way.

But his heart sank as he watched the responses of politicians in the weeks following King's assassination, and he excoriated both Johnson and Nixon, now a presidential candidate, in a May 3 address to the Texas Association of Christian Churches. Both politicians, Robinson stated, failed to show leadership in the days following King's death for fear of losing the voter base that supported them.

"I said I was not here to talk politics and that is not my purpose," Robinson told the Texan Christians. "But I can't help talking about politicians—men who set the example of acknowledging the fatherhood of God, but who find it possible, when convenient, to turn their backs on the brotherhood of man."[15]

Robinson was hoping for a substantial policy that would help the poor help themselves, especially poor blacks suffering in disproportionate numbers, and to emphasize the need for such a policy he presented a bleak picture of poor blacks.

"They see no future in an affluent, viable American industrial economy," Robinson said. So they turn to drugs, crime, rioting, and even the jungles of Vietnam. "And if they are lucky enough to come out of that war alive and physically, mentally or psychologically unimpaired, they can come back home . . . and find out that the land of the free has homes for the brave—the white brave—anywhere they can afford to live.

"It is a terrible mess, this whole situation," Robinson lamented.[16]

But he held out hope, too.

If the mess is to be cleaned up, he said, "it will only be the church and church people who will be able to do it. But it's not going to be done by just Sunday-go-to-meeting Christians, or just by Monday morning halfback Christians, or by just-let-John-do-it Christians, or 'I-don't-want-to-get-involved' Christians. It will have to be done by dedicated Christians, Christians of understanding, creating goodwill for their fellow man."[17] Robinson implored the Texans to become *active* Christians.

One day after King's assassination, Vice President Hubert Humphrey sent Robinson a brief note. "As I write this letter, our country is in such trouble," Humphrey penned. "The terrible tragedy of the assassination of Dr. Martin Luther King, Jr. has cast a shadow over our land."[18]

The vice president also took the occasion to deliver a political pitch to Robinson. "I do hope that if I should decide to be a candidate [for the presidency] that I would be privileged to have your support," he wrote.[19]

President Johnson had announced a week before that he would not seek reelection, and Robinson was not entirely displeased with that development, given what he had earlier written to Rockefeller: "While, in my opinion, [Johnson] has been the greatest influence in our domestic racial policies, he leaves so much to be desired on the foreign policy level."[20]

Vietnam was beginning to wear on Robinson, too.

Complicating matters for Humphrey, however, was that Rockefeller was now a force in the race, even though he had earlier declared that he would not be a candidate. Rockefeller defeated Richard Nixon in the Massachusetts primary on April 30.

More bad news came in May, when Robinson learned that his beloved mother, Mallie, had collapsed in the driveway of her home in Pasadena. Jackie left to be with her as soon as he could, but Mallie—the courageous woman who had taught her children that God treasures their blackness, wants them to struggle for freedom, and will always help them find a way—died before he arrived.

Robinson found it difficult to enter the room where she lay dead. "Somehow I managed to," he later recalled, "and I shall always be glad that I did. There was a look, an expression on her face, that calmed me. It didn't do anything about her hurt, but it made me realize that she had died at peace with herself."[21]

She had also died at peace knowing that she had passed her fierce faith on to all her children.

Back home in Connecticut, Robinson quickly slid back into the political thicket, this time taking on Robert F. Kennedy, who was running for the Democratic nomination for president.

Jackie had harbored resentment against Kennedy for moving to New York and defeating incumbent Kenneth Keating, a racially progressive Republican, in the 1964 senatorial race. "I cannot help but feel that Robert Kennedy is a vindictive opportunist," Robinson told Rockefeller in March.[22]

While conceding that Kennedy had made "commendable contributions" during his tenure as attorney general, Robinson emphasized that the historical record would reveal "damning things" that Kennedy had directed. "It will show how Bobby upheld the appointment of segregationist judges in the South," Jackie argued in his newspaper column. "It will show he urged the Freedom Movement to 'wait' and to 'cool off' at times when the Movement needed the moral support of all sincere men. It will show how Bobby's Justice Department persecuted the Martin King forces in Albany."[23]

On the same day that this scorching criticism appeared in print, Sirhan Sirhan, a Jordanian angered by Kennedy's support for Israel, shot the senator while he was campaigning at the Ambassador Hotel in Los Angeles. Kennedy died the next day.

Robinson felt horrible.

But he neither apologized for nor backtracked on his criticism.

He did note, however, that Kennedy was "a brilliant man, that he made some important contributions to racial progress in America and that he deserved better—as any man does—than to be gunned down because someone disagreed with him or hated him for what he stood for."[24]

Far less deserving, Robinson believed, was American society. "We have become a corrupt society," he complained. "We live in a day when, instead of gaining the victory with ballots, we seek to still dissent and opposition and the call to freedom and justice with bullets."[25]

American society had indeed become "one of the most violent 'civilizations' on the map," he added. "And the world knows it."[26]

So, too, did God. Robinson turned to Jesus' words—"He who lives by the sword will die by the sword"—to suggest that America's murderous ways deserved nothing less than divine retribution, death at the hands of an angry God. "Let us hope that a merciful God will delay the retribution which we deserve."[27]

Robinson invoked a merciful God again near the end of June, when he suffered a mild heart attack. There was no significant damage, and Robinson saw the experience as a reprieve from God.

In a letter to his friend Caroline Wallerstein, he wrote: "I guess the good Lord has a job for me, or else I could or would have had some serious heart damage. . . . I have not been too disturbed and know when it's time nothing will prevent any of us going. I don't know what it is but the good Lord has one job for me or else I would be a lot sicker than I am. I am heeding his warning and am really doing well, getting plenty of rest and reading."[28]

Hope remained one of the hallmark characteristics of Robinson's faith even in this most challenging year. "I can't imagine what else can happen to us this year," he wrote to Wallerstein. "We had our share of problems but as has been said frequently if we can stand the test all will come out fine. I am sure we have the courage. I pray we have seen the last of trouble for a while, anyway."[29]

Robinson's prayers during this time focused especially on his son Jackie Jr., now a resident at Daytop Rehabilitation Program, which was known for its rigor and discipline. "This is a tough period, only God knows how he will do," Jackie wrote to Wallerstein. "We can only hope and pray, for Jackie has lots of problems and only he can solve them."[30]

A lot more than prayer was on Robinson's mind as he faced yet another pressing problem: the Republican nomination of Richard Nixon for the presidency.

Robinson's doctors had instructed him to stay away from the Republican convention, and Jackie conceded that their advice was no doubt "all for the best."[31] Even from a safe distance, though, the convention left Robinson sickened and perplexed.

"How sickening it was to hear Strom Thurmond, an arrogant little race-baiter, declaring that Mr. Nixon had promised him and the Deep South veto power over the choice of a vice-presidential candidate," Robinson stated.[32] Nixon's selection of Maryland governor Spiro Agnew, known for his intolerance of African American demands, seemed only to confirm Robinson's fears that avowed segregationists like Thurmond of South Carolina and other Dixiecrats wielded considerable power over Nixon.

And how "incredible" and "stupid" it was, Robinson added, for the Republicans to choose Nixon—"a double-talker, a two-time loser, an adjustable man with a convertible conscience"—over the principled, honest, and progressive Rockefeller.[33]

On August 11, Robinson announced his resignation from Rockefeller's staff and his plan to campaign full-time for the Democrats.

Predictably, Robinson did not mince words at the time of his announcement. "Now he's sold out," Robinson said about Nixon, "he's prostituted himself to get the Southern vote." The Nixon-Agnew ticket, Robinson added, was "racist in nature" and "inclined to let the South have veto powers over what was happening."[34]

Robinson was angry. "The Republican Party has told the black man to go to hell," he said. "I offer them a similar invitation."[35]

On August 14, Robinson stood next to a broadly smiling Hubert Humphrey at Freedom National Bank in Harlem to announce that he was formally endorsing the liberal Democrat for president.

Republican leaders were not pleased.

Among the most vocal opponents was the ultraconservative William F. Buckley, who described Robinson as a "pompous moralizer" guilty of reverse racism.[36] Robinson delivered a fiery response, calling Buckley an "intellectual dilettante" opposed to the truth.[37]

"One truth I learned long ago . . . is that I am black first, American second and that political parties are at least as far down as third in my life," Robinson retorted. "If that is racism, so be it. I am proud to be black. I am also embattled because I am black."[38]

Barry Goldwater, the 1964 Republican nominee, wrote to protest Robinson's decision to support Humphrey over Nixon. Normally, Robinson would send a quick and pointed reply to such a letter, but Jackie Jr. was in trouble again.

On August 23, Jackie Jr. was arrested in a hotel room and charged with "using females for immoral purposes." His female companion in the room was charged with "loitering for the purposes of prostitution."[39]

Although the police reported that Jackie Jr. had pointed a revolver at them, he avoided jail time and returned to Daytop with a suspended sentence of two to four years in prison. The Robinsons prayed all the more and stayed in touch with their son as he set out, once again, on the road to recovery.

Two weeks later, Robinson sent his reply to Goldwater, explaining that it was pride in his *blackness* that fueled much of his opposition to the Republican ticket. "Because I am proud of my blackness and the progress we have made, and because I can't feel that America will continue this progress under Nixon-Thurmond rule, I refuse to support the ticket."[40]

It was this same sense of racial pride and dignity, instilled in him so deeply by his mother, Mallie, and by the Rev. Karl Downs, that led Robinson to make a surprising, even shocking, decision to stand side by side with members of the Black Panther Party in New York City. Robinson, it seemed, was moving closer to the militancy articulated so powerfully by Malcolm X.

On August 21, three Black Panthers had been arrested for assaulting a police officer, and at their hearing in Brooklyn on September 4, about 150 white men stormed the courthouse and used their fists, feet, and blackjacks to beat a dozen Black Panthers and several white sympathizers. Among the attackers were off-duty New York City police officers, and no arrests were made in the immediate aftermath of the melee.

The incident angered Robinson, who showed his support for the Panthers by speaking with them at their headquarters in Harlem. Before he did so, he held a news conference in which he depicted the Panthers as a peaceful group willing to use democratic processes to air their legitimate grievances. Robinson also sharply criticized the off-duty police officers who had participated in the violent melee.

Unlike Martin Luther King Jr., who had invoked the nonviolent teachings of Jesus even in the context of police brutality, Robinson also made a rare public admission that police brutality justified the use of force by blacks seeking to defend themselves. But Robinson certainly hoped that Panthers would not resort to violence, and to that end he sought to open an avenue of constructive dialogue between the Panthers and the office of New York City mayor John Lindsay.

Around this time, Robinson also sought to reestablish a relationship with Richard Nixon after the Republican nominee had cruised to victory in the 1968 presidential election.

Warning of a racial "holocaust," Robinson pleaded with Nixon to do something concrete to advance equality for African Americans and bridge the gap between blacks and whites. "This, Sir, is the most important role your administration must play, for a house divided unto itself cannot stand," he wrote. "Surely you see we are a divided nation searching our souls for answers. It can only come from sincere, dedicated leadership. I pray to God you have the capacity to provide that leadership."[41]

As a member of the Black Economic Council, a private group seeking to advance economic opportunities for African Americans, Robinson joined other council members in picketing the White House because of their concern that the Nixon administration would not continue to fund loan assistance for businesses in slums.

Robinson warned that Nixon had better continue funding business development in the nation's slums. "If he doesn't," he said, "I think we're in for a confrontation such as this country has never seen."[42]

In February, Robinson became interested in a program that seemed to be a perfect combination of his roots in rural Georgia and his spiritual belief that God helps those who help themselves. The developing program, begun by individuals long associated with groups such as the Southern Christian Leadership Conference (SCLC) and the National Sharecroppers Fund, called for the creation of a planned community in rural Georgia that would help poor Southerners, especially African American families, become self-sustaining farmers. The planned community, located on 4,800 acres in southwest Georgia, would accommodate eight hundred families whose members would work at intensive farming and learn skills for light industry that the community would develop.

Robinson was not opposed to welfare programs; he found them both helpful and necessary to help certain poor folks survive their deplorable living conditions. But he certainly preferred policies that would help people help themselves, and the planned community was so attractive to him that he asked his good friend Nelson Rockefeller to offer financial support to it.

"It seems whenever a real need arises I look to you," Jackie wrote. "I hope you don't consider me presumptuous. I do so only because there are so few people with your capacity, both as a humanitarian and as one who has means."[43] Rockefeller sent a check, and Robinson, steeped in his mother's stories about her impossible financial struggles in rural Georgia, was delighted.

Robinson's spiritual belief in human responsibility was also expressed at this point in his decision to found Jackie Robinson Associates, a private group of business leaders committed to providing business loans for affordable housing and minority-owned businesses. It was Robinson's effort not only to make money but also to offer a hand up to minorities struggling to enter the mainstream of the US economy. It was also his way of helping minorities avoid reliance on the government, especially the Nixon administration.

Robinson expressed deep frustration with the Nixon administration's lack of attention to minority concerns: "I'm afraid we are going to have a conflict such as this country has never seen. I think we're just a rumor away from it, unless there is concrete action—not by the black community, but by the federal, state, and local governments. The black community has no confidence in the leadership of this country today."[44]

Never one to put too much hope in politics, he had other business ventures in mind at this point, and the most significant was the Jackie Robinson Construction Corporation.

Robinson had long been interested in advancing the cause of civil rights through affordable housing for minorities. In 1954, for instance, while still with the Dodgers, Robinson sought assistance from the Eisenhower administration in securing a federal mortgage for a New York City housing project for low-income minorities. Nothing came of the project. But Robinson's dream of building affordable housing, one no doubt rooted in the stability he enjoyed in his own childhood home in Pasadena, remained strong throughout his postbaseball life. And it came to fruition in the spring of 1970.

The Jackie Robinson Construction Corporation sought to build low- and middle-income housing in the New York City area, a project that would benefit blacks and other minorities. The type of housing Robinson had in mind was large apartment buildings, and the project would include training minority contractors unfamiliar with big construction. Robinson also insisted that as much of the money as possible remain in the community where the construction was taking place.

Robinson's new office was in Englewood Cliffs, New Jersey, and because of his failing vision, he had to rely on a driver for the commute. On many days, the driver would also take Robinson around to several wholesalers so that he could collect meat and canned food for distribution at Nazarene Baptist Church in Brooklyn, a church pastored by his good friend Lacy Covington.

While the construction company reinvigorated Robinson's professional life, his personal life was eased by Jackie Jr.'s progress at Daytop. The young man slid back into drugs here and there, but his prayerful parents had noticed marked progress by the spring of 1970. And so in May, the Robinsons hosted a picnic at their home to thank Daytop for its work in helping Jackie Jr. on his road to recovery.

The best part of the day for Robinson was at the end, just before Jackie Jr. boarded the bus to head back to Daytop. The occasion reminded Robinson of the time his son had left for the army, when he hurtfully spurned his father's attempt at a hug. But this time was different. "I stuck out my hand to shake his hand, remembering the day of his departure for the service," Robinson recalled. "He brushed my hand aside, pulled me to him, and embraced me in a tight hug. That single moment paid for every bit of sacrifice, every bit of anguish, I had ever undergone. I had my son back."[45]

Sharon and David were also doing well. Sharon, following in her mother's footsteps, was studying nursing at Howard University in Washington, DC, where she met and, to her parents' pleasure, married a Howard medical student. David, an academically superior student at

Mount Hermon, a boarding school in Massachusetts, was on his way to Stanford University.

Robinson would recount these positive days in another project capturing his attention at this point, a new autobiography he would write with Al Duckett. Robinson's pitch letter for the book had described a personal evolution in terms that evoked his mother's decision to straighten her back and leave Jim Sasser's oppressive farmland.

And he let would-be publishers know that the viewpoints of others would never again lead him to bow down or remain silent. "I paid more than my due for the right to call it like I see it," Robinson explained. "And I could care less if people like me, so long as they respect me. The only way I know how to deserve respect—even if one does not receive it—is to be honest enough with oneself, to be honest with others. This is the cardinal principle I have kept in mind in making plans for this book."[46]

Random House met with Robinson about the project, but the publishing giant turned it down because Jackie insisted that the book address not only the baseball years but also his careers beyond the baseball diamond—in business, politics, and civil rights—the work he considered far more important than all of his baseball feats. But Putnam accepted the proposal, and Robinson and Duckett began to write.

However good 1970 felt at points, Robinson was dying. Plagued with advanced diabetes, his body was ravaged. His legs were hurting, his sight was failing, and his heart was struggling. Rachel was heartbroken. She had taken leave from her mental health work in New Haven in the fall of 1969, partly because she knew her husband and son would need her close by in the days and months to come. But being so close to her dying husband was not easy, especially since he refused to talk about his death, and she eventually decided to seek therapy so that she could cope with the event before them.

As his condition worsened in the new decade, Robinson made sure to pave the way for younger black leaders. He endorsed Charles Rangel over Adam Clayton Powell Jr. in the 1970 Democratic primary election to represent Harlem in the House of Representatives, and in early 1971 he offered support to the Rev. Jesse Jackson in a visit to Operation Breadbasket in Chicago.

Robinson held Breadbasket in the highest of regards and even served on its board of directors. Modeled on the Rev. Leon Sullivan's work in Philadelphia, which Robinson had long supported, Breadbasket was an SCLC campaign designed to use negotiations and the threat of economic boycotts to pressure major corporations to create jobs, and better jobs, for African Americans. With his emphasis on economic advancement, Robinson was delighted with Breadbasket's economic program.

Robinson was also impressed with Jackson's leadership of Bread-basket, and in his rallying speech in Chicago he described Jackson as a "tall, young, brave Black Moses who can take us some giant steps along the way to that Promised Land of which Dr. King spoke."[47]

Shortly after speaking in Chicago, Robinson headed to yet another sports banquet honoring his legacy. Side by side, the two events put him in a reflective mood, and in a later letter to Calvin Morris, the associate director of Breadbasket, Robinson wrote: "I left Chicago to attend a sports banquet. After my Chicago experience, the dinner was an empty affair. Imagine having to leave a Breadbasket affair where people were deeply involved in creating dignity and self-respect to attend a banquet honoring people because they were able to catch and hit a ball but not at all concerned about people."[48]

The issues of poverty and relief remained front and center in Robinson's mind in March, when Rockefeller proposed cuts to New York's welfare programs. Robinson sketched his disagreement with the governor in a letter to the *New York Post*.

"I don't think our priorities are reached when we would deny people their needs while we spend billions searching for rocks on the moon," he said. "We must care more about people and when we do, I think we will find poor people caring more about themselves. I believe dignity should be our prime target. Cutting back on welfare only indicates that we are not truly concerned about the needy."[49]

By spring, Jackie Jr. had graduated from the rigorous rehabilitation program and had even become an assistant regional director for the organization. His progress left Robinson deeply proud, as did the times when the two of them, father and son, once alienated from each other, spoke together as a team at antidrug campaigns and events.

Rockefeller took notice, and after the Robinsons spoke at a drug abuse program at a New York school district, he sent the elder Jackie a note: "I am certain you can never fully realize the impact the two of you had on the community. I thank you both for your courage and for your willingness to help others out of your own experience."[50]

Father and son also worked together, though Jackie Jr. took the lead, on an "Afternoon of Jazz" that would benefit Daytop. Scheduled for the end of June, the concert was a labor of love for the whole Robinson family.

But Jackie Jr. would not live to see the fruits of his work.

On June 17, as he was returning from New York City around 2:00 a.m., he lost control of David's car on the Merritt Parkway. The MG smashed into a fence and an abutment, breaking his neck and leaving him pinned to death in the car.

Robinson could not bring himself to identify his son's body at the morgue. "I had gone weak all over," he later wrote. "I knew that I couldn't go to that hospital or morgue or whatever and look at my dead son's body."[51]

But Robinson could not get out of breaking the horrible news to Rachel, who was away at a conference, so he and Sharon drove to Holyoke, Massachusetts, while eighteen-year-old David went to identify his brother's body in Norwalk.

Rachel collapsed on hearing the news. And when she, Jackie, and Sharon returned to their Stamford home, she bolted from the car and ran all around the property, screaming from the depths of pain that only she could know.

Jackie, too, wept openly. The pain was raw, and his hope-filled Christian faith offered some comfort.

But faith was less comforting to Rachel. According to Jackie, "She didn't want to hear about God knowing best, or any of the other clichés that people use to make you feel better. God had taken her son just at a time when he had begun to help a lot of other youngsters less fortunate than he had been."[52]

Letters, cards, and telegrams arrived at the Robinson home shortly after the news went public, and one of the letters was from the White House. "I have just learned of the tragic death of your son, and I want you to know that my thoughts and prayers are with you and Mrs. Robinson at this difficult time," Nixon wrote. "I know that nothing said could relieve the pain that this loss has brought you, but I do want you to know that Mrs. Nixon and I will be praying that God may give you the strength and courage to persevere."[53]

A family friend, the Rev. George Lawrence, conducted the funeral at Antioch Baptist Church in Brooklyn. More than fifteen hundred attended the solemn service, and gospel singer Joyce Bryant and a Daytop choir offered musical selections.

The Robinsons decided not to cancel the "Afternoon of Jazz," and more than three thousand people turned out for the lakeside event featuring Roberta Flack, Herbie Mann, Dave Brubeck, Billy Taylor, and others. Jesse Jackson spoke for more than twenty minutes and led the crowd in prayers for Jackie Jr. and the Robinson family.

The days afterward were difficult. Rachel went back to work at the hospital and then withdrew to herself on returning home. Jackie felt abandoned. Biographer Arnold Rampersad reports that the tension between the two began to dissipate only weeks later, after Sharon discovered her father weeping alone in the living room. When she asked him why, he replied: "First Mr. Rickey and my mother, then your brother. Now I wonder if I am losing my wife."[54] Rachel was reading alone in her bedroom at the time, but when Sharon told her of Jackie crying, she went to him at once. And the slow process of healing began.

Robinson also experienced a reconciliation of sorts with his former boss, William Black, who sent a generous check in support of the "Afternoon of Jazz." Robinson had left Chock full o'Nuts on unhappy terms, but he was deeply grateful when he learned of Black's gesture.

"What you are doing I shall never forget," he wrote in a letter to Black. "I am sure you must know how much your bringing me in to the Chock Full o'Nuts family in the early years meant to me and my life. While we have been apart these last few years, your influence has been a factor in many of the things I've done since that time. And now that you have made our jazz concert a success, I am even more deeply indebted to you."[55]

Several months earlier, Robinson had also reconciled with Buzzie Bavasi, who was the general manager of the Brooklyn Dodgers when Walter O'Malley decided to trade Robinson to the New York Giants. Bavasi knew that the experience had left Robinson bitter, and he attempted to heal the long-term breach, although indirectly, in a letter he wrote to Robinson in February 1971.

The occasion was Major League Baseball's decision to elect into the Hall of Fame only one player a year from the Negro leagues and to keep plaques honoring the Negro-league players separate from those of other inductees. In his letter to Robinson, Bavasi shared that he found that decision to be another example of asking blacks to "sit in the back of the bus."[56]

In Robinson's reply, he expressed his agreement and offered his own friendly gesture in return. "You know I feel strongly about this matter," he wrote. "I am pleased you are expressing yourself about the way you feel. Your action justifies the way I thought of you before the 1957 misunderstanding."[57]

As his health worsened, Robinson even adjusted his attitude toward Nixon, shifting primary blame for racial issues onto the vice president and other presidential advisers.

In early December, Nixon had written a glowing statement about Robinson's athletic prowess as his contribution to a testimonial dinner honoring him as "The Man of 25 Years in Sports." Robinson sent the president a follow-up letter gently explaining his lack of support.

"Because I felt strongly that it is not good policy for any minority to put all of their eggs in one political basket, many of us had decided it may be best to support you and your candidacy in the coming election," Robinson wrote. "However, your Vice President, Mr. Agnew, makes it impossible for me, once again, to do so. I feel so strongly about his being anti-black and anti-progressive in race relations that I dread the fact of anything happening to you and Mr. Agnew becoming President of the United States."[58]

This shift, of course, did not mean that Robinson would be silent when he disagreed with Nixon. In March 1972, he even wrote Nixon a blistering letter in which he expressed his fury at the president's call for a one-year moratorium on busing to integrate schools.

Robinson continued to seek reconciliation elsewhere as his life came to a close, and even Roy Wilkins, the NAACP head who had evoked Robinson's wrath in 1967, and Malcolm X were among the beneficiaries.

Robinson had been sharply critical of Malcolm throughout the militant's life, even after he left the Nation of Islam, but in the new autobiography he penned with Al Duckett, Robinson praised Malcolm's powerful conversion at the time of his hajj, when he came to see that Islam included people of all colors. Robinson especially liked these words from Malcolm: "If white Americans could accept the Oneness of God, then perhaps, too, they could accept in reality the Oneness of Man."[59]

Robinson also accepted a reconciliatory gesture from Walter O'Malley's son, Peter, now president of the Los Angeles Dodgers, who invited Robinson to an Old Timers Day when Robinson's number, as well as the numbers of Sandy Koufax and Roy Campanella, would be retired. With urging from Don Newcombe, Robinson accepted the invitation and ended up describing the day as one of the greatest in his life.

After the event, Robinson even told a reporter that the long-standing feud was not between him and the elder O'Malley. "The problem was never between Jackie Robinson and Walter O'Malley," he said. "It was between Walter O'Malley and Branch Rickey."[60]

But Robinson continued to have a problem with Major League Baseball, and when Commissioner Bowie Kuhn invited him to throw out the first ball at one of the games of the 1972 World Series, to mark the twenty-fifth anniversary of his shattering of the color barrier, Robinson initially declined, citing his ongoing frustration that there were no African American managers.

But Kuhn's office made it difficult for Robinson when it told him that the occasion would also honor Jackie Jr. and Daytop. Robinson relented, but in his televised speech, he delivered a jab to Major League Baseball.

With his family next to him, and a national viewing audience of sixty million before him, he said: "I am extremely proud and pleased to be here this afternoon but must admit I'm going to be tremendously more pleased and more proud when I look at that third base coaching line one day and see a black face managing in baseball."[61]

White-haired, unsteady on his feet, and virtually blind from diabetes, Robinson shocked those who had not seen him in recent years.

Rachel woke up early on October 24, 1972, nine days after the World Series honor.

After getting dressed, she headed to the kitchen to make breakfast. It was a typical day. But then she saw Jackie running down the hallway toward her. He was naked.

"So I ran out of the kitchen to meet him because I knew something was very wrong," she later recalled. "And he put his arms around me and said, 'I love you.' And he just sank to the floor."[62]

Felled by a heart attack, ravaged by diabetes, Robinson died at 7:10 a.m.

More than twenty-five hundred people—athletes, politicians, civil rights activists, and celebrities—attended the funeral at Riverside Baptist Church on 122nd Street in New York City. Rachel had asked for two-thirds of the seating to remain open for everyday citizens on a first-come, first-served basis. She also insisted, given her husband's love for children, that a special section be reserved for the young ones.

Jesse Jackson delivered the eulogy. Jackson was a longtime family friend who had asked Robinson to be the first vice president of PUSH (People United to Serve Humanity), and Jackie had accepted the offer.

In his moving eulogy, Jackson said: "When Jackie took the field, something in us reminded us of our birthright to be free."

"He was immunized by God from catching the diseases he fought," he added. "The Lord's arms and protection enabled him to go through dangers, seen and unseen, and he had the capacity to wear glory with grace."[63]

A large choir from Canaan Baptist Church sang a tribute that included "Precious Lord," "Come, Ye Disconsolate," and "If I Can Help Somebody." Roberta Flack also sang a moving spiritual, "I Told Jesus It Would Be All Right If He Changed My Name."

The funeral cortege weaved through Harlem and past Freedom National Bank before heading to Brooklyn, where a Jackie Robinson Construction Company was launching a new project, and then on to Cypress Hills Cemetery. Tens of thousands of people lined the streets to pay their respects.

Robinson was laid to rest, finally, next to his son Jackie Jr.

Today, when visitors pay their respects at the grave and look at his tombstone, they can read Jackie Robinson's spiritual approach to life: "A life is not important except in the impact it has on other lives."

Notes

Introduction

1. Lee Lowenfish, *Branch Rickey: Baseball's Ferocious Gentleman* (Lincoln: University of Nebraska Press, 2007), 125–26; Arnold Rampersad, *Jackie Robinson: A Biography* (New York: Alfred A. Knopf, 1997), 371–73.

2. Lowenfish, *Branch Rickey*, 368.

3. Rampersad, *Jackie Robinson*, 126.

4. Ibid.

5. Jackie Robinson and Alfred Duckett, *I Never Had It Made* (Hopewell, NJ: Ecco Press, 1995), 30–31.

6. Jamie Crawford, "How Church Helped Sign Jackie Robinson," CNN.com, April 14, 2001.

7. Jackie Robinson, untitled manuscript on faith, n.d., Jackie Robinson Papers,, box 12, folder 11, Library of Congress, Washington, DC.

8. Lowenfish, *Branch Rickey*, 374.

9. Rampersad, *Jackie Robinson*, 126.

10. Add Seymour Jr., "Jackie Robinson: 'Temper Like a Rattlesnake,'" Associated Press, April 14, 1997.

11. Chris Lamb, *Conspiracy of Silence: Sportswriters and the Long Campaign to Desegregate Baseball* (Lincoln: University of Nebraska Press, 2012), 25–26.

12. Rampersad, *Jackie Robinson*, 127.

13. Robinson and Duckett, *I Never Had It Made*, 30–34.

14. Lowenfish, *Branch Rickey*, 376.

15. Robinson and Duckett, *I Never Had It Made*, 32.

16. Rampersad, *Jackie Robinson*, 143.

17. Robinson, untitled manuscript on faith.

18. See Chris Lamb, "Did Branch Rickey Sign Jackie Robinson to Right a 40-Year Wrong?," *Black Ball: A Negro Leagues Journal*, June 2013, 5–18.

19. Jackie Robinson, "Trouble Ahead Needn't Bother You," in *Faith Made Them Champions*, ed. Norman Vincent Peale (Carmel, NY: Guideposts, 1954), 239.

20. Ibid.

21. "Branch Rickey Dies," *Columbus Dispatch*, December 10, 1965, 2.

22. Chris Lamb, "Jackie Robinson: Faith in Himself—and in God," *Wall Street Journal*, April 11, 2013.

23. Robinson, untitled manuscript on faith.

24. Eric Metaxas was among those who criticized Helgeland for avoiding the issue of Robinson's faith. See Eric Metaxas, "Jackie Robinson: A Man of Faith," *USA Today*, April 11, 2013.

Chapter 1: "I Put My Trust in God and Moved"

1. Jackie Robinson, untitled manuscript on faith, n.d., Jackie Robinson Papers, box 12, folder 11, Library of Congress, Washington, DC.

2. Carl Rowan interviewed Mallie Robinson for Carl T. Rowan and Jackie Robinson, *Wait Till Next Year: The Life Story of Jackie Robinson* (New York: Random House, 1960), but he did not report most of the faith-related material that appears in our chapter.

3. Robinson, untitled manuscript on faith.

4. Ibid.

5. Rowan's interview is the source for this chapter's depiction of Mallie's time on the Sasser farm and her decision to leave.

6. Carl T. Rowan with Jackie Robinson, *Wait Till Next Year: The Story of Jackie Robinson* (New York: Random House, 1960), 20.

7. Robinson, untitled manuscript on faith.

8. Ibid.

9. Arthur D. Morse, "Jackie Wouldn't Have Gotten to First Base," *Better Homes and Gardens*, May 1950, 226.

10. Ibid.

11. Rowan, notes on Mallie Robinson interview.

12. Arnold Rampersad, *Jackie Robinson: A Biography* (New York: Alfred A. Knopf, 1997), 24.

13. Rowan, notes on Mallie Robinson interview.

14. Ibid.

15. Rampersad, *Jackie Robinson*, 24.

16. Rowan, *Wait Till Next Year*, 24.

17. Rampersad, *Jackie Robinson*, 26.

18. Jackie Robinson (as told to Ed Reid), "Robinson Never Forgets Mother's Advice," *Washington Post*, August 23, 1949.

19. Ibid.

20. Morse, "Jackie Wouldn't Have," 226.

21. Rowan, notes on Mallie Robinson interview.

22. Ibid.

23. Robinson, "Never Forgets Mother's Advice."

24. Rowan, notes on Mallie Robinson interview.

Chapter 2: "To Seek to Help Others"

1. Arnold Rampersad, *Jackie Robinson: A Biography* (New York: Alfred A. Knopf, 1997), 52.

2. Ibid.

3. Karl E. Downs, "Timid Negro Students!," *The Crisis*, June 1936, 171.

4. Jackie Robinson, untitled manuscript on faith, n.d., Jackie Robinson Papers, box 12, folder 11, Library of Congress, Washington, DC.

5. Ibid.

6. Karl E. Downs, "Did My Church Forsake Me? A Negro Methodist Asks a Question," *Zion's Herald*, March 9, 1938, 308. This article is the source for the chapter's narrative of Downs's rejection at the hotel and his response.

7. "Made Good," *Time*, March 21, 1938, 61.

8. William N. Jones, "Day By Day," *Baltimore Afro-American*, April 9, 1938.

9. Robinson, untitled manuscript on faith.

10. "NAACP to Hear Carl Downs," *Baltimore Afro-American*, November 12, 1938.

11. Robinson, untitled manuscript on faith. This manuscript is the source for the following part of chap. 2, to the sentence, "We had a lot of long talks which affected me deeply."

12. Jackie Robinson and Alfred Duckett, *I Never Had It Made* (Hopewell, NJ: The Ecco Press, 1995), 20.

13. Rampersad, *Jackie Robinson*, 53.

14. Robinson, untitled manuscript on faith.

15. Ruby Berkley Goodwin, *It's Good to Be Black* (Garden City, NY: Doubleday, 1953), 10.

16. Rampersad, *Jackie Robinson*, 65.

17. Ibid., 66.

18. Gary Libman, "Rachel Robinson's Homecoming: She Recalls a Legend and Her Days in L.A.," *Los Angeles Times*, September 2, 1987.

19. Rampersad, *Jackie Robinson*, 77.

20. Libman, "Rachel Robinson's Homecoming."

21. "Interview with Rachel Robinson," *Scholastic*, n.d., www.scholastic.com /teachers/article/interview-rachel-robinson#top.

22. Libman, "Rachel Robinson's Homecoming."

23. "Interview with Rachel Robinson," *Scholastic*.

24. Robinson and Duckett, *I Never Had It Made*, 22.

25. Ibid., 23.

26. Rampersad, *Jackie Robinson*, 78–79.

27. Ibid., 79.

28. Robinson and Duckett, *I Never Had It Made*, 23.

Chapter 3: "You Are a Child of God"

1. Arnold Rampersad, *Jackie Robinson: A Biography* (New York: Alfred A. Knopf, 1997), 82.

2. Jackie Robinson and Alfred Duckett, *I Never Had It Made* (Hopewell, NJ: Ecco Press, 1995), 11.

3. Rampersad, *Jackie Robinson*, 82.

4. Ibid., 84.

5. Robinson and Duckett, *I Never Had It Made*, 12; Rampersad, *Jackie Robinson*, 84–85.

6. Rampersad, *Jackie Robinson*, 86–88.

7. Robinson and Duckett, *I Never Had It Made*, 12.

8. Rachel Robinson with Lee Daniels, *Jackie Robinson: An Intimate Portrait* (New York: Harry N. Abrams, 1996), 27.

9. Chris Lamb, *Conspiracy of Silence: Sportswriters and the Long Campaign to Desegregate Baseball* (Lincoln: University of Nebraska Press, 2012), 168–69.

10. Patrick Washburn, *The African-American Newspaper: Voice of Freedom* (Evanston, IL: Northwestern University, 2006), 144–47.

11. Lamb, *Conspiracy of Silence*, 170.

12. Rampersad, *Jackie Robinson*, 96.

13. Walter White, "White Supremacy in World War II," in *A Documentary History of the Negro People in the United States*, ed. Herbert Aptheker (New York: Citadel, 1974), 4:80.

14. Lamb, *Conspiracy of Silence*, 176.

15. John Vernon, "Jim Crow, Meet Lieutenant Robinson: A 1944 Court Martial," *Prologue* 40, no. 1 (Spring 2008), www.archives.gov/publications/prologue/2008/spring/robinson.html.

16. Rampersad, *Jackie Robinson*, 95.

17. Ibid., 97.

18. Vernon, "Jim Crow, Meet Lieutenant Robinson."

19. Ibid.

20. Ibid.

21. Rampersad, *Jackie Robinson*, 100.

22. Vernon, "Jim Crow, Meet Lieutenant Robinson."

23. Rampersad, *Jackie Robinson*, 104–5, 109. Rampersad, 104–18, is the source for the part of chap. 3 that runs from this note to the sentence that ends, "his junior year at UCLA, when he hit .097."

24. See Brian Carroll, *When to Stop the Cheering? The Black Press, the Black Community, and the Integration of Professional Baseball* (New York: Routledge, 2007).

25. Lamb, *Conspiracy of Silence*, 249–53.

26. Ibid., 260–61.

27. Ibid., 263.

28. Ibid., 264–66.

29. Wendell Smith, Wendell Smith Papers, Baseball Hall of Fame, Cooperstown, NY.

30. Lamb, *Conspiracy of Silence*, 263.

31. Rampersad, *Jackie Robinson*, 116–17.

32. Robinson and Duckett, *I Never Had It Made*, 24.

33. Rampersad, *Jackie Robinson*, 118.

34. Ibid.

35. Jules Tygiel, *Baseball's Great Experiment: Jackie Robinson and His Legacy* (New York: Oxford University Press, 1997), 63.

36. Ibid.

37. Ibid., 41.

38. Smith, WSP.

39. Rampersad, *Jackie Robinson*, 124, 125.

Chapter 4: "I Have Kept My Promise"

1. Lee Lowenfish, *Branch Rickey: Baseball's Ferocious Gentleman* (Lincoln: University of Nebraska Press, 2007), 17.

2. Ibid., 15–16.

3. Ibid.

4. Ibid., 17.

5. *St. Louis Globe-Democrat*, September 30, 1930.

6. E-mail correspondence with Lee Lowenfish, July 10, 2016.

7. Bill Horlacher, "The Man Who Integrated Baseball," *Moody*, July–August 1987, 18.

8. Lowenfish, *Branch Rickey*, 16.

9. Ibid., 14–15.

10. Ibid., 19.

11. A. S. "Doc" Young, "The Black Athlete in the Golden Age of Sports: Branch Rickey Launched Negroes to Stardom with Signing of Jackie Robinson," *Ebony*, November 1968, 156.

12. Lowenfish, *Branch Rickey*, 21–22.

13. Murray Polner, *Branch Rickey: A Biography* (New York: Atheneum, 1982), 7.

14. Carl T. Rowan with Jackie Robinson, *Wait Till Next Year* (New York: Random House, 1960), 105–6.

15. *Miami Herald*, October 24, 1945. Quoted in Chris Lamb, "Did Branch Rickey Sign Jackie Robinson to Right a 40-Year Wrong?," *Black Ball: A Negro Leagues Journal* 6 (2013): 5.

16. Lowenfish, *Branch Rickey*, 24.

17. *Miami Herald*, October 24, 1945. Quoted in Lamb, "40-Year Wrong?," 2.

18. Mark Harris, "Branch Rickey Keeps His 40-Year Promise to a Negro Dentist," *Negro Digest*, September 1947, 4–7.

19. Arthur Mann, "The Life of Branch Rickey, Part 1," *Look*, August 20, 1957, 79. Quoted in Lowenfish, *Branch Rickey*, 23.

20. David Lipman, *Mr. Baseball: The Story of Branch Rickey* (New York: G. P. Putnam and Sons, 1966), 10.

21. Young, "Black Athlete in the Golden Age," 154.

22. Arnold Rampersad, *Jackie Robinson* (New York: Alfred A. Knopf, 1997), 121–22.

23. Jules Tygiel, *Baseball's Great Experiment: Jackie Robinson and His Legacy* (New York: Oxford University Press, 1997), 52.

24. Lowenfish, *Branch Rickey*, 24; and "Says Rickey Hit Jim Crow During Life at College," *Cleveland Post Call*, August 9, 1947.

25. Harris, "Promise to a Negro Dentist," 4.

26. Tim Cohane, "A Branch Grows in Brooklyn," *Look*, March 19, 1946.

27. Ibid.

28. Fredrick Faber, "There's a Wideness in God's Mercy," 1862.

29. Lowenfish, *Branch Rickey*, 26–27.

30. Ibid., 36.

31. Ibid., 29.

32. Winthrop G. Martin, Brooklyn and Queens YMCA, to Branch Rickey, letter, November 6, 1942, Branch Rickey Papers (hereafter cited as BRP), box 68, file 8, Library of Congress, Washington, DC.

33. Branch Rickey to Paul Hayward, YMCA, Fort Worth, Texas, telegram, January 11, 1947, BRP, box 68, file 8.

34. Lowenfish, *Branch Rickey*, 30. Lowenfish, 30–59, is the source for the part of chap. 4 that describes the rest of Rickey's playing career and his time outside baseball until the St. Louis Browns asked him to be their business manager.

35. Wesley H. Hager to Branch Rickey, letter, October 22, 1952, BRP, box 59, folder 11.

36. Horlacher, "Man Who Integrated Baseball," 16.

37. Frederick Lieb, "Games Loses Beacon of Progress," *Sporting News*, December 25, 1965.

38. Lowenfish, *Branch Rickey*, 280.

39. Jackie Robinson, untitled manuscript on faith, n.d., Jackie Robinson Papers, box 12, folder 11, Library of Congress, Washington, DC.

40. Ibid.

41. Lowenfish, *Branch Rickey*, 289.

42. David Pietrusza, *Judge and Jury: The Life and Times of Judge Kenesaw Mountain Landis* (South Bend, IN: Diamond Communications, 1998), 411.

43. Chris Lamb, *Conspiracy of Silence: Sportswriters and the Long Campaign to Desegregate Baseball* (Lincoln: University of Nebraska Press, 2012), 13–14.

44. Lowenfish, *Branch Rickey*, 280.

45. Pietrusza, *Judge and Jury*, 365.

46. Lowenfish, *Branch Rickey*, 309.

47. Lamb, "40-Year Wrong?," 8–9.

48. Art Rust Jr., *Get that Nigger Off the Field* (New York: Delacorte, 1976), 6.

49. Ibid.

50. Lowenfish, *Branch Rickey*, 354.

51. *Amsterdam News*, December 26, 1942. Quoted in Lamb, *Conspiracy of Silence*, 223.

52. Arthur Mann, *Branch Rickey: American in Action* (Boston: Houghton Mifflin, 1957), 212–13; Tygiel, *Baseball's Great Experiment*, 56; Lowenfish, *Branch Rickey*, 326.

53. Lowenfish, *Branch Rickey*, 349.

54. Rampersad, *Jackie Robinson*, 122.

55. Tygiel, *Baseball's Great Experiment*, 56–57.

56. Lamb, *Conspiracy of Silence*, 225.

57. Lowenfish, *Branch Rickey*, 359.

58. Red Barber, *1947: When All Hell Broke Loose in Baseball* (New York: Da Capo Press, 1984), 49–50.

59. Ibid., 52, 63.

60. Ibid., 63–64.

61. Lamb, *Conspiracy of Silence*, 271.

62. Lowenfish, *Branch Rickey*, 368.

63. Lamb, *Conspiracy of Silence*, 232.

64. Lowenfish, *Branch Rickey*, 377; Lamb, *Conspiracy of Silence*, 273.

65. Lamb, *Conspiracy of Silence*, 274.

66. Lowenfish, *Branch Rickey*, 378.

67. Chris Lamb, *Blackout: The Untold Story of Jackie Robinson's First Spring Training* (Lincoln: University of Nebraska Press, 2004), 43, 48.

68. Lamb, *Conspiracy of Silence*, 291.

69. *New York Herald Tribune*, October 25, 1945. Quoted in Lamb, *Conspiracy of Silence*, 295.

70. Rowan, *Wait Till Next Year*, 39.

71. Lamb, *Blackout*, 66.

72. Lipman, *Mr. Baseball*, 142.

73. Lowenfish, *Branch Rickey*, 386.

74. Mann, *Branch Rickey: American*, 230–32.

75. Branch Rickey to Wendell Smith, letter, January 8, 1946, Wendell Smith Papers, Baseball Hall of Fame, Cooperstown, NY.

76. Ibid.

77. Lamb, *Blackout*, 63–65.

78. Ibid., 75–76.

79. Rampersad, *Jackie Robinson*, 133.

80. Rachel Robinson with Lee Daniels, *Jackie Robinson: An Intimate Portrait* (New York: Harry N. Abrams, 1996), 40.

81. Rampersad, *Jackie Robinson*, 133.

82. Rachel Robinson, *Intimate Portrait*, 43.

Chapter 5: "God Has Been Good to Us Today"

1. Chris Lamb, *Blackout: The Untold Story of Jackie Robinson's First Spring Training* (Lincoln: University of Nebraska Press, 2004), 5.

2. Gilbert King, "The Most Dangerous Place to Be Black," *Pacific Standard*, August 7, 2013, www.psmag.com/books-and-culture/the-most-dangerous-place-to-be-black-64206.

3. *Chicago Defender*, February 23, 1946. Quoted in Lamb, *Blackout*, 61.

4. Carl T. Rowan with Jackie Robinson, *Wait Till Next Year* (New York: Random House, 1960), 131.

5. Rachel Robinson with Lee Daniels, *Jackie Robinson: An Intimate Portrait* (New York: Harry N. Abrams, 1996), 46.

6. Rowan, *Wait Till Next Year*, 132.

7. Rachel Robinson, *Intimate Portrait*, 46.

8. Rowan, *Wait Till Next Year*, 133.

9. Ibid. See *Chicago Defender*, February 23, 1946. Quoted in Lamb, *Blackout*, 13.

10. Lamb, *Blackout*, 13, 14.

11. Ibid., 15, 16.

12. Jackie Robinson and Alfred Duckett, *I Never Had It Made* (Hopewell, NJ: Ecco Press, 1995), 42.

13. Lamb, *Blackout*, 90.

14. Telephone interview with Billy Rowe, March 10, 1993. See Lamb, *Blackout*, 19.

15. Lamb, *Blackout*, 16, 18, 19.

16. Ibid., 83.

17. Arnold Rampersad, *Jackie Robinson: A Biography* (New York: Alfred A. Knopf, 1997), 142.

18. Lamb, *Blackout*, 88.

19. Ibid., 88, 89.

20. Rowan, *Wait Till Next Year*, 94.

21. Lamb, *Blackout*, 95.

22. Lee Lowenfish, *Branch Rickey: Baseball's Ferocious Gentleman* (Lincoln: University of Nebraska Press, 2007), 392.

23. Arthur Mann, *Jackie Robinson Story* (New York: Grosset and Dunlap, 1950), 142.

24. Lamb, *Blackout*, 67.

25. Robinson and Duckett, *I Never Had It Made*, 45.

26. *Pittsburgh Courier*, April 20, 1946. Quoted in Lamb, *Blackout*, 164.

27. Rachel Robinson, "I Live with a Hero," *McCall's*, March 1951.

28. Rampersad, *Jackie Robinson*, 144.

29. Ibid.

30. Ed Charles, information presentation (Daytona Beach, FL, 1996). Quoted in Lamb, *Blackout*, 93.

31. Lamb, *Blackout*, 103, 104, 105.

32. Jackie Robinson, untitled manuscript on faith, n.d., Jackie Robinson Papers, box 12, folder 11, Library of Congress, Washington, DC.

33. Lamb, *Blackout*, 103.

34. Ibid., 103, 104, 105.

35. Jackie Robinson and Wendell Smith, *My Own Story* (New York: Greenberg, 1948), 78.

36. Ibid., 79.

37. Lamb, *Blackout*, 154–55.

38. Ibid., 166.

39. Ibid., 171, 172.

40. Wendell Smith, "It Was a Great Day in Jersey," *Pittsburgh Courier*, April 27, 1946.

41. Ibid.

42. William G. Nunn, "American Way Triumphs in Robinson 'Experiment,'" *Pittsburgh Courier*, April 27, 1946.

43. Rampersad, *Jackie Robinson*, 153.

44. Patrick Sauer, "The Year of Jackie Robinson's Mutual Love Affair with Montreal," *Smithsonian*, March 5, 2016, www.smithsonianmag.com/ist/?next= /history/year-jackie-robinsons-mutual-love-affair-montreal-180954878/.

45. John Wilson, *Jackie Robinson and the American Dilemma* (New York: Longman, 2010), 73.

46. Ibid., 73.

47. Sean Kirst, "Jackie Robinson in Syracuse: For Opening Day, Honoring Deep Ties and One Essential Moment," Syracuse.com, April 10, 2013, www .syracuse.com/kirst/index.ssf/2013/04/jackie_robinson_in_syracuse_on.html.

48. Lester B. Granger, "Manhattan and Beyond," *New York Amsterdam News*, June 8, 1946.

49. Rampersad, *Jackie Robinson*, 154.

50. Lowenfish, *Branch Rickey*, 397.

51. Jules Tygiel, *Baseball's Great Experiment: Jackie Robinson and His Legacy* (New York: Oxford University Press, 1997), 122.

52. Ibid., 129.

53. Rampersad, *Jackie Robinson*, 154.

54. Ibid., 155.

55. *Pittsburgh Courier*, undated article, Wendell Smith Papers, Baseball Hall of Fame, Cooperstown, NY (hereafter cited as WSP).

56. Rampersad, *Jackie Robinson*, 156.

57. Ibid., 157.

58. *Pittsburgh Courier*, October 12, 1947. Quoted in Lamb, *Blackout*, 173.

59. *Pittsburgh Courier*, March 15, 1947, WSP.

60. George Mitrovich, "Without Montreal, There Would Have Been No Brooklyn," *Montreal Gazette*, January 30, 2015, montrealgazette.com/sports

/baseball/opinion-without-montreal-there-would-have-been-no-brooklyn-for
-jackie-robinson.

61. Lamb, *Blackout*, 66.

62. "33 Brooklyn Leaders Here Aided Jackie," *New York Amsterdam News*, October 25, 1947.

63. Rampersad, *Jackie Robinson*, 161; Robinson and Duckett, *I Never Had It Made*, 56; Jonathan Eig, *Opening Day: The Story of Jackie Robinson's First Season* (New York: Simon and Schuster, 2007), 36, 37.

64. Eig, *Opening Day*, 36.

65. Rampersad, *Jackie Robinson*, 161.

66. Robinson and Duckett, *I Never Had it Made*, 56.

67. Eig, *Opening Day*, 37.

68. Ibid., 36–38.

69. Rampersad, *Jackie Robinson*, 162.

70. Ibid.

71. Ibid., 164.

72. Ibid., 166.

73. Jackie Robinson, "Batting It Out," *Pittsburgh Courier*, March 22, 1947.

74. *Pittsburgh Courier*, April 5, 1947, WSP.

75. Eig, *Opening Day*, 47.

76. Rampersad, *Jackie Robinson*, 168.

Chapter 6: "I Get Down on My Knees and Pray"

1. Jonathan Eig, *Opening Day: The Story of Jackie Robinson's First Spring Training* (New York: Simon and Schuster, 2007), 48.

2. Ralph Branca, "The Strength to Turn the Other Cheek," *Guideposts*, n.d., www.guideposts.org/positive-living/inspiring-entertainment/sports/the-strength
-to-turn-the-other-cheek?nopaging=1.

3. Ibid.

4. Eig, *Opening Day*, 61.

5. Ibid., 73.

6. Jackie Robinson and Alfred Duckett, *I Never Had It Made* (Hopewell, NJ: Ecco Press, 1995), 59.

7. Ibid., 60.

8. Arnold Rampersad, *Jackie Robinson: A Biography* (New York: Alfred A. Knopf, 1997), 173.

9. Eig, *Opening Day*, 77.

10. Gil Jonas, *Freedom's Sword: The NAACP and the Struggle against Racism in America, 1909–1969* (New York: Routledge, 2004).

11. Eig, *Opening Day*, 87.

12. Rampersad, *Jackie Robinson*, 179.

13. Eig, *Opening Day*, 217.

14. Rampersad, *Jackie Robinson*, 174–75.

15. Wendell Smith, *Pittsburgh Courier*, undated article, Wendell Smith Papers (hereafter cited as WSP), Baseball Hall of Fame, Cooperstown, NY.

16. Ibid.

17. Eig, *Opening Day*, 86.

18. Ibid., 97.

19. John Sexton, *Baseball as a Road to God: Seeing Beyond the Game* (New York: Gotham Books, 2013), 189.

20. Eig, *Opening Day*, 4–5.

21. Rampersad, *Jackie Robinson*, 179.

22. Ibid., 175.

23. E-mail interview with Lee Lowenfish, April 4, 2016.

24. Rampersad, *Jackie Robinson*, 175–76.

25. Ibid., 172.

26. Branca, "Turn the Other Cheek."

27. Carl Erskine and Burton Rocks, *What I Learned from Jackie Robinson: A Teammate's Reflections On and Off the Field* (New York: McGraw-Hill, 2005), 29.

28. Rachel Robinson with Lee Daniels, *Jackie Robinson: An Intimate Portrait* (New York: Harry N. Abrams, 1996), 72.

29. Rampersad, *Jackie Robinson*, 176.

30. Robert C. Cottrell, *Two Pioneers: How Hank Greenberg and Jackie Robinson Transformed Baseball—and America* (Washington, DC: Potomac Books, 2012), 39.

31. Wendell Smith, "The Sports Beat," *Pittsburgh Courier*, May 24, 1947.

32. Rachel Robinson, *Intimate Portrait*, 72.

33. Wendell Smith, *Pittsburgh Courier*, undated article, WSP.

34. Eig, *Opening Day*, 3.

35. Erskine and Rocks, *What I Learned*, 87.

36. Eig, *Opening Day*, 223–24.

37. Ibid., 5.

38. Chris Lamb, presentation (Parkland Library, Parkland, FL, March 20, 2006).

39. Robinson and Duckett, *I Never Had It Made*, 70; Rampersad, *Jackie Robinson*, 193.

40. Rampersad, *Jackie Robinson*, 186–87.

41. Dan Burley, "Jockeying Worse Than Phillies; Fails to Affect His Playing," *Pittsburgh Courier*, October 4, 1947.

42. Ibid.

43. The Rev. John Curren to Jackie Robinson, October 7, 1947, Jackie Robinson Papers (hereafter cited as JRP), box 12, folder 11, Library of Congress, Washington, DC.

44. Robinson and Duckett, *I Never Had It Made*, 70, 71.

45. Wendell Smith, "Sports Beat," *Pittsburgh Courier*, February 28, 1948.

46. Jackie Robinson, untitled manuscript on faith, n.d., JRP, box 12, folder 11.

47. Jules Tygiel, *Baseball's Great Experiment: Jackie Robinson and His Legacy* (New York: Oxford University Press, 1997), 323.

48. See Martin Bauml Duberman, *Paul Robeson* (London: Pan Books, 1989), 358.

49. Robinson and Duckett, *I Never Had It Made*, 86.

50. Rampersad, *Jackie Robinson*, 212–16.

51. Ibid., 219.

52. Ibid., 220.

53. Ibid., 230.

54. "Jackie Robinson Featured in Go-To-Church Advertising," *Los Angeles Sentinel*, November 2, 1950.

55. "Jackie Robinson in Liberty Group," *New York Amsterdam News*, June 30, 1951.

56. Jackie Robinson, "This I Believe," n.d., JRP.

57. "Jackie among Donors Aiding New School," *New York Amsterdam News*, November 3, 1951.

58. "Brooklyn Pastors United to Aid Concord Efforts," *New York Amsterdam News*, February 14, 1953.

59. "Jackie Robinson to Lead Parade at Methodist Meeting," *Chicago Defender*, March 31, 1956.

60. Rampersad, *Jackie Robinson*, 204.

61. Ibid., 220.

62. E. J. Cadou, "Jackie Robinson Writes Little Boy Who Wishes He Was White," *Pittsburgh Courier*, March 13, 1954.

63. Rampersad, *Jackie Robinson*, 261–62.

64. Louis A. Radelet to Rachel Robinson, February 16, 1954, JRP, box 7, folder 19.

65. "Harmful Critic," *Indianapolis Recorder*, August 11, 1956.

66. "Bill Keefe Says We're Ape-like," *Pittsburgh Courier*, August 25, 1956.

67. Rampersad, *Jackie Robinson*, 297.

68. Samuel Haynes, " 'High Point of My Career'—Jackie of Spingarn Award," *Afro-American*, December 8, 1956.

69. Ibid.

Chapter 7: "Hoeing with God"

1. Jackie Robinson, untitled manuscript on faith, n.d., Jackie Robinson Papers, box 12, folder 11, Library of Congress, Washington, DC.

2. Arnold Rampersad, *Jackie Robinson: A Biography* (New York: Alfred A. Knopf, 1997), 322. This chapter's narrative is indebted to Rampersad's book.

3. Robinson, untitled manuscript on faith.

4. Michael G. Long, ed., *First Class Citizenship: The Civil Rights Letters of Jackie Robinson* (New York: Times Books, 2007), 11. All the letters quoted in

the present book can be found in *First Class Citizenship*, which documents the location of each letter cited. For instance, the book notes that the November 25, 1953, letter from Robinson to Eisenhower is in the Dwight D. Eisenhower Library, President's Personal File, box 798, folder 47. The present book will cite only Long's edited collection.

5. Rampersad, *Jackie Robinson*, 287.

6. *The Autobiography of Martin Luther King, Jr.*, ed. Clayborne Carson (New York: Warner Books, 1998), swap.stanford.edu/20141218230026/http://mlk-kpp01.stanford.edu/kingweb/publications/autobiography/chp_8.htm.

7. Jackie Robinson and Alfred Duckett, *I Never Had It Made* (Hopewell, NJ: The Ecco Press, 1995), 224–25.

8. Long, *First Class Citizenship*, 28.

9. Ibid., 40.

10. Ibid.

11. Ibid., 41.

12. Felix Belair Jr., "Eisenhower Bids Negroes Be Patient about Rights," *New York Times*, May 13, 1958.

13. Rachel Robinson with Lee Daniels, *Jackie Robinson: An Intimate Portrait* (New York: Harry N. Abrams, 1996), 161.

14. Alison Leigh Cowan, "Archive Shows Robinson as Moderator on Morality," *New York Times*, December 24, 2010.

15. "Eisenhower Cites Integration Goal," *New York Times*, April 18, 1959.

16. James Wechsler, "A New Column on All Subjects: Jackie Robinson to Write for the *Post*," *New York Post*, April 24, 1959. Robinson's column for the *Post* was titled "Jackie Robinson" (hereafter cited as JR). Some of the most important Robinson columns are collected in *Beyond Home Plate: Jackie Robinson on Life after Baseball*, ed. Michael G. Long (Syracuse, NY: Syracuse University Press, 2013).

17. JR, May 29, 1959.

18. JR, June 12, 1959.

19. JR, July 6, 1959.

20. JR, July 6, 1959.

21. JR, July 15, 1959.

22. JR, July 27, 1959.

23. JR, July 27, 1959.

24. JR, October 28, 1959.

25. JR, October 28, 1959.

26. JR, December 28, 1959.

27. JR, January 6, 1960.

28. JR, February 20, 1960.

29. JR, March 11, 1960.

30. "Truman Says He'd Oust Disrupters in His Shop," *New York Times*, March 20, 1960.

31. JR, March 25, 1960.

32. JR, April 25, 1960.

33. See Rampersad, *Jackie Robinson*, 351.

34. Long, *First Class Citizenship*, 125.

35. Ibid., 127.

36. Robinson's first column for the *New York Amsterdam News* appeared on January 6, 1962. The column was first titled "Jackie Robinson Says" but quickly changed to "Home Plate" (hereafter cited as HP).

37. "'I Won't Crawl to the Hall of Fame'—Jackie Robinson," *New York Amsterdam News*, January 12, 1962.

38. "Hall of Fame 'My Greatest Thrill'—Jackie Robinson," *New York Amsterdam News*, February 3, 1962.

39. "Ex-Dodger Happy: Robinson Recalls Humble Beginning," *Spokane Daily Chronicle*, January 24, 1962.

40. Rampersad, *Jackie Robinson*, 364.

41. HP, July 14, 1962.

42. Jackie Robinson, untitled manuscript on faith.

43. Rampersad, *Jackie Robinson*, 365.

44. HP, August 11, 1962.

45. HP, August 18, 1962.

46. HP, August 18, 1962.

47. Martin Luther King Jr., "Hall of Famer," *New York Amsterdam News*, August 4, 1962.

48. Ibid.

49. Ibid.

50. Ibid.

51. HP, September 22, 1962.

52. HP, February 2, 1963.

53. HP, February 2, 1963.

54. HP, February 2, 1963.

55. HP, February 9, 1962.

56. HP, February 9, 1962.

Chapter 8: "Do You Know What God Did?"

1. Jackie Robinson, "Home Plate," *New York Amsterdam News*, March 30, 1963 (hereafter cited as HP).

2. HP, April 30, 1963.

3. Michael G. Long, ed., *First Class Citizenship: The Civil Rights Letters of Jackie Robinson* (New York: Times Books, 2007), 168–69.

4. Arnold Rampersad, *Jackie Robinson: A Biography* (New York: Alfred A. Knopf, 1997), 374.

5. HP, June 22, 1963.

6. HP, June 22, 1963.

7. Long, *First Class Citizenship*, 173.

8. HP, July 13, 1963.

9. United Church of Christ, "Minutes, Fourth General Synod, Denver, Colorado, July 4–11, 1963," ed. Fred S. Buschmeyer, 86–87. Reproduction provided from the General Synod Collection of the United Church of Christ Archives, Cleveland, Ohio.

10. Jackie Robinson, "Address by Mr. Jackie Robinson, Fourth General Synod of the United Church of Christ, Wednesday, July 10, 1963, Denver, Colorado," Jackie Robinson Papers, box 13, folder 3, Library of Congress, Washington, DC.

11. Ibid.

12. Ibid.

13. United Church of Christ, "Minutes, Fourth General Synod."

14. Ibid.

15. Ibid.

16. HP, July 27, 1963.

17. HP, July 27, 1963.

18. HP, July 27, 1963.

19. HP, September 7, 1963.

20. HP, September 7, 1963.

21. HP, September 7, 1963.

22. "Six Dead after Church Bombing," *Washington Post*, September 16, 1963.

23. Jackie Robinson, "America's Blowin' in the Wind," *New York Amsterdam News*, September 28, 1963.

24. Ibid.

25. Ibid.

26. Ibid.

27. HP, November 30, 1963.

28. "Muslims Reject 'Hundreds' of White Applicants," *Jet*, November 21, 1963, 51.

29. Rachel Robinson with Lee Daniels, *Jackie Robinson: An Intimate Portrait* (New York: Harry N. Abrams, 1996), 194.

30. HP, June 13, 1964.

31. HP, July 11, 1964.

32. HP, July 11, 1964.

33. HP, July 11, 1964.

34. HP, July 18, 1964.

35. "Clay Says He Has Adopted Islam Religion and Regards It as Way to Peace," *New York Times*, February 27, 1964.

36. HP, March 14, 1964.

37. HP, March 14, 1964.

38. HP, July 4, 1964.

39. Jackie Robinson, "The G.O.P.: For White Men Only?," *Saturday Evening Post*, August 10–17, 1963, 10.

40. Ibid., 14.

41. HP, October 31, 1964.

42. HP, October 31, 1964.

43. John Herbers, "Dr. King Rebuts Hoover Charges," *New York Times*, November 20, 1964.

44. HP, December 5, 1964.

45. Rampersad, *Jackie Robinson*, 400.

Chapter 9: "The Good Lord has Showered Blessings on Me and This Country"

1. Jackie Robinson, "Home Plate," *New York Amsterdam News*, January 2, 1965 (hereafter cited as HP).

2. See Michael G. Long, ed., *First Class Citizenship: The Civil Rights Letters of Jackie Robinson* (New York: Times Books, 2007). Long's edited collection is the source for all letters quoted in the part of chap. 9 from this note to "he fired off a letter to the vice president, beginning with an uncustomary greeting of 'Sir,'" (see pp. 207, 212–16).

3. Martin Luther King Jr., "Our God Is Marching On" (speech, Montgomery, AL, March 25, 1965), Martin Luther King, Jr. Research and Education Institute, Stanford University, kinginstitute.stanford.edu/our-god-marching.

4. "Transcript of the Johnson Address on Voting Rights to Joint Session of Congress," *New York Times*, March 16, 1965.

5. Long, *First Class Citizenship*, 129.

6. Arnold Rampersad, *Jackie Robinson: A Biography* (New York: Alfred A. Knopf, 1997), 398. This chapter's narrative is indebted to Rampersad's book.

7. Long, *First Class Citizenship*, 221.

8. Ibid., 222.

9. Tom Wicker, "Johnson Pledges to Help Negroes to Full Equality," *New York Times*, June 5, 1965.

10. Rachel Robinson with Lee Daniels, *Jackie Robinson: An Intimate Portrait* (New York: Harry N. Abrams, 1996), 194.

11. Victor Free, "Man of Parables," *Pittsburgh Press*, February 18, 1968.

12. Mike Recht, "Branch Rickey Laid to Rest," *Nashua (NH) Telegraph*, December 14, 1965.

13. Jackie Robinson, "It's Like Losing a Father," *New York Amsterdam News*, December 18, 1965.

14. Ibid.

15. "Branch Rickey Calls for End to Racial Bias," *Pittsburgh Courier*, August 30, 1952.

16. "Son Hurt in Vietnam; Jackie Urges D.C. Home Rule Now," *Washington Afro-American*, December 7, 1965.

17. Ibid.

18. HP, February 5, 1966.

19. HP, February 19, 1966.

20. HP, February 19, 1966.

21. HP, May 28, 1966.

22. HP, May 28, 1966.

23. Rachel Robinson, *Intimate Portrait*, 147.

24. HP, June 6, 1966.

25. HP, April 16, 1966.

26. HP, April 16, 1966.

27. HP, July 30, 1966.

28. Adam Clayton Powell, *Keep the Faith, Baby!* (New York: Simon and Schuster, 1967). Powell is the source for all quotes in the part of chap. 9 from this note to "must demand and have a proportionate share of the responsibilities of running the communities, the cities and the states in which they live" (see pp. 9–11, 16–17).

29. HP, October 22, 1966.

30. HP, October 22, 1966.

31. HP, October 22, 1966.

32. HP, March 11, 1967.

33. Robert Lipsyte, "Clay Refuses Army Oath; Stripped of Boxing Crown," *New York Times*, April 29, 1967.

34. See Howard Bingham and Max Wallace, *Muhammad Ali's Greatest Fight: Cassius Clay vs. the United States of America* (Lanham, MD: M. Evans, 2000), 149–50.

35. Ibid.

36. HP, October 14, 1967.

37. HP, October 14, 1967.

38. HP, March 25, 1967.

39. Martin Luther King Jr., "Beyond Vietnam" (speech, New York City, April 4, 1967), Martin Luther King, Jr. Research and Education Institute, Stanford University, kingencyclopedia.stanford.edu/encyclopedia/documentsentry/doc_beyond_vietnam/.

40. Ibid.

41. Ibid.

42. HP, May 13, 1967.

43. HP, May 13, 1967.

44. HP, May 13, 1967.

45. Long, *First Class Citizenship*, 252.

46. HP, July 1, 1967.

47. HP, July 1, 1967.

48. HP, July 1, 1967.

49. HP, October 21, 1967.

50. HP, October 21, 1967.

51. HP, August 12, 1967.

52. Jackie Robinson, "Cast the First Stone," October 15, 1967, Jackie Robinson Papers, box 8, folder 3, Library of Congress, Washington, DC.

53. Homer Bigart, "Rap Brown Calls Riots 'Rehearsals for Revolution,'" *New York Times*, August 7, 1967.

54. Rampersad, *Jackie Robinson*, 417.

55. HP, October 7, 1967.

56. HP, December 2, 1967.

Chapter 10: "I Guess the Good Lord Has a Job for Me"

1. Rachel Robinson with Lee Daniels, *Jackie Robinson: An Intimate Portrait* (New York: Harry N. Abrams, 1996), 201.

2. William Borders, "Jackie Robinson, Jr. Is Arrested on Heroin Charge in Stamford," *New York Times*, March 5, 1968.

3. Ibid.

4. Ibid.

5. Michael G. Long, ed., *First Class Citizenship: The Civil Rights Letters of Jackie Robinson* (New York: Times Books, 2007), 273.

6. Ibid., 275.

7. Martin Luther King Jr., "I've Been to the Mountaintop" (sermon, Memphis, TN, April 3, 1968), Martin Luther King, Jr. Research and Education Institute, Stanford University, kingencyclopedia.stanford.edu/encyclopedia/documentsentry/ive_been_to_the_mountaintop/.

8. Martin Luther King Jr., "The Drum Major Instinct" (sermon, Atlanta, February 4, 1968), Martin Luther King, Jr. Research and Education Institute, Stanford University, kingencyclopedia.stanford.edu/encyclopedia/documentsentry/doc_the_drum_major_instinct/.

9. Jackie Robinson, "Home Plate," *New York Amsterdam News*, April 13, 1968 (hereafter cited as HP).

10. William Cowper, "Light Shining Out of Darkness," Poems of William Cowper, www.puritansermons.com/poetry/cowper8.htm.

11. Martin Luther King Jr., "The Ways of God in the Midst of Glaring Evil, Sermon Delivered at Dexter Avenue Baptist Church," in *The Papers of Martin Luther King, Jr.*, vol. 4, *Symbol of the Movement: January 1957–December 1958*, ed. Clayborne Carson, Sarah Carson, Adrienne Clay, Virginia Shadron, and Kieran Taylor (Berkeley: University of California Press, 2000), 109.

12. Ibid.

13. HP, April 13, 1968.

14. HP, April 13, 1968.

15. Jackie Robinson, "The Church and the World" (speech, May 3, 1968), Jackie Robinson Papers (hereafter cited as JRP), box 8, folder 3, Library of Congress, Washington, DC.

16. Ibid.

17. Ibid.

18. Long, *First Class Citizenship*, 276.

19. Ibid., 276–77.

20. Ibid., 275.

21. Jackie Robinson and Alfred Duckett, *I Never Had It Made* (Hopewell, NJ: The Ecco Press, 1995), 275.

22. Long, *First Class Citizenship*, 275.

23. HP, June 8, 1968.

24. HP, June 22, 1968

25. HP, June 13, 1968.

26. HP, June 13, 1968.

27. HP, June 13, 1968.

28. Arnold Rampersad, *Jackie Robinson: A Biography* (New York: Alfred A. Knopf, 1997), 429. This chapter's narrative is indebted to Rampersad's book.

29. Ibid.

30. Ibid., 430.

31. HP, August 17, 1968.

32. HP, August 17, 1968.

33. HP, August 17, 1968.

34. "Jackie Robinson Splits with G.O.P. over Nixon Choice," *New York Times*, August 12, 1968.

35. HP, August 17, 1968.

36. Rampersad, *Jackie Robinson*, 431.

37. HP, September 7, 1968.

38. HP, September 7, 1968.

39. Rampersad, *Jackie Robinson*, 430.

40. Long, *First Class Citizenship*, 283.

41. Ibid., 291–92.

42. "Robinson Cautions Nixon on Slum Aids," *New York Times*, January 30, 1969.

43. Long, *First Class Citizenship*, 294.

44. Rampersad, *Jackie Robinson*, 434.

45. Ibid., 439.

46. Long, *First Class Citizenship*, 303.

47. "Remarks of Mr. Jackie Robinson at SCLC Operation Breadbasket Saturday Morning Meeting," January 23, 1971, JRP, box 13.

48. Long, *First Class Citizenship*, 305.

49. Ibid., 308.

50. Ibid., 309.

51. Robinson and Duckett, *I Never Had It Made*, 256.

52. Ibid., 259.

53. Long, *First Class Citizenship*, 309–10.

54. Rampersad, *Jackie Robinson*, 449.

55. Long, *First Class Citizenship*, 310.

56. Ibid., 305.

57. Ibid., 306.

58. Ibid., 311.

59. Robinson and Duckett, *I Never Had It Made*, 193.

60. Rampersad, *Jackie Robinson*, 456.

61. Ibid., 459.

62. *Jackie Robinson*, directed by Ken Burns, Sarah Burns, and David McMahon (Arlington, VA: PBS Distribution, 2016), DVD.

63. Jesse Jackson, "He Made Us Proud to Be Black," *New York Amsterdam News*, October 28, 1972.

Index

499416BV00001B/3/P